The Sporting Alien

The Sporting Alien
English Sport's Lost Camelot

Mihir Bose

MAINSTREAM
PUBLISHING
EDINBURGH AND LONDON

First published in Great Britain in 1996 by
MAINSTREAM PUBLISHING COMPANY (EDINBURGH) LTD
7 Albany Street
Edinburgh EH1 3UG

ISBN 1 85158 745 4

A catalogue record for this book is available from the British Library

Typeset in Garamond
Printed and bound in Great Britain by Butler and Tanner Ltd, Frome

In memory of Ian Marshall, not only for providing me with my first chance in journalism and making it fun, but proving that you can defy conventions and break moulds, and to Gareth Hewitt, who continues to prove that what matters is not differences in race, culture or background but a shared humanity that can bind us together.

Books by the same author

Contents

Preface

This book was conceived in El Vino's. If anyone had told me when I first came to London that one day a publisher would commission me to write a book, while sipping wine in El Vino, I would have laughed it off as even more fanciful than my dream of scoring a hundred on my Test début at Lord's, the century coming in 17 balls. Then, as I first walked down Fleet Street, drinking in the names of the great newspapers that had their home there, entering El Vino was like reaching the outer door of heaven.

By the time Bill Campbell of Mainstream ordered the chilled white wine and agreed to pay me an advance for *The Sporting Alien* much had changed. The journalists had long gone and El Vino's, where almost every table once saw a famous reporter, had long since become the abode of lawyers and stockbrokers.

Maybe this unhinged Bill, who, in that excess of emotion over cold hard judgement – supposedly foreign to Scots – decided to lay out his firm's money for this book. But then Bill does have a touch of that expansiveness and sense of adventure that marked some of his Scottish ancestors. The exception is that those remarkable imperialists saw their risk being rewarded by pots of gold as they ventured into places such as my own birthplace, Calcutta. I cannot believe Bill will earn much money, let alone a pot of gold, from *The Sporting Alien*. So my first thanks to Bill for asking me to write it.

Of course, I would not have been in any position to take up his offer but for the help and encouragement of many others over many decades.

Father Fritz was the first person to make me believe that one day I might earn a living from writing. It is one of the great regrets of my life that he never lived to see the fruits of what he planted.

Intoxicated, perhaps, by what Fritz had said I fantasised that one day I would become a journalist of the stature of James Cameron, Neville Cardus, John Arlott and I.F. Stone. Now, when modern, particularly tabloid, journalism depresses me I look up Cameron's *What a Way to Run A Tribe*, and marvel how he he conjured up such vivid word pictures, often struggling against impossible deadlines and primitive post-war communications. To think that many of the pieces were written either for *The Daily Express* or papers that have since died shows how much our journalism has changed – often for the worse.

I shall never write a single article that could match anything Cameron, Cardus, Arlott or Stone wrote, but my consolation is that I did meet all of them – Cardus and Stone just before their deaths, and had the privilege of working for some years in the same press box as John Arlott. In choosing them as my role models I may have set impossibly high standards but, as the wise man said, if you do not aim for Everest, you may not even reach the top of your neighbourhood skyscraper.

Ian Marshall, who gave me my first job in journalism in that brief period of joy and discovery during the first summer of LBC's broadcasts, will always be in my thoughts. I would like to thank his successors, Mervyn Hall and Mike Lewis. There are others who deserve thanks for seeing in me something they felt was valuable.

Peter Roberts gave me my first job at *The Sunday Times*, more than 20 years ago. As he took me to lunch, he pointed out William Shawcross and said that one day Shawcross would be the next editor of *The Sunday Times*, succeeding Harry Evans. It has not quite come true but Roberts had not made many false predictions and I am grateful he took a gamble with me. John Lovesey was the first sports editor of the paper to let me loose on the sports pages and his example was followed by his successors: David Robson, Chris Nawrat and Nick Pitt. As nearly all of them would say, they could never have indulged in the luxury of employing me but for the miracles the subs did on my copy and I am grateful to a whole generation of *Sunday Times* subs, not least for so quickly understanding that when I said Manchester Untied I meant Manchester United. Two of the backbench deserve special mention: Jim Pegg and Stan Levenson.

During the course of my career I have met with much kindness from fellow sports journalists. To name all of them would be impossible but I ought to single out David Foot, who remains the great gentleman sporting journalist; Brian Glanville, who is truly an institution; Brian Scovell, who belies appearances by showing an uncanny knack of bridging cultures; and Nigel Dudley for that rare combination: understated English passion and truth.

I am also grateful to my present sports editor at *The Daily Telegraph*, David Welch and his team, in particular, Keith Perry and Brian Oliver for putting up with me.

In the course of writing this book I have incurred many debts. Sally Hibbins of Parallax took time off from her busy schedule to help me understand her television programme about black footballers and let me use transcripts of her full interview with Ron Noades. Vicky Woods explained the background of her article on Imran Khan in *The Sunday Times* and allowed me to quote from it. A great many people voluntarily gave their time to talk to me: Jas Bains, Luther Blissett, Brian Stein, Garth Crooks, Dwight Marshall, David Pleat, Colwyn Rowe, Shahed Sadullah, Brian Swain, Simon Wilde, Alex Williams, Graeme Wright and Trevor Westley.

I would also like to thank Nayanesh Desai who kindly read the book with a beady lawyer's eye helping me avoid some of the obvious pitfalls.

Part of this book was written in Toronto while I was on holiday there and my thanks, as ever, to Panna – no man could ask for a more understanding sister – her husband, Tapan, and their daughter, Anjali, for allowing me the freedom of their lovely home.

I cannot thank enough my nephew, Abhijit, who so generously allowed me to use his flat in North London which, besides providing me with the room to be messy without getting into my wife's hair, has proved a marvellous haven to get away from other distractions.

My father warned me that journalism would never make my fortune and it is too early to say if I shall have to deliver the same warning to my daughter, Indira. She is only six and has yet to be tempted by my profession. By the time she grows up I hope the sporting Camelot that eluded me will truly belong to her. Who knows, by then Tottenham, with whom she has already fallen in love, may even win the championship. However, that must be considered more improbable than my scoring a hundred in 17 balls at Lord's, or winning another contract at El Vino's.

London
Summer, 1996

CHAPTER ONE

Not the Man from the *Southall Express*

Ten minutes before the start of the match, the season ticket-holder sitting a couple of rows behind the press box tapped me on the back and asked me the question which made me realise I was a sporting alien. The surprise was that it needed his intervention to provide confirmation – after all, I should have known all along. Now, nearly 20 years later, I still dine out on the story and get a laugh with the punchline.

It was Chelsea versus Tottenham Hotspur and, as the official programme reminds me, it was 'Football League Division One Season 1978–79, Saturday, 18 November, 3 p.m.'. I do not need much reminding of the match or the score – a 3–1 victory for Tottenham – although I had forgotten the exact date and I had certainly forgotten that the programme cost 25 pence. Scanning it now, it comes as a surprise to learn that, amidst all the hysteria about marketing being the product of the Thatcherite '80s, there were match sponsors – in this case a computer consultancy group – even then, in the last days of the Callaghan Government.

For all I know individual players were also sponsored. Why else would I have noted Betty and Denis Dodswell's name next to John Bumstead, the Chelsea sub that day? The programme, dug out from underneath the mound of cuttings in which it has lain ever since, reminds me that however much the hype may have changed, society has not. The first page of the Chelsea programme had an injunction against foul language and dirty songs, warning that 'from letters received, it is clear they are harming our Club'. And if Sky's introduction of live television on Monday nights led to the innovation of American-style cheerleaders before the match, even Chelsea in 1978 had a pre-match show. On that November afternoon, however, when Mrs Thatcher was still an aspiring housewife, instead of girls with pompoms showing us their legs we had dogs – Royal Air Force police dogs that jumped through hoops before the match and were supposed to return at half-time to provide a 'criminal attack' display. I cannot recall if they did. But even if I jump through imaginable hoops, I cannot for the life of me understand what I meant by writing on the back of the programme, just above the line-up, 'Max for Spurs, Zapp for Chelsea and Sailor for Chelsea' and next to Max's name this comment: 'a little too large for a colour photograph month of training and considerable'. The way the sentence trails off suggests I had been interrupted before I could complete it. The names may have been those of the mascots, but I suspect they were what the Alsatians were called.

It was just after the last of the Alsatians, Sailor perhaps, had jumped through the hoops that I received that tap on the shoulder. In fact, I had been expecting a tap not so much from a Chelsea season ticket-holder as from somebody far more important and it was a worry that had been with me from almost the moment that I left Mr Ghosh's house in Wood Green that morning to travel to Stamford Bridge. I had come to the match in a state of dread which, if not like the feeling my journalist guru, James Cameron, felt every morning as he stared at the blank page and feared they would rumble him, was just as real and quite distracting. Instead of taking the Piccadilly Line all the way to Knightsbridge, which would have been the logical route to Chelsea, I somehow found myself on the Circle Line heading for Liverpool Street, as if my destination was Upton Park or White Hart Lane. In the end I gave up and took a taxi to Stamford Bridge. I justified this to myself on the grounds that the portable typewriter I had borrowed from Rose was rather bulky but the fact is that I did not quite know how to approach the reporting of the game. Not that I was a virgin reporter. Far from it. I had been to grander stages than Stamford Bridge and covered international events. In the previous four years I had covered three Test series involving England, written on a variety of subjects ranging from archaeology through accountancy (for which I had even won a prize), to society and politics. My book on Keith Miller was about to be published and I was just finishing a heavyweight political biography.

But as the taxi dropped me near Stamford Bridge and I fished out the Chelsea press pass that said 'Sunday Times, Season 1978–79'. I knew that this journalistic occasion was different. I had barely go to the press box, on the upper tier of the then new East Stand and much better located than the present one, when I realised that whatever the virtues of Rose's typewriter is was quite the wrong thing for this place. The desk in front of me was far too small, so it balanced precariously with half the carriageway and the row of letters beginning A and Z hanging in mid-air.

The cover seemed so large that when I placed it in the aisle next to me I could fairly have been accused of causing an obstruction. At press boxes at Old Trafford, Lord's, Leeds, the Oval or even Bombay similar portable typewriters were the norm but now I realised that by bringing it to Stamford Bridge I was merely drawing attention to myself as the sort of journalist who did not quite belong there. Everyone else seemed to have a slim W.H. Smith notebook neatly tucked away in a gabardine raincoat. As conspicuous as I had felt carrying it up three flights of stairs, I felt an even greater fool as I replaced the cover and tried to hide the typewriter underneath my seat. The scene had all the markings of a Bateman cartoon.

Even without Rose's typewriter, the feeling that thousands of eyes were boring into me would have been hard to shake off. If sport introduces you to a special club, then sports reporting is even more specialised. To the sporting world at large sportswriters are often seen as a privileged minority – alternatively feared and resented. The vast majority of sports followers, having failed to become sportsmen themselves, see sportswriting as something they could easily do and despise those of us who have become supporters with typewriters – or now laptops – as ignorant and lazy. Football reporting is even more specialised, a niche even in this special interest club, and long before I arrived in Stamford Bridge I knew that for all my pretension to be a real journalist I could not claim to belong. This, after all, was my first time in a football press box. But the real reason I felt so self-conscious was that I feared that any moment somebody might discover the extraordinary circumstances which had brought me there. It felt like a very heavy secret, far heavier than Rose's typewriter.

Just six weeks earlier I had boarded an Air India plane in Bombay still unsure whether I should continue my curious double life of chartered accountant and part-time writer. Accountancy gave me the sort of lifestyle that the English had fashioned for themselves in India when they owned the place. My life, working as a partner of S.R. Batliboi & Co, the Indian accountancy operation of Arthur Young McClelland Moores, was not dissimilar to the one Imran Khan now condemns as the contemptible world of the brown sahibs. Housework was unknown to me as there were servants who cooked, cleaned and washed my clothes. The journey from home to office broadcast my status as a brown sahib. The servant carried my briefcase to the car, the chauffeur drove me to the office and, as the car drove up the driveway to the covered entrance of the tall multi-storeyed tower block by the warm sea that laps Bombay, a tall, uniformed man complete with beard, cap and baton, opened the door. Then, from somewhere underneath his armpit, a short little man, more of a boy, one of the office peons, shot out, grabbed my briefcase and ran in front of me to hold open the lift door. All the while people in faded beige uniforms, doormen and liftmen saluted me murmuring, 'Salaam', which I acknowledged with the distracted nod of the head I had so often seen my father employ.

Before I reached my desk I passed the outer office where a large telex machine clattered away all day and next to which was another desk with a typewriter and a young lady with long, twittering eyelashes ready with notebook to take dictation. In my spacious room there was a sofa where I could seat important clients and next to my desk a buzzer which would fetch peons eager to do my every bidding – Nirad Chaudhuri has written that nowhere else in the world but on the Indian sub-continent can a man be made to feel aristocratic quite so easily. What elsewhere would be a simple journey to the office made me feel like royalty.

When all this paled there was the rest and recreation that the English had bequeathed the Indians – the clubs. The firm paid for membership of the Saturday Club, where a decade earlier no Indian could become a member, and of South Club, home of Indian tennis, where the lawns had so impressed Tilden that he had pronounced them to be the best outside Wimbledon.

Occasionally the lady with the twittering eyelashes would be asked to break away from audit reports and ritual communications starting, 'Dear sir, we thank you for your letter dated, etc', to take down my mock imitation Tolstoy-style rumblings. I had, at one stage, put a typewriter on my desk, the sort of heavy manual typewriter then common in offices and newsrooms. But when I came back the next day I found the peon had moved it to the secretary's room and it had proved a source of some commotion. What was meant to spur me to write had been seen by my secretary as a gesture of rebuke. She felt that by placing a typewriter on my desk I was making an implied comment on her typing. After all, in her experience, who had ever heard of a boss typing his own letters? So my writing was done in stolen moments away from boring audit files and spurred by the hope that one day it would enable me to write that one great book we all believe we have within us and, by winning something or becoming sufficiently noticed, proclaim myself a full-time writer and with one bound escape accountancy.

This remained a closely guarded secret. I kept my writing world very separate from accountancy. It helped that most of my journalism and writing was for English newspapers and magazines so that hardly anybody in the office, or for that matter in India, knew that I wrote at all. My writing efforts and the fantasies I built round them were confined to my flat. I had a small electric typewriter in a corner of my living-room and next to it I stored one of the few perks of being a *Sunday Times* stringer – precious copies of the airmail edition of *The Sunday Times*. When the paper first started sending me copies I was tempted to imitate the character from the Somerset Maugham novel who always made sure he read the paper on a day that matched its print day. So Maugham's character always read Monday's *Times* on a Monday, irrespective of the day he received the paper in his lonely Malay outpost, his reason being that it made him feel he was really in England. However, this was too much like denial for me: I was always impatient to know how Tottenham or Surrey had done and, if their results were good, then I read and re-read them many times before cutting them out, much to my houseboy's chagrin.

In a marvellous example of recycling, old newspapers can always be sold to Indian paper merchants who then make them into paper packets to be sold by roadside vendors. When *The Sunday Times* first started arriving, the houseboy's eyes had lit up. He knew his tip from a newspaper from England would be higher than that from recycling *The Times of India*. But the first time he tried to sell my copies of *The Sunday Times* the paper merchant opened the paper and found gaping holes where match reports of Tottenham and Surrey had been. The houseboy got away by saying, 'Oh, the baba [child] in the house must have cut up the papers. I shall speak to the sahib.' There was, of course, no such baba and he never did speak to me. But after that whenever he saw me poised with the scissors he would come and stand by, very silently taking in the scene. On the first occasion I had asked, 'Do you want something?' He just shook his head and I treated it as one of those inexplicable things that some servants are apt to do. It was only much later I learned the reasons from my aunt, but by then it was too late.

As the chauffeur drove me that September night to Bombay's Santa Cruz airport for the trip to London, I was still enjoying the report of Tottenham's 2–1 away victory over Leeds which had gone some way to make up for the shock 7–0 defeat in the fourth match of the season at Liverpool. And, like my writing, the enjoyment was made all the greater because, as the car sped through the dark Bombay night, nobody, certainly not the servant in the front seat carrying my briefcase or my mother next to me, was privy to my mental attempts to picture how Lee and Taylor might have scored the two Tottenham goals. Mother was, in any case, busy offering her prayers to whatever gods she could reach. The route to the airport offered her many opportunities, taking us first past the giant statue of the Hindu goddess Lakshmi and then the church of St Mary at Bandra. My mother, who has never had any hesitation in offering prayers to all gods of whatever religion, folded her palms and bowed her head as we passed both shrines. Then, aware that I was not a great believer, she touched her folded palms to my forehead as if passing on the blessing. Praying came as naturally to my mother as conceding goals must have done that dismal Anfield afternoon for Tottenham, on this occasion, however, judging from her comments, her prayers were laced with a fervent plea that I would not return from England with a mem-sahib, an English wife. The idea of having an English daughter-in-law alarmed her even more than Balu, the little servant boy, cheating her with the milk money every morning.

As my mother asked the god's help in turning my mind away from irresistible English women, I debated Keith Burkinshaw's wisdom of dropping Hoddle – he had returned that very Saturday in a lucky 1–0 victory over West Bromwich Albion – combined with the slightly more personal thought of dropping myself from the Batliboi partnership and not returning at all to India.

In my suitcase was the half-completed manuscript of a political biography, along with supporting books and documents collected from such diverse places as the National Archives of India in Delhi, the Public Record Office in Kew and the Italian and German Foreign Ministry. They easily outweighed my clothes. As I paid the excess luggage bill, I knew I had a choice to make. My biography of Keith Miller, after some problems, was finally being published, having been rescued at Calcutta airport by Rose's brother, Mark. The political biography was also due to be published, although neither book offered a fortune. My advance on the Miller book was a mere £400 and, while the advance on the political biography was a bit more, already my research costs had exceeded the figure received. There was also a cloud surrounding its publication in that the publishing firm was no longer owned by William, who had commissioned me on a previous visit to London. That moment produced an indescribable sense of inner giddiness of joy and triumph and for many months, and even years, when accountancy drove me to the brink of despair, I saw that moment with William in the pub as encapsulating all the release I had imagined writing had to offer. One minute you are just a storyteller hoping to keep your end up until the next round, the next moment you have a contract and are being hailed as a possible best-selling author.

In my long years of studying and practising chartered accountancy I had secretly pined for that moment of release when the world would finally recognise me as a great writer. And quite like the way the national lottery lures its customers by promising sudden riches, I fantasised about the moment that would proclaim my worth and free me from the chains of audit files and certificates – unlike the lottery advertisements, however, I did not imagine it would take the form of a pointed finger dropping from the sky: I liked to think I was more of a realist and imagined the news would come in the form of a letter.

I had carefully choreographed my reaction to the news. I would go to the office and behave absolutely normally – hang my overcoat on the coat rack, settle down as normal at my desk – and then say quietly, 'I have just won the Booker Prize.' Then, while my fellow accountants gasped, I would push the file of audit papers away with such force it would land on the floor. I would yank back the chair, stand up erect and walk slowly to the door. I could not quite make up my mind whether I would leave my overcoat on the coat rack or in a final gesture lift it from the hook, roll it in a ball and toss it out the window. It was irritating not to be able to fix that detail, but that was the sort of minutiae which always gave me problems. Long before my literary fantasies, when I only nurtured sporting ones, I had never been able to make up my mind whether my Test century on my début at Lord's would come in 17 or 19 balls. The rest of my fantasy was pictured in meticulous detail.

I saw myself emerging from the Long Room on the first morning of a Test match with the score reading nought for four. The fourth wicket would have fallen with the last ball of an over. The next over would be a tense maiden. I would hit the first five balls of the first over I faced for six. But just as I did not know what to do with my coat, I could not decide whether I should hit a six off the last ball as well, which would mean equalling Gary Sobers' six sixes in an over – something that has never been done in a Test match (Sobers achieved it in a county match). My quandary was that this would mean I would lose the strike, so I settled for a three off the last ball of the over which meant I faced the first ball of the next over. The next over would see a repeat: six, six, six, six, six, three which would leave a third over of six, six, six, six, six and a final six to reach 100 and, of course, to hit six sixes in an over. I considered this scenario slightly more likely than scoring five goals in four minutes to turn a Cup final that my team were losing 3–0, with six minutes to go, into a 5–3 victory. My cricketing fantasies would end with a shout from my mother as my intended six chipped a piece of bedroom furniture; my literary fantasies with the cold print of a rejection slip.

That October evening at Heathrow, as Air India finally landed, it was the immigration officer who introduced the necessary dose of reality. I was what the immigration laws defined as an R/R, a returning resident. Although I had lived in England for many years before my return to India, I had never acquired a British passport. But my passport was stamped with the crucial words: 'The time limit on the holder's leave to enter the United Kingdom is hereby removed.' So I could come and go as I pleased and even vote in UK elections. But R/R imposed obligations as well. If I left the UK, I had to be back within two years. If I stayed away a day more than that, I lost my right to be a resident. Having left England in 1975, I had been away for more than three years, but I had preserved my precious R/R status by a brief visit of a month in October 1976. That had involved another subterfuge, if only a partial one. I had told my friends and relatives in India that I was going to England to collect a journalistic prize, which was true except that I did not need to collect the prize in person. I made the journey simply to retain my right as a resident. In the dim recesses of my mind was the thought that escape from accountancy might one day involve using R/R.

Now I was returning almost two years to the very day since that visit in 1976, reassured by the British Deputy High Commissioner in Bombay that there would be no problems. I waited with a sense of superiority as the long line of passengers from India disgorged from the Air India jumbo. The people in front of me were what my aunt called the '*lota, kambal* army', her sneering depiction of what she saw as the Indian peasantry. Whenever she saw them travelling she expressed surprise that they could afford to and was even more condescending about their habits of carrying a *kambal*, a blanket, and a *lota*, a pot. My instincts, shaped by the Jesuits and then by the *New Statesman*, was to rebuke her for her crude prejudices but when it came to waiting on immigration officers at Heathrow, or elsewhere, I could not help sharing some of my aunt's contempt. In colour they may look like me, but why, they couldn't even speak English, and although I would never admit it publicly, I derived some sardonic amusement from their linguistic struggles with the immigration officer as they tried to explain why they wanted to enter the country.

As far as I was concerned the worst I expected from an immigration officer was a muttered, 'Welcome home', then, after a meaningful pause, 'Sir', indicating that even as he was reconfirming the right of abode in my passport, he did not really consider that England was my home. For me that was how petty officials behaved the world over and I harboured no fears.

But this time, while the *lota, kambal* brigade' I had secretly derided went through, I waited and waited at the immigration desk. The officer scanned my passport. Instead of picking up the stamp which would mark R/R, he turned to a file of important-looking papers and kept turning the pages back and forth. Suddenly my stomach muscles knotted and, as I began to feel I was much worse off than the '*lota, kambal* brigade', I heard with something approaching shock that my precious R/R had lapsed. I was no longer a resident. The officer reasoned that my stay outside the UK for three-and-a-half years, despite the month-long visit in October 1976, meant I had lost my right to live in this country. I was using R/R as a flag of convenience and my absence away for all but three years clearly indicated I had no desire to live in the UK and could not claim to be a true resident.

So whereas in the past my passport had been stamped as given leave to enter for an indefinite period, he now stamped: 'Leave to enter the United Kingdom is hereby given for six(6) months.' It was the sort of stay visitors are given and I knew the imprecise fantasy of resigning my partnership at Batliboi and retreating to a garret somewhere behind Russell Square to finish my novel was no longer feasible. But the immigration officer's decision had also thrown down a challenge. Had he reconfirmed my R/R I might, after a month, have gone back to India content to postpone my literary fantasy. Now the die was cast. The more I looked at the wretched stamp the more determined I was to fight it, to prove that I genuinely wanted to live in the UK. I could hardly do that if, after a month, I returned to India. It was soon obvious to me that if I was to get even closer to the Booker Prize fantasy I had not only to give up accountancy but also India. Within a week there was an added reason to remain. Serena.

She was one of the many who had replied to my advertisement for a secretary to type up the political biography. We met one evening. A drink led to a meal and as we emerged from the Italian restaurant outside Finchley Road tube station, she offered me her very full and inviting lips. During the meal she had offered me her fingers to hold and half an hour later, back in her flat, there was much more of her wonderful anatomy to explore. Now as I cajoled the Home Office to reconfirm my resident status, her flat above the supermarket and bang opposite the Swiss Cottage Odeon provided all the solace, not to say prompting, that I needed.

I doubt if Serena typed even a page of the manuscript but she did type the letter I wrote on 6 November 1978, within days of the Home Office returning my right to live in this country that the immigration officer had confiscated. The letter was to my partners in India. Addressing them as 'Gentlemen' I described how I was writing 'probably the most important and difficult letter of my life', informing them of my decision to give up accountancy for writing. William would later read the letter and say, 'Rather theatrical, I think. Don't you? I suppose you wrote it for posterity to read.'

If truth be told, nearly two decades later it does not read quite so well, although the sentiment that writing was the only true vocation of my life was a genuine one. I did and still do feel remorse that I had not taken to journalism at 17 when I left school instead of trying first to be an engineer, which meant I ended up at Loughborough, then eventually fleeing to London to become a member of the English Institute of Chartered Accountants. Re-reading it now I can hardly believe what I wrote to my sweet, unsuspecting Indian partners: 'I have been feeling uneasy about my life and career for some time. It is only now, at the age of 31, that I realise I have done nothing. If I should die tomorrow, who will remember me? Nobody except a few generous relatives who have put up with my appalling behaviour and a few kind friends. This may sound grandiloquent nonsense for me. But I do believe that if I take writing seriously I can leave some work behind that future generations will find useful. As an accountant I have nothing to offer.'

If that was not bad enough, I was even more theatrical in my letter to my parents, asking them to consider me dead and disinherit me, but at the time it all seemed to make wonderful sense. I can still picture Serena, her skirt riding high, sitting at her desk in front of her new electric typewriter of which she was so proud, and where a little golf ball kept pace with her manicured fingers, while next door her father arranged and rearranged his array of dentures. And as the words poured out, Serena murmured her approval, which meant a lot then but now makes me realise that the touch of melodrama I showed was not confined to Hindi movies of my youth.

I may have heightened the melodrama because I was aware that I was reversing the usual scenario for such dramatic partings. Exile in the Indian tradition is very much like in any other: the banishment comes as a result of failure, misdemeanour or betrayal. Indians tend to prefer betrayal as a theme for banishment and had there been an Indian version of the Oscar Wilde story then some dark satanic betrayal would have figured very strongly. Not long before I composed my letters, a popular Indian film had, for the first time, treated the question of divorce where the hero and heroine find their life ruined by the heroine's scheming rich relations who despised the husband's poverty. In the final scene the heroine tries to return to her true love but when she knocks on his door she discovers he has gone away. The people who now live there tell her he has gone to England to recover from his broken dreams. Many years later when one of my accountancy colleagues came to London on a visit he asked me why I had left. When I told him it was to write, he listened then tapped me on the arm and said, 'I understand. You have to say this. I heard there was a betrayal. That partner [he mentioned a name] resented your success as an accountant and conspired against you.' I could not shake him from his conviction that I must have given up my houseboys, servants, peons, secretary, chauffeur-driven cars and membership of various clubs for something more than the hope of bashing out words for a newspaper. Perhaps I might have made him understand had I told him that this was, in effect, a belated bid for freedom. But I could not tell him, any more than I could my partners or parents, fearing they may not understand or feel very insulted.

English writers like V.S. Pritchett have told us how they made their dash for freedom but in this case it was at the age of 20 and all it required was getting on a train to the Gare du Nord. I was doing it at 30 and, unlike Pritchett in Paris, there was no Mr Hotchkiss waiting for me in London. I did have just over £700 in the bank but no prospect of regular income and nowhere to sleep except the sofa in Mr Ghosh's living-room. Fortunately, I soon discovered that although I had forsaken accountancy I could still write about it and a couple of weeks before my journey to Stamford Bridge I had begun to write for a magazine aimed at accountants. And there was *The Sunday Times*, whose stringer I had been in India for the previous three years, and who were now quite eager that I write for them.

These events brought me to Chelsea that day, although I could hardly have anticipated the circumstances. Just before leaving India I had done the radio commentary on a football match between a local Calcutta team, Mohun Bagan, and Cosmos, the New York side which included Pele. The great man's arrival in Calcutta had caused such a stir that the newly elected local Marxist government declared it would rebuild Calcutta's roads – an almost impossible promise, given the state of Calcutta's roads – and at midnight 30,000 people turned up at Calcutta airport to welcome Pele. Almost 100,000 attended the match and I wrote a story about Pele in Calcutta for *The Sunday Times*.

Although I had written for various sections of the paper, the Pele piece was the first for the sports pages and when I got to London I found that

John Lovesey, the sports editor, who had an eye for offbeat stories, was taken by it. Once I had sorted my R/R and got to Gray's Inn Road he was quite keen to use me as a match reporter. I could easily have gone to a rugby match but I expressed a preference for football, and so it was that I was at Chelsea that Saturday.

But while had I played the game since my schooldays and followed it in India and England for almost 20 years, this was the first English football match I reported. I was that odd reporter: a journalist with experience but a virgin to English league football. This was the mental baggage that had accompanied me to the Chelsea press box and at any moment I expected all of it to come tumbling out. So when, just after the dogs had retired and just before the public announcer gave the teams, the season ticket-holder tapped me on the back I was not surprised.

What I was not prepared for was his question: 'Who are you reporting this match for – *The Southall Express*?'

For a moment I thought it was a wind-up from a colleague in the press box – there was another row of press seats behind me – but I turned round to find a man leaning forward from the rows of season ticket-holders behind the press box, wearing a leather jacket and a smile that was more a smirk than a true laugh.

It did turn to laughter when I replied, 'No, *The Sunday Times*.'

'Cor blimey! Brian Glanville must have changed colour.'

Was he perhaps making a wide, wittier reference to the growing presence of immigrants in football? After all that was the first time Osvaldo Ardiles appeared at Stamford Bridge – his signing along with Ricky Villa by Spurs at the beginning of the season was still something of a sensation. Villa was a sub that day and his name was considered so unfamiliar that as the announcer gave the line-up he spelled it out. For the next hour and a half I did not have much time to think about what the man had said; soon the teams had taken the field and there was the consuming struggle to make sure I got the semicolons in the right place.

The Sunday Times insisted – and still does – that teams be filed in the formation they assume on the field. Not for *The Sunday Times* just listing the teams as they are printed on the programme. What they wanted to know was how they had lined up: was it the usual English flat back four signified by 4–4–2 or the rarer 4–4–3 or some other formation? The accepted style was to distinguish the group making up the back four from the midfield by a semicolon. So, as my programme notes show, I busily scribbled down the numbers on the players backs and placed semicolons after them. Chelsea: 3–5–6–2 semicolon, 7–8–10 semicolon, 11–9–7 semicolon, which indicated a 4–4–2 formation. Spurs in contrast had: 2–4–5–3 semicolon, 7–8–6 semicolon and 10–9–11 semicolon, which meant a 4–3–3 formation with Hoddle playing as a sort of third striker, supporting Lee and Taylor.

It was only after five o'clock when I had returned to the warmth of the pressroom and John, the short, rather sweet pressroom steward, had given me a large whisky that the full import of what the season ticket-holder said struck me. Even more slowly I realised that it could be turned to my advantage. This may have been my very first football match report for *The Sunday Times* but I had for many years diligently memorised all those tips on how to become a writer. Rule One, read the publication you want to write about: I had read the match reports endlessly and often. Brian Glanville got some 800 words and actually appeared to tell you what happened in a match; none of the other match reporters got more than about 350 words, which seemed to be an excuse for the writer to tell a few jokes and ignore what happened in the match. It made the match reporter a cross between a comic turn and a social reporter and I was attracted by the genre.

I had been particularly taken by the style of Chris Lightbown, who had written a match report on Manchester United versus Spurs. The match was a bore so Lightbown decided to ignore it completely and devoted his entire piece to the number of flags and boxes round Old Trafford. The subs of *The Sunday Times* were also given their head in those days and this report was headlined: 'Flags 43, Boxes 27, United 0'. Even more than this I liked his piece which painted the picture of the Wolves press box. The players or the play hardly featured. Instead, Lightbown made the veteran local reporter the hero of his report. Lightbown described how, throughout the match, he rarely if ever looked up from his book of crosswords except to utter, 'Brains in their balls', when Wolves played badly, which they did for most of the afternoon. Once, when they scored, he did look up to ask, 'What time? Who scored? Who passed the ball?' noted it down and went back to his crossword. The Sunday after Lightbown's 'report' appeared *The Sunday Times* carried a little paragraph saying, much as they do in the credits for movies or on the inside jackets of novels, that any resemblance between the local reporter mentioned in Lightbown's piece and the real life reporter was purely incidental. Clearly the local reporter had complained, although *The Sunday Times* apology made it seem as if Lightbown had imagined a fictional reporter and transposed him to Molineux.

I could not quite match this feat but as the six o'clock deadline neared, and fortified by a second stiff whisky from John, I felt sufficiently bold to lead my report with a recital of the conversation with the Chelsea season ticket-holder. Then, desperately searching to find a connection between that and the game I had to report, I went on, 'Good London wit also found expression in this London derby. English football is alive and well, if still requiring the help of immigrants.'

This was the cue to contrast Ardiles's play with that of the Englishmen on the field and after all that it was relatively simple to describe the match with the result that it seemed as if the goal that Langley had scored to give Chelsea the lead added to the two Lee scored and the one Hoddle hit to give Tottenham the 3–1 victory all seemed to flow from my having been mistaken for the reporter from *The Southall Express*. I ended my report by saying that, as well as Spurs played, 'what they will have to do to get in *The Southall Express*, I don't know'. Lightbown's apology suggested he had created a mythical reporter; I had no need for such fiction but thanks to the season ticket-holder's question I had the next best thing to work on – a denial that I worked for a mythical newspaper.

I had expected a reaction, a chortle perhaps, even an 'oh', when I dictated the copy but the lady who took it down said nothing. She was probably exhausted by her efforts to understand how my name was spelled – in the end it was misspelt and appeared in the paper with an imaginary 'h' in Bose. When I rang the desk for my check call half an hour later, this time fortified by another whisky in the pub opposite Stamford Bridge, I felt I could be the subject of yet another Bateman cartoon: the man who tried to tell a joke but could not get the audience to react. Certainly I got no reaction from the man I came to know so well, Stan Levenson, then the football editor of *The Sunday Times*. His first words to me were, 'You overwrote.'

'Sorry.'

'We wanted 350 words, not a novel. But never mind. That is what we have subs for.'

'Er,' I mumbled, desperate to find out what had happened to the introduction, 'I started that way because I thought . . .'

'Oh that,' he cut in brusquely, 'very funny.' Then a sudden 'Got to go' and he had put the phone down.

That evening I was tortured by the thought that the introduction may have been left on the cutting-room floor and just to make sure it got an audience I narrated the story over dinner to Dominic and his soon to be wife. Dominic was much taken by the tale which eased my anguish, although this was also helped by the quite breathtaking physical gifts, Thelma, the waitress, brought to the serving of the meal. Enough to last me through the night and even overcome my phobia of dogs as I crashed out on Dominic's living-room with Hamish and Kazan, his two Alsatians, in close attendance.

Next morning, as I lay petrified and still while they nuzzled near my mouth, Dominic burst in with *The Sunday Times*, threw it in my direction and said, 'See, they used your intro. I knew you would get colour in somehow, you old racialist.' We laughed uproariously. But now that I look back, I should have questioned Dominic's use of the word racialist. I had not meant to make a racial point when using the story in *The Sunday Times*, merely to introduce the sort of humour that I thought would match Lightbown and impress Lovesey. The supporter was making an unmistakable reference to the general stereotype of the sub-continental immigrant – Paki, therefore must come from Southall; in the press box, so let's have a crack about *The Southall Express*, they must have a paper like that, mustn't they? On reflection, it seems more an expression of the bewilderment he felt in seeing a man with my obvious background in that situation. After all, I was the only person with a genuine suntan in the press box and, probably, in the entire ground. Remember, this is 1978, Viv Anderson has yet to play for England, and the idea of half or more of a league team being black would have sounded bizarre to everyone connected with English football. That day, needless to say, neither Chelsea nor Tottenham had a black player.

Much has changed in the 18 years since then. I have been to many football press boxes. Chelsea is by no means unique and a lot better than most. Not all the experiences have been unpleasant. Indeed, now when I go to Chelsea, with the press box much nearer the fans, I am even recognised and pleasant words are exchanged. Many of the experiences have been extremely happy and rewarding, although a few have been so unnerving that I have come close to abandoning football reporting. I have been chased by Arsenal fans, mocked by Manchester United fans, told to go back to Bangladesh – a country I have never been to – by Watford fans, spat at by Leeds fans and assaulted by Chelsea fans. I have seen the face of hate but I like to think I have acquired sufficient detachment to even try and explain this very English phenomenon to those who may not be familiar with it.

Yet in this, the people's game, the game that Arthur Hopcraft described not as a sport but as something 'inherent in the people . . . built into the urban psyche, as much a common experience to our children as are uncles and schools', I remain the outsider. For me the promise the English game seemed to hold out when I had fallen in love with it as I opened the pages of *The Times of India* that May day in 1961 has yet to be fulfilled.

It is this gap between promise and reality that is the burden of this book, although the betrayal of promise is not merely racial. Indeed, the English sporting alienism of which I speak is a much wider phenomenon where the question of race can often be peripheral or arise in ways that are not immediately obvious. It affects not merely those who are black or brown but even people of the same colour and extends to those who run the English game. It is about a sporting culture that has never been able to come to terms with its own creations, let alone understand how these creations affect others. It is the gap between an England which, just as it acquired an Empire in piecemeal fashion, also, almost accidentally, created games that have since gone round the world and captivated millions. Yet the echoes of their journey into other countries never seem to have returned to the mother country, never seem to fill England with pride about the wonder it has wrought; the English never consider that the unique sporting games they devised have changed the lives of millions who, like me, fell in love with them and, therefore, England.

This was vividly brought home to me, yet again, during the course of writing this book. A press visit took me to Antigua in the company of some cricket writers and the conversation turned to football. One of my fellow journalists, a gentle, kindly man who had spent many years reporting northern football before turning to cricket, mentioned how on one of his trips following Manchester United to Eastern Europe he had been with Bobby Charlton and was astonished to hear the young people of the city chanting his name, 'Bobby, Bobby'. 'I couldn't understand how they knew Charlton's name,' he commented, still mystified after all those years. As he told me the story I thought of my friend, Umesh, and how 30 years ago he might have been such a boy had Charlton visited Bombay.

It is the sporting equivalent of what Nirad Chaudhuri in his autobiography *Thy Hand, Great Anarch!* calls the greatest failure of British imperialism in India. Chaudhuri's point is that British rule in India renovated and revitalised a Bengali culture that had 'become almost fossilised culturally. British rule, by bringing European cultural influences to bear on Indian life, created what was virtually a new culture'. It led to the Bengali renaissance and in turn to the Indian renaissance, which gave rise to modern Indian ideas of nationhood and nationalism.

But even as the Indians took to British culture, the British resented it. 'With the exception of a very small number of very wise British administrators, and the missionaries generally, this new culture and its creators, i.e. the Bengalis, were hated by the local British. They did not like the adoption of their culture by the Indians, and displayed throughout British rule an unmeasured rancour against the activity. In this lay the greatest failure of British imperialism in India, for no empire can last without practising cultural proselytisation. The British in India rejected this role. Their attitude presented a total contrast to that of the Romans, who were true imperialists . . . They felt proud to have given peace to the Mediterranean world, but were not ashamed to confess that the conquered Greeks conquered them culturally. The British were not required to adopt Indian culture, and were expected only to spread their own culture. Even this inspired them with horror, and their abuse of the Bengali and other Indians who were assimilating European culture was not only unrestrained but indecent and aggressive. This behaviour is unparalleled in the history of all civilised peoples in ancient or modern times.'

In the sporting context there had been not so much horror as total ignorance about the idea of any people other than the English adopting the games England had created. And when Englishmen have encountered love and understanding for the English game in far corners of the world, they have come back surprised, unable to believe what their eyes have seen or their ears heard.

Nobody has expressed this English bewilderment better, albeit unwittingly, than Arthur Hopcraft. His book, *The Football Man*, is a classic of the game. It focuses on the 1960s but with some of the characters like Ken Bates still around, it has tremendous contemporary relevance. When I first read it, I kept admiring Hopcraft's facility with the language and his ability to express the complex emotions I have felt when watching soccer. That is until I came to the last paragraph of page 220.

This is a chapter devoted to what Hopcraft calls 'Football and Foreigners'. Here Hopcraft goes over the by now familiar story of how English soccer had for years been insular, shunning both the World Cup and European competitions until, led by Matt Busby, they were forced to change. Writing just after the 1966 World Cup, Hopcraft is convinced that English footballing insularity has been overcome at last and, as evidence, cites the crowds which turned up at Liverpool, Goodison and Villa Park to watch World Cup matches not involving England. Then, having painted the picture of a new, aware English soccer, he turns to the North Koreans, in many ways the surprise team of the tournament: 'And then there was the delirious affection which the Middlesbrough crowd developed for the tiny North Koreans, with their extraordinary three-part names – Li Chan Myung, Han Bong Zin, Lim Zoong Sun, Oh Yoon Kyung – who were billeted at the local airport . . . When they beat Italy 1–0 to win a place in the quarter-finals, the crowd fell upon them in hysterical acclaim. My lasting memory from that match is of a tall British sailor lugging two Koreans off the pitch, one under each arm, like prizes . . . These World Cup matches had all the anger, the soaring tension, the love of triumph and the pathos of defeat that attend the football which British crowds follow week by week. Watching these crowds absorbed as if personally involved in these confrontations of foreign teams, it seems unbelievable that only a few years before the national leadership of our game had turned a cold shoulder to organised international competition. This public response confirmed conclusively that football belongs to the people, that it is the conflict and the setting which possess them in their ownership. In a matter of days a dark, slant-eyed footballer with a name like a nonsense rhyme can be adopted as a personal representative by a Middlesbrough labourer just because he is expressing hope and liberation through the one art the labourer fully comprehends . . . East and West are undoubtedly linked at Middlesbrough.'

Until I read those words I thought Hopcraft had been speaking to me personally. It is always the hallmark of a good writer and a great book – and in the football context Hopcraft's book qualifies on both counts – that he or she makes you feel you are the only reader in the world to whom the words are addressed. I had experienced that emotion from the moment I read Hopcraft's first two sentences: 'Sport can be cruel to men. Football can make a man more ridiculous even than drink can.' As I read further I nodded my head in agreement and not a little envy that he had found the words that expressed my own feelings so well.

But, as I read about dark, slant-eyed foreigners with names that evoked nonsense rhyme, I realised that Hopcraft was not speaking to me at all. Remove the reference to slant-eyed, and those North Koreans could be me. I am, if anything, darker and my name does not even have the consolation of sounding like nonsense rhyme. It is so difficult that for many years when I telephoned *The Sunday Times* copytakers and told them my name – 'I have some football copy and I am Mihir' – they would interrupt me to say, 'Me here, do you say? I know you are there, but what is your name? You can't just say "Me here", we have got to put your name.' Then, after I had slowly spelled it out: 'M for mother, O for orange, etc', I would proceed to give copy, although even then it required vigilant subs to make sure I was not spelled Mickhail or even Micky Booze. Sometimes copytakers proved so obdurate that there were occasions when I thought that maybe it would have been preferable to have changed places with the North Koreans and been lugged away under some Middlesbrough sailor's arms.

Don't get me wrong. My point about Hopcraft's book is not that it is not politically correct. I have never laid any great store by such wretched modern terms. Hopcraft clearly means well and he is entitled to describe the North Koreans or, for that matter, Indians or any race or nationality in any way he sees them. What jolts is the realisation that the world I thought belonged to me for 220 pages turns out on page 221, suddenly, without warning, not to be mine at all. It is like being on a train that is meant to take me to Brighton, say, then finding at Haywards Heath, where the train divides, that only the first four coaches are bound for Brighton. What is more, the Brighton portion has gone and I, being in the fifth, have been left behind at Haywards Heath and find myself bound for Lewes.

More fool you, you say. Why didn't you look before you got on the train which coaches were going to Brighton? The answer is that unlike British Rail trains no such sporting warning was ever given to me when I fell in love with English sport. Nobody told me, 'Beware! You are falling in love with games and teams which, while having a universal feel about them, are really very parochial expressions of a particular, intensely nationalist, country and, what is more, the country may not care whether you play its games or not.'

More significant and worrying is that even a writer of such sensitivity as Hopcraft fails to appreciate, let alone tackle, the fact that English soccer, like other English sports, such as cricket, rugby, tennis or golf, has by spreading across the world acquired a dimension that makes it no longer purely English. Like the Romans, the English created an imperialism, a sporting imperialism which civilised and taught the nations of the world the team games they should play, how they should play them and the joy, burdens, obligations and ethics these wonderful creations can impose. But, unlike the Romans, who dubbed everyone drawn into their civilisation as a Roman, irrespective of their origin or colour, the English seem bewildered and surprised that the world should play their games, or even know anything about them.

Of course it could be argued that if football, cricket and other English games have been taken up by the rest of the world, surely that is their responsibility. Why should the English and their sports be burdened by the consequences? If these countries have not had the wit or the imagination to devise their own games, it only shows how superior the English are. I am quite happy to concede that the English ability to invent these games does prove their sporting superiority, at least as far as team games are concerned. But the fact remains that these games were propagated as part of the imperial adventure, and just as the imperialists had a duty to spread the

English culture, to make sure the people they were conquering and civilising took to British ways, so the people who organised the games of England had, and have, a duty to take into account the effect their creations have had beyond England. Or, if that is asking for the moon, at least to be aware that many millions who never having seen England would know, or feel they know, about it by reading descriptions of Tottenham at White Hart Lane and by listening to Henry Blofeld describing the number ten bus going down Harleyford Road in the course of a day's play at the Oval.

Here, a story from Roman Britain, as told by Sheppard Frere in *Britannia: A History of Roman Britain*, might make my point. In the small town of Borough on the Humber (Petuaria) a Roman citizen, M. Ulpius Ianuarius, gifted a theatre and erected a tablet in honour of the Domus Divina of Antoninus Pius and the deified emperors. It was a very Roman scene but outside the town the Celts had buried the local priest. The burial rite was inhumation accompanied by a native iron-bound wooden bucket and two sceptres. It was a traditional rite and to emphasise its non-Roman character the two sceptres had been intentionally bent and broken to devitalise them for the journey to the otherworld. Frere writes, 'Nothing could illustrate better the dual character of Roman-British civilisation. Outwardly it was Roman, inwardly it remained Celtic, yet it would be wrong to suppose an inner conflict between the two aspects. The result was a synthesis, intended by Rome, and welcomed by the British people as they came to realise the advantages of peace and wealth conferred by membership of the empire.'

I had long ago accepted the advantages of belonging to the English sporting empire. I knew no other and cared nothing for any indigenous sports the Indians might have had – the only one we ever played at school, *kabbadi*, was treated as a joke on a par with marbles. My problem was on growing up to discover that there is no English sporting M. Ulpius Ianuarius who, let alone tolerate a synthesis, is even prepared to accept that I, and many people like me, may have a claim to membership of this sporting empire; the most glorious and unique in the annals of the sporting man.

It has been said that the creator or coloniser often knows little of what he has created. C.L.R. James in *Beyond a Boundary* had only to ask the question, 'What do British people know of what they have done there?', to answer it. What I didn't realise until much later was that I had fallen for an export-only version of English sport, one that proclaimed a universality but whose allure concealed an insularity that could turn ugly. This meant that people like me would always be somewhat outside, always somewhat alien. Whatever we did and however much we proclaimed our love, we would be the untouchables of the English sporting scene, like those shunned for centuries by my high caste Hindu ancestors and treated much as my mother treated the sweeper who came to clean our toilets at home. Every morning a small door away from the kitchen would be opened and a small bow-legged woman would come and clean the loos, have a cup of tea in a special cup, squatting on her haunches on the kitchen floor, and depart. Never did she enter the main house and while my mother recognised she was useful – nobody else would clean the loos and she had therefore to be tolerated – it did not mean she had to be accepted as equal.

The only difference between the sporting exclusion I speak of and the one my mother practised on the sweeper was that if I had ever taxed my mother about it she would proclaim that it was not discrimination at all but part of the ancient Aryan code as laid down in the hoary old Manu Smriti. English sport, in contrast, held out the promise of a worldwide membership, equal in every way to the rights and privileges available for people in this country. But when we decided to take it up and demanded those rights they expressed surprise and astonishment.

In that sense our position was not very different to the American blacks who, having read in their constitution that all men are born equal, had to struggle against the fact that the men who wrote these words themselves employed slaves and saw no contradiction between their words and their deeds. I realise we should guard against the ease of the rear-view present-day look at the past. As the South African writer Alister Sparks has pointed out, slavery was tolerated by all societies, black, white or brown, and all religions from the pagan to the High Church, until it became a great issue of conscience in the early part of the 19th century.

Nevertheless, the sporting contradiction remains and is the burden of this book – the contradiction that a country which has the genius to devise the most beautiful and intricate of sports, beyond the imagination of any other country, games that can instantly appeal to millions round the world, cannot appreciate how its sporting creations have affected those people and why they should claim them as their own.

Kipling had branded my Bengali ancestors who had so eagerly taken to English education as Calibans. In 1913, as Rabindranath Tagore became the first Asian to win the Nobel Prize for Literature, Kipling, instead of glorying in the fact that it was the English education Bengalis had received which had produced Tagore, wrote to Rider Haggard denouncing Macaulay's policy of producing Indians who were English in everything but the colour of their skin.

Many years after I had taken to English sport I realised that there is a sporting equivalent to his literary reaction. We had fallen in love with English sport expecting to be welcomed to a sporting Camelot, only to find ourselves treated as sporting Calibans.

CHAPTER TWO

The Making of a Sporting Camelot

The day the doors of English sporting Camelot opened for me was 8 May 1961. It was a Monday and *The Times of India* featured a photograph showing the Spurs double team parading the Cup and League trophies through the streets of north London. The trophies were being carried on an open-top double-decker bus that looked very like the BEST (Bombay Electric Supply and Transport) buses so familiar to me – no wonder, for Bombay had bought the old buses that London Transport did not need.

Recently I looked up the photograph and it was as I remembered, grainy black and white, except that I had forgotten how startlingly white the bus looked, as if it had been coloured in with crayon, and even whiter than the two hand-painted white signs reading, 'Private, Private'. As it makes its way up the Tottenham High Road between Edmonton and Tottenham Town Halls the bus seems to be escorted by a line of policemen shepherding a large, happy crowd who look more curious than boisterous. Behind them are council flats packed with people and overhead are the tram cables. Ron Henry holds the championship trophy and Peter Baker the FA Cup. I cannot in all honesty claim I remembered all those details and my devotion to Tottenham has never reached that of Irving Scholar, the former chairman. His test for every aspiring girlfriend was: can you name the double team? And if they couldn't instantly recite Brown, Baker,

Henry, Blanchflower, Norman, Mackay, Jones, White, Smith, Allen, Dyson, the relationship did not progress much beyond the initial cocktails.

But my love for Tottenham was sufficiently strong that the following season the first thing I turned to on Monday mornings was the results of the previous Saturday's English League matches – they came too late for inclusion on a Sunday – only to find a club called Ipswich, a place I had to look up on the map, had deprived Tottenham of a second consecutive double. It saddened me but also in a curious way strengthened my loyalty for I was used to my favourite sporting teams 'flattering to deceive', a phrase I had often seen in *The Times of India.* Having fallen in love with Tottenham, I was determined not to abandon it even when my friend, Umesh, challenged me with his adoration of Manchester United. We argued long and hard about the respective merits of Denis Law and Jimmy Greaves, having followed Greaves's unhappy move to Milan and return to Tottenham. How I raged when Ramsey dropped Greaves in the final stages of the 1966 World Cup.

The only truce I had with Umesh was when the name of Bobby Charlton came up. Much as I loved Tottenham, Charlton was like a god who occupied a special plane, epitomising the promise the English sporting world held out to me, the promise to open the door to the unique, wondrous world where skill reigned supreme and sportsmanship was never in doubt; a world I had first glimpsed when as a nine-year-old I saw Tom Graveney score a hundred in each innings of a friendly match at the Brabourne Stadium. The beauty Graveney produced was so great that not even Fred Trueman, who broke the fingers of Vijay Hazare – my favourite Indian batsman – could dim it. Trueman may have been a great English devil who ate Indian batsmen for breakfast but my mind was filled with Graveney, the English enchanter. I can still see him elegantly stretch his left leg and stroke the ball through the covers so sweetly that he had hardly finished the stroke before it was hitting the concrete just in front of the East Stand where I sat. Elegant, said the retainer my father had assigned to escort me to the match, and elegant repeated I, not quite sure what the word meant but certain it was a term of approval.

Not long after this a cousin gave me Graveney's *Cricket Through The Covers* as a birthday present and I read and re-read it many times, not least his praise of my hero Subash Gupte and his prediction that in 1959 Gupte's leg spin would devastate England. I raged when it did not come true but that was nothing like the anger I felt when someone, I believe the servant who every morning dusted the furniture with a piece of felt cloth, tipped a pot of ink on the book. Despite this and the fact that it stained a horrible dark blue, including the picture of W.G. Grace, I kept the book and refused to let my mother throw it away. Around that time I had also become a Surrey supporter – they were in the middle of their seven championships in a row sequence – and eagerly lapped up Jim Laker's *Over To Me*, although I wasn't sure how to take his criticisms of Peter May. However, when Surrey banned Laker from the Oval, I felt personally slighted.

Besides that, of course, at school and at home I had received a whole host of signs which made England seem all the time like the land of super sportsmen, the veritable factory of sporting dreams. After I played in my first football match at my Jesuit school, Father Fritz, who took us for sports and English (his advice to Sunil Gavaskar, two years my junior, was: block the good length ball, the rest wallop), fixed a photograph on the school noticeboard purporting to be from the match. It turned out to be a photograph of an English first division game which had been reproduced in an Indian sports magazine and, if my memory serves me right, showed Dave Mackay tackling some other burly player. Fritz had just scratched out their names and replaced them with those of two of my school team-mates. He explained it was not meant to deceive. He wanted us to look at the photograph of those huge English players, study their technique and seek to emulate them.

Even without Fritz's bizarre way of providing an English role model, reports and descriptions of England at play were all about us. Every week there was the *Sport and Pastime*, the awkward-looking A5-sized magazine, which you could not slip too easily under the bedclothes for reading after the lights were put out. Full of action photographs of English sport – football in winter, cricket in the summer and all-year-long reprints of articles from the English press – it made us feel we were not 6,000 miles away but in the grandstand. Since these articles were often from newspapers like the *Daily Express* and the *Daily Mail* they were an early introduction of the popular style of reporting so different to the almost Victorian prose used in *The Times of India*.

In the summer even *The Times of India* easily, effortlessly, allowed English sports like cricket and tennis to take over its sports pages. In general foreign news always took precedence over domestic news – 500 deaths from cholera a small news item, 16 miners killed in Belgium meriting big headlines. Writers like Naipaul have seen this as a sign of the displacement of Indians in their own lands, people trying to mimic mature societies, but the summer emphasis on English sport seemed most natural and it fitted in neatly with the rhythms of the sporting season in India.

Indians may play sports all the year round but the major events take place mostly in winter. That is the time for Tests and domestic cricket, the important tennis competitions including the Davis Cup and also the major hockey, football and other sporting tournaments. Come May, and with it the unbearable heat, domestic sports carried on but in a much lower key.

The rains saw Bombay take to soccer and the Harewood League – the city's football league – but it was useless to pretend it could match the lure of a Lord's Test or Wimbledon tennis. So from early May through to September the sports pages of *The Times of India*, while reporting local sports, often led with English sporting stories. This was all the more convenient as one of the newspaper's former sports editors, an Englishman who had retired to England, carried on writing about English sports as if he was still editing the paper. Every now and again there was an Indian interest. At this time, in the early 1960s, there was always the Indian hope that Ramanathan Krishnan, who twice reached the Wimbledon semi-finals in 1961 and 1962 – both times losing to the eventual winner – would actually win the tournament. But even in the years when he failed, Wimbledon made the headlines. And English Test cricket always made a lead, even in 1960 when South Africa were the visitors.

Nothing could have illustrated England's sporting hold on us more emphatically. On the editorial pages *The Times of India* hardly had a kind word to say about South Africa, which was hardly surprising given that it was in the middle of bolstering its hated apartheid policy. And we were all aware that white South Africa did not want to have anything to do with us Indians. It had never played us, did not want to play us and it treated people of our colour abominably. But as far as the sports editor of *The Times of India* was concerned the fact that South Africa were playing England was not the issue, what mattered was that this was Test cricket from England and deserved not just a mention but often the top billing. So through that 1960 series I followed South Africa's progress, including the amazing throwing controversy of Griffin who finally ended up being no-balled at Lord's by Syd Buller.

Even when we read about Indians' progress in sports like cricket it was often refracted through English eyes. Vizzy, the Indian prince who looked like an owlish Indian Billy Bunter and despite being no more than a club cricketer had intrigued his way into the captaincy for the 1936 Indian tour of England – his most noteworthy feats were to arrive in England with 36 items of personal luggage and two servants, and to send the best Indian player home – had now become a commentator. One of his assistants carried a thick book to every Test which was full of cuttings from Cardus.

Every time Vizzy wanted to describe a stroke his assistant would open the book, Vizzy would select the appropriate Cardus phrase and recite it over the airwaves. Many years later I was to learn that this produced a quite extraordinary incident during the 1963–64 England tour of India. Vizzy had donated the pavilion at Delhi's Kotla ground where Test cricket is played, which entitled him to about four seats at the press box. However, on the day before the Test, E.M. Wellings, the correspondent of the *London Evening News*, along with John Clarke of the *Evening Standard*, arrived and selected the seats they would occupy for the next five days. The ones they chose were the seats Vizzy and his entourage normally used.

When Vizzy arrived with his party on the day of the Test, led by the assistant carrying the book of Cardus cuttings, to find Wellings and Clarke in occupation of their traditional seats, it produced a memorable scene. To Vizzy's request that the Englishmen move, Wellings replied, 'You may be the Maharaja of Vijayanagram but as far as I am concerned you are the Maharaja of fuck all. Now fuck off.' That seemed conclusive enough and it resulted in a sort of Mexican stand-off. It was made clear to Wellings that if he did not vacate the seat he would find himself barred from the ground the next day and the matter would be brought to the attention of Gore-Booth, the British High Commissioner who was also a great authority on Sherlock Holmes and Moriarty. But before Gore-Booth was called upon to solve the problem, Wellings saw sense and moved. However, he could no longer partake of Vizzy's hospitality – Vizzy, as was his custom, had put up a marquee during the Test, where the English cricket journalists were invited for lunch and tea – and had to get Ian Todd, a young reporter for *The Daily Herald*, to smuggle him back some food.

The story is now told as evidence of the cussed nature of Wellings but had I heard it as a schoolboy in Bombay it would only have confirmed my low opinion of Vizzy. Despite quoting Cardus, his unfortunate speaking voice, not remotely suited to radio – somewhere between a hoarse whisper and a strangulated cry – meant he more often than not sounded quite comical. We preferred our Cardus straight, as for instance his essay on Ranji which was part of our prescribed reading at school, or relayed to us through K.N. Prabhu, *The Times of India*'s legendary cricket correspondent. Not only did Prabhu often quote Cardus but his attempts to explain India, even our own Bombay, meant borrowing English imagery. Thus Shivaji Park, the vast, teeming ground in congested central Bombay which has produced a whole galaxy of cricketers who have played for India through to the present day Sachin Tendulkar, became in Prabhu's prose, the Pudsey of Indian cricket. It did not seem at all incongruous to us that we could appreciate Shivaji Park, which we passed on the way to the airport and where my father often took us because it housed his favourite Bengal Club, only by comparing it to the cradle of Yorkshire cricket which we had never seen. As far as Prabhu was concerned, by calling Shivaji Park the Pudsey of Bombay, Shivaji Park had been properly categorised, even redeemed. After all had not Pudsey produced Len Hutton, the ultimate batsman? Not having images and metaphors of our own, we borrowed shamelessly from England and even began to feel that they were part of our traditions.

In time this made us feel that things that were wholly English really belonged to us and we had as much, if not more, claim to them as the English. So every April when *Wisden* announced its five cricketers of the year, the *Evening News of Bombay* would prominently carry the names of the chosen five along with their photographs. If, on the odd occasion, an Indian was honoured, it would make the front page. But if there was no Indian, not only was there disappointment but a sense of anger. One leading sportswriter would always use the occasion to denounce *Wisden* and question its selection of the five cricketers of the year. If the list included a county cricketer who was not that well known in India, he would ask how his merits could outweigh the claims of some Indian cricketer who might have had an outstanding international season. This, in turn, would provide a launch pad from which to criticise *Wisden* for devoting quite so much space to English schools cricket when Indian cricket was dismissed in a couple of pages. The fact that *Wisden* was an English annual, whose primary task was to report and record English cricket, including schools cricket, made no impression on us. We felt that though the English may have created *Wisden* as their cricket annual, it belonged to us.

There was a perfectly good Indian equivalent of *Wisden – Indian Cricket* – but it has never acquired anything like the prestige of *Wisden* and I certainly never pined to buy a copy. So desperate was I to get my first *Wisden*, however, that I even allowed myself to be cheated. The bookseller to whom I had given my carefully hoarded money kept promising he would get me a copy then, as the summer was coming to an end, he disappeared never to return. Although my 16 rupees (then equivalent to one pound sterling) could hardly have been a factor, in my anger and confusion I imagined it was a conspiracy to deny me. I had to wait until I travelled to London where almost the first thing I did was buy a *Wisden* and feel I had at last achieved a great ambition.

Even when India played in England – all too rarely and all too disastrously – we heard about the Tests through English voices, listening to World Service's ball by ball commentary, and experienced it via English writing. So while Prabhu often covered tours abroad, when India went to England, as during the 1967 tour, he stayed at home. Ian Woolridge wrote about it for *The Times of India*. In the traditional opening match for the Indians against Indian Gymkhana he wrote rather tenderly of a corpulent Indian Gymkhana leg-spinner, clearly an expatriate Indian, who had troubled the Indian team. I read and re-read that passage many times, thinking how sweet it was of Woolridge to take the trouble to produce an extra touch which he knew would appeal to his Indian readers. Many years later, when I finally arrived in Fleet Street, I learned that Woolridge was still waiting to be paid for his dispatches, but by then I had realised that that was a common fate for those who wrote for Indian papers. Indian editors were inclined to think that writing was its own reward and did not require any financial compensation.

This, in turn, fitted in neatly with the other pictures of England that were constantly crowding in. I had been introduced to the BBC World Service and all its wonders. The World Service news, which was followed alternatively by commentary about the day's events or news about Britain, was soon a must for me. In those days the ten-minute news featured only one newsreader, there were no other voices during the bulletin, with the newsreader at most saying, 'A correspondent in a dispatch to the BBC says, etc'. I could barely sit through the All India Radio news which was so boring and so predictable. The prevailing joke was that if World War Three broke out it might just make the closing headlines after the latest production figures for rice and wheat. To listen to the BBC news was to feel that I was a citizen of the world and I can remember my excitement when I heard that the Russians had erected a wall in Berlin. I rushed in to tell my father and his friend, who gazed at me in wonder, curious to know how I had discovered this amazing information.

The shining jewel of the World Service was the Saturday Special, the sports programme presented by Paddy Feeney. It would start at round about half past four Indian time on a Saturday afternoon and end late at night with the Sports Round-Up. Then with the streets of Bombay hushed for the first time, and a single overhead lamp burning over my desk, I would listen to a stentorian voice reading the English football results. As the voice said League Division One I stopped everything I was doing and tried to picture the matches that had been played that Saturday. Just before this I would have listened to a second-half football commentary which as often as not turned out to be a Scottish game. So not long after falling in love with Tottenham I also fell in love with Celtic. Their European Cup victory in 1967 brought great joy and I imagined the moment when I would celebrate a similar triumph for Tottenham.

About the time that I fell in love with Tottenham the man I knew as my grandfather – although in reality he was my father's uncle – came through on one of his periodical visits from Poona (he was on his way to a Rotary election) and presented me with two William Brown books. If I remember right they were *Just William* and *William in Trouble*. Soon I was progressing through my own English world of letters: Biggles, followed by Sherlock Holmes, Agatha Christie and finally, the grandest of them all, P.G. Wodehouse and the Jeeves books.

My father often used to tell me that it was good to eat fish. Once I had read the first Jeeves story I needed no further inducement. After all, was that not why Jeeves was so bright? Needless to say I did not see myself as Jeeves. I imagined that once I got to London I, like Bertie Wooster, would belong to a club like Drones and get a manservant like Jeeves to whom I would feed the Bengali delicacy of *Hilsa* specially flown in from India.

If following Tottenham and Surrey made me feel I knew how my two favourite games were meant to be played, then the William books reassured me that life in England was not all that different from India. After all, did not William have a cook, housemaid and servants and did he not tussle with his parents about school as much as I did? I recently recounted my love for William books and how I imagined everyone in England lived like that to an Australian friend. But what about William's dropped aitches said the friend, did that not strike you as odd, he asked? I had never noticed it as odd. I was amused by it but it did nothing to shake my conviction that everyone in England spoke like Alvar Liddell. The one exception was John Arlott, but then Arlott was God and like any true god he was allowed to be idiosyncratic.

The more we read and heard about England the more easily we imagined ourselves to be part of it. This was particularly so when the *Sport and Pastime* serialised extracts from the memoirs of cricketers, footballers and even English jockeys. It was here that I learned from Scobie Breasley, who in the late '40s had just failed to win the Derby with the horse owned by the Maharaja of Baroda, that the Derby came too early in the English season. Not long afterwards, when a friend of my father came to our house and discussed horse-racing, I stunned him by repeating it. When asked, 'Have you been in England in early June?' I had to shamefacedly accept I had not. When my father's friend went on to say Breasley was Australian and did not know much about England it was my turn to be stunned.

But that did not stop me from claiming a superior intelligence based on knowledge of English sports. When a friend of mine discussed the deeds of the then leading Indian jockey, Pandhu Khade, I said with some authority, having read it in *Sport and Pastime*, that Khade could not possibly match Breasley, who was a fine judge of speed and the best jockey to engineer a win by a short head. Unlike my father's friend, my friend did not ask, 'Have you seen Breasley ride?', probably because he too passed on opinions of English sport he had garnered from the *Sport and Pastime* as his own. Both of us knew that in the eyes of our contemporary it made us important, marked us out as men of the world.

This was all the more relevant because, although we would never have quite put it like that, we felt Indian sport, like Indian life, was deficient, not quite complete. It could only be completed by knowledge of England and the more we knew about it the more superior we felt, a superiority already guaranteed to us by the fact that we went to what was called an English-speaking school, where the language of instruction was English, as opposed to most other schools where students were taught in Hindi, Marathi or other Indian languages.

About this time my uncle, who had become a prominent Congress politician, came from Calcutta to attend the annual session in Bombay. There had been atrocities against Hindus in the then Eastern Pakistan. My uncle was unhappy about it and more so about the Indian Government's rather weak response. He wanted to make a tough speech. I eagerly volunteered to be his speech writer. Summoning all the words I had recently learned, and fortified by Fritz's praise of my command of the English language, I poured them into the speech, talking of genocide of the Hindus and appeasement of Pakistan with suitable references to Chamberlain, Munich and Hitler. With Nehru, who was to die a few weeks later, watching, my uncle delivered the speech in his best oratorical style and it quite electrified that staid Congress session. Afterwards Congressmen gathered round complimenting him. He generously pointed out that I had drafted it and that I was only 16. One of his Congress colleagues, an old man, patted me on the back and said, 'Genocide, appeasement, very appropriate words. You write like an Englishman.' It may have been a perfect illustration of Naipaul's mocking description of our mimic societies but at that moment I felt so proud.

This was India of the early '60s, almost 15 years after its much cherished independence from England. The Indian Constitution had laid down that in 1960 Hindi would replace English as the national language but this raised such a protest that the Constitution was amended to allow

English to co-exist with Hindi. We would hear of Indian politicians, who had themselves been educated at Hindi-speaking schools, sending their children to convents. Our contempt for those who could not speak English fluently was cruel and shameful. Much later I realised it was a typical colonial reaction, a way of looking at England as the mother country, the source of goodness, the provider of knowledge to validate our experience.

'I am craze for foreign, just craze for foreign,' Mrs Mahindra told V.S. Naipaul when renting out a room to him in Delhi. Interestingly Naipaul was visiting India in the very season I was puzzling over the achievements of Ipswich and mourning Tottenham's surrender of its crown, and like so much in his *Area of Darkness* he had caught the mood just right. We were all 'craze for foreign' – foreign degrees, foreign foods, above all, approval of foreign opinion. And England stood at the very apex of our foreign craze.

The evidence was all round us. Our flat was in the most famous street of Bombay, Hornby Road, renamed Mahatma Gandhi after the father of the nation, at the centre of which stood the fountain to Flora and from where roads radiated away in all directions, connecting every important landmark of the city: here the road that led to the sea, there the road that led to the Victorian High Court and the Brabourne Stadium, another that led to a neo-Victorian railway station and, just behind our house, one that opened up to the wide boulevards of Ballards Estate, the location of offices once owned by the English and since taken over by Indians, and then Bombay's docks named after the daughters of Queen Victoria. All roads led to our flat, said my father, and they all end up in my kitchen, moaned my mother, often in exasperation as visitors and guests poured in all day, every day – looking for tea and chat and staying for dinner.

But if we felt ourselves to be at the centre of Bombay the streets below and around echoed to cries that made us aware we were very peripheral figures on a world stage. The cries were, 'Foreign, imported novelty', as the street vendors enticed us with items, imported and smuggled, from England and other parts of the world. The vendors did not need much to persuade us that if an item was made in England then it must by definition be better than anything India had to offer.

Strange as it may seem in 1996, in our eyes it was Japan that was suspect and England beyond reproach. My father's most telling example of the shoddiness of Japanese goods was derived from his own experience from the '30s when the streets of Bombay had been flooded with cheap Japanese imitations of Western goods. This memory of Japan as the home of badly made goods never left him. If you wanted quality, said my father, you bought English. Japanese may be cheap but it was rubbish.

In his business – the company made raincoats – there could be no higher quality than Gabardine and Burberry. And for him the only car worth possessing was an English car. He had great faith in Fords – Ford Anglia, Ford Popular– although Ford was an American company, the cars we had were made in Dagenham. 'Whatever happens,' he would say, 'an English car will always start first thing in the morning.' His best friend had a Sunbeam sports car and while my father did not approve of the flashiness he was reassured that it was English. To even write this now is to invite mockery, given there is no English car industry left, but in India of the late '50s and early '60s such sentiments were commonplace and evoked no comment, let alone derision.

It was not merely that British goods were more reliable, but also England had a superior moral system. My father's favourite example of this was the way Edward VIII had not been allowed to ascend the throne because he wanted to marry a divorced American woman. For my father it showed how family life was valued by the Royal Family. Had he been alive today the recent events with Diana would have left him bemused.

My love affair with Tottenham had begun at a crucial time for me. I had just turned 14 and felt I was an aware teenager who could hold his own in any argument. The previous winter we had an unseasonal holiday in Calcutta to see my grandmother – we usually went in the summer – and on the long 36-hour train journey, just days before the 1960 American presidential election, I poured over papers debating the fortunes of Kennedy and Nixon and argued with my father that Kennedy would be better for India. We were aware of its great power and influence and America fascinated us. Many of my schoolfriends were planning to go there to study. I myself sat the SSAT exams for American universities and in time MIT and Harvard were talked about as much as Oxford or Cambridge, though they could never equal Oxbridge in prestige. In the early '60s the Indian balance of payments made foreign travel very difficult – any venture outside India required Form P for travel, a Kafkaesque bureaucratic nightmare, and anyone leaving India received just £3. But for those who got admission to Oxford or Cambridge there was never any problem for the Reserve Bank of India giving foreign exchange. The civil servants who decided such things were themselves from Oxbridge; the two universities set a standard which Yale or Harvard could not match – as did almost everything in England.

The Madras Brahmin who, on reading O'Hara's *From the Terraces*, had told Naipaul, 'You couldn't get a well-bred Englishman writing this sort of tosh', echoed many of our feelings about the powerful but crude

Americans. At school the poetry and almost all the prose we read derived from English writers – Shakespeare, of course, but Shelley, Wordsworth, Walter de la Mare, Chesterton, Robert Lynd. The only American we ever read in our school was Mark Twain. That was his essay on Bombay and then largely to point out how dreadfully certain foreigners can get things wrong about India. Fritz used to almost foam at the mouth when he referred to Twain's passage describing the Indian crow.

My father admired American marketing skills. Alfred Tack's book on selling was one of the few he had read diligently. And I was much impressed when a friend at school suddenly turned out to be a salesman for *Time* magazine and even got my father to subscribe to it. But while *Time* was useful – I noted down the difficult words I read there in a notebook – for real writing we all preferred the English. I felt I had stolen a march there for about this time I discovered a very special British library which none of my friends even suspected existed. I was still chaperoned wherever I went. If for some reason my father's chauffeur could not take me to school then he would detail one of his many company peons. To take me to Tests at the Brabourne Stadium there was always one of his clerks, Mr Kandalgoakar, who had played some cricket at Shivaji Park and considered himself an expert on the game. But on Thursdays, when our school had a midweek holiday, after lunch I was allowed to wander out into Hornby Road on my own. There I stumbled across the offices of the British Deputy High Commissioner, just opposite our flat and the other side of Flora's fountain, located on the second floor of a marvellous white stone building – the rest of it was occupied by the Hong Kong and Shanghai Bank. I found that it had a small library which housed all the latest English papers, printed on paper so thin I felt I could eat them, let alone read them.

My reading was voracious and undiscriminating and the high point was the *New Statesman* and the political commentaries of Anthony Howard. Harold Macmillan was then immersed in political problems – soon the Profumo scandal would break – and Howard wrote in a style that was at once so intelligible and accessible. Political commentaries were not unknown to me. *The Times of India* carried one almost every day and once a week the editor wrote his long piece that took up almost the entire leader page, setting right the nation and the world. But they were written in a heavy neo-Victorian style that was quite difficult to fathom. Howard was like a ray of sunshine cutting through a dense fog.

As I read I imagined him to look like David Niven, our idea of the typical Englishman. I had been fascinated by *Guns of Navarone* which, along with *My Fair Lady*, was easily the most popular film of my early teens. Of particular interest was the character of the British explosive expert played by David Niven. A friend of mine, with whom I played cricket, was in the habit of declaiming Niven's speech to Gregory Peck as he urged him to kill the traitor in their midst. Niven told Peck, 'Do it for England', and every time we batted together, and very often just after I had played and missed five times in an over, Edwin would come down the pitch and, leaning on his bat, say, 'Do it for England'. The tone, far from mocking, was reverential and I'm convinced Edwin did think he was Niven talking to Peck.

The journey to the library was like going to the source of the river. *The Times of India* had a weekly 'Letter from London' from its correspondent on the goings on in Whitehall and Downing Street. But far from carrying any of the verisimilitude that Alastair Cooke's 'Letters from America' have always had, they read poorly, sounded contrived and, as I soon realised, were no more than a summary of the British press. This feeling strengthened when I read the originals and began to detect a phrase or two *The Times of India* man had lifted, without attribution, from the *London Times* or the *Guardian*.

Perhaps what gave me the most pleasure about visits to the library of the British Deputy High Commissioner was that I knew it was like a secret treasure trove to which I alone had the key. Of course there were many in Bombay who knew about it but they were grown men and women. I alone of my contemporaries and schoolfriends knew of this library and its treasures. We all knew of the much more famous and bigger library run by the British Council. The idea of free public libraries is taken for granted in Britain but it is unknown in India and membership of the British Council library, which was the nearest equivalent, was the great prize of our youth. But such was the demand that the British Council had rationed membership and we had to wait until we were 16 before we could become members. Of course we could become members of the United Startes Information Service, but it had boring books on the threat of Soviet Communism, or why collective farming was not working in Poland, by writers we had never heard about. The British Council library offered us access to the writers who were part of our school syllabus but in a more abundant and complete form.

My discovery of the Deputy High Commissioner's little library meant that while my friends waited to be 16, I felt I had already got access to part of the kingdom. The Deputy High Commissioner's library had no Wodehouse or Shaw that I could take home to read but the compensation was that I could always read book reviews discussing Wodehouse and Shaw.

My interest in that library was not merely intellectual; the sensual side was also catered for. The Sixties were upon us and the English girls of the High Commission had taken to wearing short skirts – if not quite mini, certainly much shorter than anything to be seen in Bombay. Lunchtime was a good time to go because just after two they all returned in one group. I only had to look up from that week's Anthony Howard political commentary to see a generous flash of thighs as they paraded past. The combination of Howard's astringent prose and the promise of those thighs made me long for Thursdays to come around.

But just as the promise of the thighs never turned into reality, and I never imagined they would, so for very different reasons I was shocked when years later I got to London and made my pilgrimage to the *New Statesman* offices at Great Turnstile. I was ushered into Howard's office. He received me with great kindness but I could hardly take in anything he said. Far from looking like Niven he looked like one of our Nepali servant boys and to my utter shame – although I did not say this to him – as I left his office I told myself, 'How can a man who looks like Ramu write so well?'

Yet all this did not mean a wholesale acceptance of anything and everything English, indeed, our love for English sport was also a contradiction, except that at that age we saw no contradictions. It was only much later, after I had read C.L.R. James and then returned to Nirad Chaudhuri and his autobiography – the two representing, as Naipaul put it, the delayed and imperfectly understood cultural boomerang from the colonies – that I began to appreciate the moral and political confusion from which our love of English sport had sprung.

I shall have more to say about James and Chaudhuri a bit later but it is worth emphasising that our longing for the English sporting world was mixed with our loathing for what we saw as the iniquitous way, for instance, the English cricket world treated Indian cricket. Indeed, when it came to international sporting contests it was Australia rather than England that claimed us. England playing Australia would have us all rooting for Australia and Australia got our support even when they played the West Indians. The only time we wanted Australia to lose was when they played India.

Our fanatical support for Australia was nourished by Test cricket commentaries from that country. After BBC cricket commentaries our great joy was to tune in to these cricket broadcasts from Australia by Alan McGilray and Lindsay Hassett. They were carried on Radio Ceylon, a sort of Indian sub-continental Radio Caroline. It combined advertisements, profiting from the fact that in those days All-India Radio refused to carry any, with Hindi film songs and BBC World Service news. When Australia played a Test series at home, Radio Ceylon relayed cricket commentaries from the Australian Broadcasting Commission. The time difference was perfect. Whereas listening to BBC cricket commentaries meant sitting up late, often as late as 11.30 p.m. – difficult on schooldays – the Australian Test would start at six in the morning Indian time and finish by lunchtime.

I first began to appreciate this during the West Indian tour of Australia in 1960–61, the one that produced the first-ever tied Test. The last Test saw a narrow Australia win by two wickets and they took the series 2–1. The reaction of the Australians was unprecedented. As the West Indians left Melbourne, a quarter of a million inhabitants of the city crowded the streets to bid them goodbye. It was the first series where the West Indians had been captained by a black man, Worrell, and it was the most memorable series of all. Jack Fingleton would declare that it saved Test cricket and his book, *The Greatest Test of All*, soon became a favourite, almost displacing Graveney's *Cricket Through The Covers*.

By the time I read the book I had followed almost every ball of that series on the radio. Just before the series began I had finally persuaded my father to get me a proper radio that could receive shortwave broadcasts. My father had resisted this in the past because he felt it would distract me from my studies. So, during the series I would wake early and before going to school listen to all the pre-lunch session of play. So did most of my schoolfriends and during that series much of our discussions would centre round events in Sydney, Melbourne, Brisbane and Adelaide. However, I had an advantage over them. Whereas they had to have their lunch at school, my father's chauffeur would drive me home for lunch. Before that series began it was a routine event. During the series it acquired tremendous significance. It meant that while my schoolmates speculated on the score I could catch the last few overs before the close of play.

I would return after lunch full of myself, aware that I was the only one in school who knew what the close of play in Australia was. Just before the master arrived I would stride up to the podium on which the master's desk perched. Behind the desk, and just underneath a large cross, hung the class blackboard. I would take the chalk from the monitor and write the score in large capital letters. This often produced comical moments. The monitor usually had the names of boys who had misbehaved and should be caned by the master. Now next to their names would be 230 for two or some such score. In the fourth Test, when the last-wicket pair of Mackay and Kline batted for over an hour to deny the West Indians victory, I, to the bemusement of the cook, missed lunch and sat glued to the radio as

Hassett and his fellow commentators described quite the most absorbing closing overs of a match I have ever known. Then I rushed back to give the news to the class. The Australian victory in the final Test in Melbourne, which led to the ticker-tape parade, saw me proclaim Australia's triumph from the blackboard in class VIII to the cheers of my classmates.

We saw no contradiction in our love for Australian cricket and our vision of England as a sporting paradise. We knew nothing about Australia and were completely ignorant of its treatment of the aborigines, or even its white Australia policy which meant most Indians could not migrate to that country. Even had we known it would have made no difference. I think the only piece of non-cricketing news about Australia I ever heard at school was that very few Australians went to university. Australia meant great cricketers and, what is more, unlike top English cricketers, they were willing to tour India.

In general, Australia would get its cricket teams to stop off in India on the way back from an England tour. They often beat the Indians but this policy meant we did see all the great post-war Australian cricketers and we respected them for treating us as equals. In contrast, through the '50s and '60s England sent what were very nearly 'B' teams to India. May, Trueman, Bedser, Bailey, Laker, Evans, Tyson, Hutton and even Compton – although he had played in India during the war – never toured India with England. Before an England visit we would read how England's best players preferred to have a winter's rest rather than tour India and India always produced a new captain for England. The ultimate insult had come in 1951–52 when Nigel Howard led the side to India. He had never played for England, never played again and is that rare Test player who played for his country only as captain. It was not until 1976 that a reigning England captain, Tony Greig, took a team to India. It meant that India often defeated England in India, but we felt the victory was hollow as it was clearly not against the best English side. In contrast, with Australia we saw Benaud, Miller, Lindwall, Harvey, O'Neill, Simpson, Lawry and Burge. They may have had as many tummy problems as the Englishmen but they came and, often, conquered both on the field and off.

So, unlike C.L.R. James, we did not see nationalism in sporting triumphs. James felt exuberant about the 1960–61 Australia-West Indies series which, despite the West Indian defeats, was an essential part of nation building. I can see the point James is making. The West Indians, a people without a history, saw cricket as the vital cementing factor. The history of the island is dismal – slavery until 1834, indentured labourers until 1917 – so the cricket code of gentlemanliness, fair play and teamwork was something to hold on to. As Naipaul has said, in the West Indies they filled a need. 'In islands that had known only brutality and proclaimed greed, cricket and its code provided an area of rest, a release for much that was denied by the society: skill, courage, style; the graces.

But we did not need cricket to supply us a history – if anything Indian history was often suffocating. For us the series was merely enduring proof of the superiority of Australian cricket. James says that when he left school he had educated himself into a member of the British middle class with literary gifts. We had no such ambition. We were the first generation of Indians to grow up free of the Raj and our love of India and Indian nationalism was strong and vibrant. James says he saw himself as a Greco-Roman. We did not. Indeed, any such suggestion would have been strongly stamped on. Views that Indian drama may have been derived from ancient Greece were strongly rebutted. A book claiming that was the subject of a long, critical article in the Sunday edition of *The Times of India*. On the contrary, said the reviewer, it was the Greeks who had borrowed from ancient Hindus – just like the Arabs who had carried the number theory to the world by borrowing from the ancient Indians the all important concept of zero. Even Fritz, so keen to encourage us to seek English role models in cricket and football, was a strong nationalist. Unlike the West Indies we had no dearth of history for us to fall back on and, unlike James, no reason to envy the English for Drake or Nelson.

I did wish that some of the medieval Indian warriors had had somebody like Drake or Nelson by their side. When I came to the chapters in Rawlinson's *History of India* dealing with India's appalling medieval history, I would quietly close the book and fantasise myself into an Indian medieval warrior king ready to refight the lost battles of Panipat. The problem for me was that while Panipat may be the Indian Hastings, unlike the accursed south of England battlefield, Panipat has seen not one but a whole host of battles which have proved to be turning points in Indian history. So I was spoilt for choice when deciding which battle I should refight.

There were other contradictory currents in our nationalism. My grandfather had served with the British in Singapore. But there was also the example of Subash Bose who, organising an army from the defeated Indian soldiers left behind by the British in Singapore, had fought the British under Japanese auspices. For him it was a revolutionary struggle to free India from British yoke. Bose had died in an air crash at the end of the war but many Indians refused to believe this. Two government enquiries have since examined the matter but while we were growing up the fantasy was strong that he would suddenly emerge and rescue the country from its problems. Despite the similarities of our names, he was not related but we knew his family well. His brother was my father's friend and his brother's wife, whom we called aunty, was a great friend of my mother's.

And then every year, just after the rains ended, we Bengalis celebrated Durga Puja and rewrote history, making Robert Clive a scoundrel. One of the plays that was always staged was the one showing how Clive had defeated Siraj-ud-daullah, the Nawab of Bengal, at the Battle of Plassey in 1757 and thus founded the British Empire in India. The play presented Siraj as the tragic hero and Clive as the cheating Englishman. It was an historical travesty. My Bengali ancestors had quite correctly decided that in any battle between Siraj and Clive, Clive was infinitely preferable. I would now unhesitatingly accept that view and can see the play as part of our attempt to create the myth of an Indian nationalist history. However, when we were growing up, plays like that were treated as representing hard historical facts and uncritically accepted.

So, unlike James, our love of English sport was not because we adored the English political nation, let alone accept what it had done in India, but almost despite it. James presents his love of English cricket as a complete whole. In my case the connection was not quite that simple.

Also, we had our own Indian teams. If I loved Tottenham and Surrey I also loved Bombay and East Bengal. Both had much to offer. Bombay's winning sequence in the Ranji Trophy – for 15 successive years – is unparalleled in domestic cricket anywhere in the world. In Rannath Kenny, the slim, stylish batsman who, much in the style of Ranji, always batted in silk shirts buttoned down to his wrists, we had an ideal hero to emulate. East Bengal invoked the lands of my fathers and played the sort of passing, dribbling football I loved. I doted on Balaram, the slim player who could turn defenders almost at will, and my joy when East Bengal came to play football at Bombay's Cooperage was great. My father's friend, Mr Mitra, who ran soccer in Western India, gave us special tickets and an East Bengal victory was the icing on the cake. My joy was complete on the afternoon when East Bengal beat Mohun Bagan, the other great Indian football club, and went on to claim the Rovers Cup. But much as I loved Balaram or Rannath Kenny, I could not believe that their deeds could ever match those of my Tottenham or Surrey heroes. Cooperage was a ground of many happy memories – I always won the Christmas race for my age group there – but I would never have dreamt of comparing it with Wembley. And much as I loved the Brabourne Stadium and considered it unique, it wasn't Lord's.

In all this I felt very like the old Indian retainer who had served both the Raj and their Indian successors. In 1961, when the Queen came on a royal visit to India, the first since the Raj had departed, this old retainer was still employed at the Viceregal Palace built by Sir Edwin Lutyens. It was now the home of the Indian President and a reporter asked the old retainer about the royal visit. 'Ah,' he said, 'at last the real owner is coming back.' The implication was clear. His new boss may be the Indian President and the Viceregal Palace may be called Rastrapati Bhavan, President's House, but he was still a usurper, not quite like the real English masters who had created it. That is how I felt about cricket and football in India. However wonderful the Indian settings might be, nothing could displace Lord's and Wembley as my true footballing and cricketing heavens.

Over the years I had every reason to be grateful to cricket and English cricket, more so when it won me a totally unexpected free trip to Israel. Just after the Six-Day War the Israelis decided they wished to promote their image as peacemakers and organised an international youth festival. Two delegates were selected from India, with the one from Bombay chosen on the basis of an elocution contest. I spoke on the marvels of cricket, the wonder of Lord's and ended up quoting J.M. Barrie and Peter Pan. The Israeli Consul in Bombay knew nothing about cricket but was so impressed by my speech that he selected me.

Not long after that I came to England thinking I knew all that there was to know about English sport. It was some years before I realised that I had been deluded by too many glossy advertisements seeking to portray an English sporting world that did not exist and, probably, never had. By that time many of the ideas and loyalties I had acquired in my childhood were being questioned.

In my last year at school my boxing hero was the Swede Ingemar Johansson, whose blond good looks I admired as much as his boxing skills and whose victory over Floyd Patterson gave me great joy. In the rematch, when Patterson fairly bludgeoned Johansson to defeat, I was so sickened that at the annual school debate I proposed the motion: Boxing should be banned. One of my school chums questioned my support for Johansson, saying, 'You know Patterson is black.' I looked at him as if he had spoken in a language I did not understand. 'What do you mean by that?' To me the fact that Patterson was black and Johansson was white was of no significance, I just liked him as a boxer. It was no different to my support for Australian cricket, whatever the colour of their opponents, except, of course, when they played India. Now, after more than a quarter of a century in England, I would instantly understand what my schoolfriend had meant to convey.

This was brought home to me in April 1995 when I was in Antigua for the second Test between the West Indies and Australia. The first at Barbados had seen Australia win by ten wickets in three days. On the first day of the Antigua Test the West Indies bowled Australia out cheaply and over breakfast the next day a West Indian official assured me that the usual West Indian dominance would be reasserted. It was a Sunday and by the time I got to the ground I was aware that Tottenham's Cup semi-final against Everton was about to start at Elland Road. I kept one ear cocked to news from Elland Road as Brian Lara and Richie Richardson set about the Australian bowling. Just as Everton scored the first goal, Richardson got out and just as the final, numbing score from Elland Road came, 4–1 to Everton, Lara got out.

I did not know then that Daniel Amokachi had scored two goals. Tottenham had no black players and that season was the first in which Everton had a black player, but even if Everton had fielded all 11 black players and Tottenham never played a black man, it would make no difference. I would still sing with joy when Tottenham won and weep when they lost. In contrast, I realised at Antigua that I no longer felt the same loyalties towards Australian cricket I had had since the 1960–61 series. In Antigua, as the West Indian wickets fell, I did not rejoice but wanted to be distracted and decided to explore the ground and then Antigua itself. It started to rain. I took shelter in a bar nursing my twin defeats – Tottenham and the West Indies – while the local policeman went to look for a cab. As I headed back to my hotel, I thought of what a man had once said to me in a London club when England, under David Gower, were beaten 5–0 by the West Indies.

'You must be be celebrating,' he said.

'Why?' I asked.

'Because,' the man started to say, then checked himself.

'Because we both share a dark skin,' I interjected. 'I am not West Indian.' The supposition that just because my skin colour was close to the West Indians' I would automatically support them angered me. But now in the taxi back what else could explain my sorrow at the fall of the West Indian wickets? Yet what could explain my continued support for Tottenham despite the fact that they hardly have a black player these days? Arsenal have many more but that has never tempted me to change my allegiance, let alone rejoice in their triumphs. I can only do so when they are beaten.

The answer is not simple and it would be too easy to say that my apparently contrasting reactions to these two sporting teams is the result of my years of living in this country. Familiarity may breed neither contempt nor children but it can dramatically change the way you look at some things, even things you thought you knew well.

CHAPTER THREE

Not Counting Sporting Niggers

(with apologies to George Orwell)

I say my love for English sport was born out of sporting and national confusion. As I write this I see that English sport itself, particularly in its remarkable worldwide spread, conveys a very English confusion. What is more this confusion transcends sports and enters almost all aspects of national life.

We can best appreciate this if we first consider one of the most perceptive essays written by probably the greatest political writer and essayist of this century: George Orwell. In July 1939, with the world sliding towards war, Orwell wrote an essay in the magazine Adelphi entitled 'Not Counting Niggers'. In the course of the article he reviewed a book entitled *Union Now* by an American writer, Clarence K. Streit. Streit had argued that the only way to combat the dictators was by forming a peace bloc. This bloc, he said, would initially be formed by 'fifteen democracies' and their union would be similar to the bonds that tied together the different states of the United States with a common government, common money and completely free internal trade. Such a bloc, he argued, would so unnerve the dictators that they would crumble even before a shot was fired in anger. At a time when many people wanted to defeat Hitler but did not want war, it was an immensely attractive idea.

Remember this is 1939, the British and French empires are still intact and there is no question of withdrawal from the colonies. Streit admitted that the so-called democracies had dependencies full of coloured inhabitants but he saw no contradiction in democracies with colonies, who had no intention of giving those colonies freedom, claiming to fight fascism in the name of freedom for mankind. Streit saw these colonies as continuing in the form they were, in other words deprived of freedom, vote and voice. So, although India then had more people than all his 'fifteen democracies' put together, Streit dismissed the country in a page and a half and was convinced that it was not fit for self-government. It would still have to be ruled by Englishmen. Orwell, with his sharp mind, immediately saw what was missing in Streit's argument. 'The unspoken clause is always "not counting niggers". For how can we make a "firm stand" against Hitler if we are simultaneously weakening ourselves at home? In other words, how can we "fight Fascism" except by bolstering up a far vaster injustice? For of course it is vaster. What we always forget is that the overwhelming bulk of the British proletariat does not live in Britain, but in Asia and Africa. It is not in Hitler's power, for instance, to make a penny an hour a normal industrial wage; it is perfectly normal in India, and we are at great pains to keep it so. One gets some idea of the real relationship of England and India when one reflects that the per capita annual income in England is something over £80, and in India about £7. It is quite common for an Indian coolie's leg to be thinner than the average Englishman's arms. And there is nothing racial in this, for well-fed members of the same race are of normal physique; it is due to simple starvation. This is the system which we all live on and which we denounce when there seems to be no danger of it being altered. Of late, however, it has become the first duty of a "good anti-Fascist" to lie about it and help to keep it in being. What real settlement, of the slightest value, can there be along these lines? What meaning would there be, even if it were successful in bringing down Hitler's system in order to stabilise something that is far bigger and in its different way just as bad?'

As Orwell had predicted Streit's idea remained a literary one. War came and while the dictators were defeated, the British and French empires could not be preserved. However, people with Streit's bend of mind still exist and it is interesting to note that some of the discussions in the wake of the 50th anniversary of VE-Day had echoes of the 'not counting niggers' attitude. This was particularly noticeable during debates centred round the possibility of making peace with Hitler in 1940 or at least 1941. Among those who debated this question were men like Alan Clark and the historians Andrew Roberts and Correlli Barnett. Clark, in particular, felt strongly that Britain's failure to make peace with Hitler in 1941 was a big mistake. But in the process he completely ignored the question Orwell had posed: what would have happened to the empire? Would it have remained, in Orwell's phrase, a 'mechanism for exploitation of cheap coloured labour'? Just as Streit did not think niggers or Indian coolies came into the argument, so Messrs Clark, Roberts and Barnett did not think they were worth considering. Their position seemed to be that they were English historians discussing what was good for England; who cared what niggers – albeit under England's heel – thought about it, let alone how they might have been affected by such a peace?

A similar indifference to niggers also seems to underlie attempts by the British who were Japanese prisoners of war during the Second World War to get compensation for the way they were treated by the Japanese. The VJ-Day anniversary saw much prominence given to their agitation. There is no doubt the Japanese attempt to set up an East Asian empire was marked with great cruelty in the course of which they committed many atrocities. But the point nobody made was: what were the British doing in that part of the world then? Were they not there because they were holding down millions of people? The British empire may never have reached the barbaric level of the Japanese but it was still a colonial, coolie empire populated by peoples who had no voice in whether they wanted to belong to Britain. If the British prisoners of war had a case against the Japanese, what about the far vaster injustice, to quote Orwell, that a whole host of other peoples – the Malays, the Burmese, the Chinese and the Indians – suffered at the hands of the British?

Many hundreds of words were written about the VE/VJ-Day anniversaries and the bravery of the Allied troops in freeing these areas from Japanese rule. Nobody asked: was this freedom not illusory? Did freedom from Japanese occupation not mean that these areas returned to slavery of the British empire? Raise such a question and the answer is that you cannot talk of the British empire being slavery, or compare the British to the Japanese – entirely different, old boy. This is a bit like saying there is no point of comparison at all – I emphasise at all – between the Ford open prison and, say, the chain gang prisons that used to be operated in the American South. True, there are two very different kinds of prison and if you have to go to prison, Ford open prison is the one to choose. But for those who have no choice in the matter – as the colonial peoples did not – they both represent a denial of freedom.

This political point about not counting niggers has a sporting application and to fully appreciate it we must be aware of how writers have seen this country's sporting legacy. Let me take a recent example. In 1994

Claudio Veliz, a professor of history at Boston University, wrote *The New World of the Gothic Fox*, a book comparing the legacy of Spain and England in the Americas. Borrowing the idea of foxes and hedgehogs devised by Isaiah Berlin – to whom the book is dedicated – Veliz asked: why has the English legacy in North America been so much more powerful and productive than the Spanish legacy in South America? The question is all the more pertinent because in the 16th and 17th centuries Spanish Indies was one of the world's greatest secular powers, while English North America was little more than scattered settlements. Yet today it is English North America that leads the world, while Spanish Latin America is a Third World disaster area.

Veliz's answer is that the English brought to the New World a stubborn ability to thrive on diversity and change, forged by the industrial revolution and reflected in their vernacular Gothic style. Their descendants became the 'foxes' of Berlin's metaphor, characteristically independent, pluralistic and adaptable, qualities that today continue to sustain their technological and scientific prowess.

The English achievement in inventing modern sports figures large in this thesis and Veliz devotes several pages to describing with some pride how England, as a by-product of the industrial revolution, created the world of sports we all know and enjoy. Even the Germans acknowledged England as the mother country of sports. So overwhelming was England's sporting mastery that in 1936 the German writer Agnes Bain Stiven wrote that English sporting technical terms have become 'the common possession of all nations in the same way as Italian technical terms in the field of music'. For Veliz, seeking to prove English superiority over the Spanish, this is a rich seam to mine and he mines it deeply. Veliz goes on to say that, 'these sporting activities of English origin engage the attention of more people, at more frequent intervals, and in more different places than any other cluster of comparable activities. Moreover, their importance and acceptance are everywhere increasing, they can now claim the status of national sport in an astonishingly large number of countries, and it is becoming difficult to think of any in which the more popular games are not of English origin.'

Now this is all very well. It confirms our opinion of a certain kind of England and Veliz sounds exactly the sort of colonial I could identify with. I have no arguments with his view that England is the mother country of sports. I do not need a professor from Boston to tell me what the dear old Times of India had drilled into me all those years ago.

But there is a problem that Veliz does not tackle. Why and how did the games spread round the world? What was the thinking of the English when they took their games to far-flung corners of the globe? It is not enough to say, as Veliz does, that soccer reached Brazil when British sailors first played the game there. For some reason he does not mention that cricket reached India a century before Brazilians took to soccer, when British sailors played in the Gulf of Cambay – the navy has clearly a lot to answer for. As we now know, the natives both of India and Brazil first gawked at these sailors in much the same manner the natives of the Americas gawked at the ships of Columbus, then realising the wonder of the games and aware they had nothing comparable to offer, they took to them. Over time they have done more than merely copy. Both the Indians with cricket and the Brazilians with soccer have added dimensions to their adopted games which make them quite a bit different from the original English version. Nevertheless they could not have done so had the English not created the model in the first place.

However, the point Veliz does not even consider is the most important, namely that the sailors were not part of a great imperial adventure. This was not part of a great English philosophical drive to make these sports world cultural symbols. These were individual Englishmen indulging in their favourite games. The taking up of cricket and soccer by the natives of India and Brazil happened not because of the English but in spite of them.

Why is this important? It is important precisely because Veliz is using the fact that we all play these English sports to ascribe moral ascendancy to the English. The English creation of sports that the world plays is part of his proof of the superiority of English thinking and way of life over the Spanish, one of the reasons why the English, not the Spanish, have left the more important, enduring legacy in North America. If we are to accept his thesis then surely we must explore the thinking behind the English creation of these games? What was the moral basis for them? What was the philosophical underpinning for such a remarkable spread of ball games and team contests? It is abundantly clear they were not seen as mere bodily activities. They were, are, supposed to convey a moral message. They were, are, supposed to transcend the physical actions and convey a wider meaning about the higher purpose of life.

Let us ask: did William Webb Ellis, in that memorable moment at Rugby, pick up the ball and run with it – thus creating the game of rugby – have any thought that this game would one day serve to unite the races of South Africa and be a metaphor for how peoples of all races and all creeds in all climes can come together? No, of course he had no such thought. However, the people who made rugby, cricket, football and many others national games did proclaim that they were meant to serve a higher moral purpose. What was this purpose? In answering this question Veliz's argument begins to fall apart. We find that the creators of English sports had no grand world vision. The sports they created were not only not meant for anybody who was not English, they were born to satisfy the insular, even racist, needs of the times. They were there to help the English at a particular moment in their history. The fact that the world took to them says more about the world than about the English. The fact they are now played by everyone and are, according to Veliz, next to sex the most universal thing in our lives, does not mean that the English inventors of these games had a universal, cosmopolitan approach.

Writers writing about English sports have consistently missed the point. At times they have gone to great lengths to obscure it through what in effect has been a clever little trick. The trick is to link the English invention of games to the ancient Greeks and see it as sanctified by history and part of a continuum, albeit interrupted by 1,500 years. The Greek link to English sport is important. We know the ancient Greeks were the fount of modern Western thought, the most political of ancient people, the inventors of the ideas of free speech, assembly and democracy. We also know that the Greeks not only invented the Olympic Games but elevated sports and athletes to the highest level of public life. Fifteen hundred years later the English inherit the Greek mantle of civilising the world. They are now the proud possessor of an empire and as they expand and rule this empire they invent team games and spread them around the world. Nobody has made the connection between the Greeks and the English better than C.L.R. James in *Beyond a Boundary*.

One of the classics of our age, this is probably the most challenging book on sport, one where James comes in various guises – novelist, critic, social historian – to argue that cricket is art. A good deal of the book is taken up by the men who made sports and, in particular, cricket so prominent in 19th-century England. James has a holy trinity of sporting heroes. They are Thomas Arnold of Rugby, the creator of the public school system, his acolyte, Thomas Hughes, who wrote *Tom Brown's Schooldays* and was, in effect, Boswell to Arnold's Johnson; and W.G. Grace, the man who revolutionised cricket. James's thesis is that their achievements put them on a par with the statesmen and thinkers of that age.

James is a beautiful writer and makes his arguments powerfully, even movingly. There is much to stimulate and provoke but at the heart of his thesis about the English and their sports legacy lies a terrible, cruel fallacy, one that is such a gross distortion as to be quite amazing. These are serious charges to make about a great writer, so let me start by saying where I entirely agree with James. I have no problems with him when he says that through cricket you learn much about life, or even when he tries to present cricket as art. I can echo his view that 'the British tradition soaked deep into me was that when you entered the sporting world you left behind your sordid compromises of everyday existence'.

My problem arises when James seeks to link English sport to the ancient Greeks and argues that the creators of English sport sought to propagate ideas of universal brotherhood and fellow feeling for all mankind. Let us follow him through this complex argument.

James speaks of how his love for cricket and English literature was akin to that of boys in ancient Greece combining poetry and games. 'If, for them, games and poetry were ennobled by their roots in religion, my sense of conduct and morals came from my two, or rather my twin, preoccupations, and I suspect that it was not too different with a Greek boy.' So much so that when James left school he felt he would be more at home in ancient Greece. 'If I had been French or German or African I would have thought differently. But I was British, I knew best the British way of life, not merely in historical facts but in instinctive responses. I had acquired them in childhood and, without these, facts are merely figures. In the interval of my busy days and nights I pondered and read and looked about me and pondered and read again. Sport and Politics in Ancient Greece. Sport and Politics in 19th-century Britain . . . the luminous glow of the Greek city-state seems to penetrate more searchingly into every corner of our civilisation. Into the immeasurable chaos of his Guernica, lit by the electric chandelier, Picasso introduces a Greek face with an extended arm which holds a primitive oil-lamp. The Greek lamp burns today as steadily as ever. They who laid the intellectual foundations of the Western world were the most fanatical players and organisers of games the world has ever known.'

James, having set himself the self-imposed task of getting Greece clear, seeks to demonstrate that the ancient Greeks treated sports very seriously. While the Greek states fought each other unceasingly, every four years a truce was called to stage the Olympics. They became the centre of Greek intellectual life. Even a philosopher like Lucian, who sneered at the Games, could not but, through the mouth of Solon, speak of the 'courage of the athletes, the beauty of their bodies, their splendid poses, their extraordinary suppleness, their tireless energy, their audacity, their sense of competition, their unconquerable courage, their unceasing efforts to win a victory'.

James's point is that if the ancient Greeks took athletic activity seriously, and honoured athletes, then so should we. It is sheer intellectual snobbery, he says, to disregard the achievements of men such as Grace or Headley or Bradman. Their cricketing achievements were not mere sporting ephemera and extended beyond the cricket field. All this may be accepted as fair, even unarguable.

However, in the process, James confuses many things about the Greeks or rather does not allude to them. The effect is to create a false impression, first of Greek invention of sports and then of the way the English took up the Greek baton. True, the Greeks did think sport was important, but they would have made nothing of a team game like cricket because, to them, sporting glory meant individual glory. The Greek Olympics had no team games. For them glory shared was glory spoiled. The other point is that the Greek only cared about winning. Modern sports is about creating and breaking records. A game like cricket is about style, records and many other things. We like David Gower not because he won many matches for England, but for the beauty and grace of his batting. The Greeks would not have cared for him unless he won, and their attitude would be like the one English selectors displayed towards Gower when they cruelly discarded him because he was not felt to be a winner.

In cricket, victory, while always welcome, can sometimes mean less than a stylish innings in a losing cause. Or, as with Michael Atherton's great innings in the Johannesburg Test, an effort that saves a match can mean as much as a victory. The Greeks would have been nonplussed by such a view. It is surprising that James does not appreciate this for he makes many such cricketing references, particularly when he is talking of his hero, Headley. To the Greeks, much of what James says of Headley would have made no sense. At their Olympic Games there was no precise timekeeping. They did not care whether the victory had been won by .03 of a second slower than the previous year. It was enough that the athlete had won.

James does accept that, contrary to what Victorian headmasters liked to pretend, Greek sportsmen won more than the mere garland of wild olives. But his passage describing how the Greeks treated winners is written in such a fashion that it obscures the fact that the Greeks were very materialistic when it came to sports. The Greek victor would get a cash award equivalent to several years pay and free meals for life. In addition to all this there was fame and probably even a cult status after death.

James is right to stress that the ancient Greeks would have laughed at our hypocritical assertion it is only a game. For them sport was very much a part of life, part of the whole man. Unlike modern man, who divides and specialises, the Greeks saw things as an organic whole. So Solon was a political and economic writer, a man of business and a poet. H.D.F. Kitto, in his book The *Greeks*, has written, 'The sharp distinction which the Christian and the Oriental world has normally drawn between the body and the soul, the physical and the spiritual, was foreign to the Greek – at least until the time of Socrates and Plato. To him there was simply the whole man . . . The Greek made physical training an important part of education, not because he said to himself, "Look here, we mustn't forget the body", but because it could never occur to him to train anything but the whole man. It was as natural for the polis to have gymnasia as to have a theatre or warships, and they were constantly used by men of all ages, not only for physical but also for mental exercise.'

But if we accept this view that for Greeks sports was an integrated part of their existence, we must ask what was the ancient Greek conception of the whole man? And this is where James begins to fall apart. The Greeks were a very exclusive people. Not only did they have slaves but they treated foreigners with great disdain. Sparta admitted foreigners, but only grudgingly, and from time to time expelled them. Athens was more liberal, but again there was no question of naturalising foreigners. And as far as the actual Olympic Games were concerned, they were a men-only affair with strong homosexual overtones. All the participants had to be naked. This may explain why married women were not even allowed to watch – although virgins were.

James does not mention any of this. Instead he is so taken by the idea of being the heir to Greek civilisation that he says we will be able to answer Tolstoy's cry of what is art, 'only when we learn to integrate our vision of Walcott on the back foot through the covers with the outstretched arm of the Olympic Apollo'. The imagery is typical of James but quite absurd. The fact is had Walcott found himself in ancient Greece he would have been treated worse than a slave and certainly there would have been no question of him taking part in the ancient Games, let alone playing of the back foot. The Greeks only allowed people of pure Greek blood to take part in the Olympics.

However, for James, his very selective recreation of the myth of Greek sports is vital because he wants to link it to the rise of cricket and other sports in 19th-century England. In particular he uses his own version of ancient Greece to argue the case for his trinity of Arnold, Hughes and Grace. James cannot praise these men often enough, or more wondrously, and he ends his book by linking them to the West Indies tour of Australia in 1960–61, and particularly to Worrell. Recall it has been a magical tour. The West Indians have been beaten but they have won the hearts of the

Australians and none more so than Frank Worrell, the first black captain of the West Indies. James is transfixed by the effect Worrell has had on the Australians. Now read the closing lines of James's book: ' He expanded my conception of West Indian personality. Nor was I alone. I caught a glimpse of what brought a quarter of a million inhabitants of Melbourne to the streets to tell the West Indian cricketers goodbye, a gesture spontaneous and in cricket without precedent, one people speaking to another. Clearing the way with bat and ball, West Indians at that moment had made a public entry into the comity of nations. Thomas Arnold, Thomas Hughes and the Old Master himself would have recognised Frank Worrell as their boy.'

No thought could be more absurd. The idea that either Arnold or Hughes would ever have claimed Worrell as their own is preposterous. It is extremely doubtful whether even Grace would have accepted him. For a start, unlike the picture James presents of Arnold, he was very far from being the 19th-century creator of games. Arnold created the public school but did not care much about games and thought they were a waste of time. He was part of a movement that would be described as muscular Christianity – a decree to fashion an empire. But, as author Ian Buruma has said, he was more concerned with Christianity than muscles. And while Hughes, whose writing helped crate the impression that Arnold was the creator of games, was clearly a moralist. his values were very parochial and narrow.

Early on in *Tom Brown's Schooldays*, Tom Brown talks about his native Berkshire village and regrets the passing of parochial loyalties. Addressing his readers in the direct style then much favoured, Hughes puts these words in Brown's mouth: 'We were Berkshire, or Gloucestershire or Yorkshire boys and you're young cosmopolites, belonging to all counties and no countries. No doubt it is all right, I dare say it is. This is the day of large views and glorious humanity, and all that; but I wish backsword play hadn't gone out in the Vale of White Horse, and that that confounded Great Western hadn't carried away Alfred's Hill to make an embankment.'

As Buruma has pointed out: 'Here we have a quintessentially 19th-century sentiment. Railways, empire, cosmopolitanism, large views and glorious humanity – I dare say it's all right, but . . . what about native values? What about moral discipline? How about community spirit? This is where sports came in, to restore such morals and values.'

The point cannot be overemphasised. Arnold and Hughes were working to a particular agenda – one that, unlike the picture James presents, did not include all of humanity. Here is Buruma again: 'Sport built character, specially the character of empire builders. The empire was built on the belief in racial superiority. Just as the Germans did later, British sports enthusiasts often identified themselves as the true heirs of the ancient Greeks. And just as the Greeks confined their Olympics to athletes of pure Greek blood, Englishmen in the 1890s talked of holding an "Anglo-Saxon Olympiad". This scheme, wrote the main promoter J. Astley Cooper, "ought to act as an antidote to the debilitating effect of luxury, wealth, civilisation, for, should it be carried out in its full conception, the honours which it afford should be those for which the flower of the Race would chiefly survive".'

It is interesting to follow through how this 19th-century English view of sports finally inspired the modern Olympic movement. Pierre de Coubertin, not having any French sporting examples to choose from, had to choose between the German sporting traditions, which were largely derived from gymnastics, or turen, as they were called, or Arnold's English public school model. Coubertin could not quite take up the Germanic sporting ideal, not after the traumatic defeat suffered by the French at the hands of the Prussians in 1871. Instead he turned to the public school sporting ethos which, thanks to Hughes, was now seen as Arnold's legacy. Coubertin even came to Rugby and literally worshipped at the tomb of Arnold. A sincere, if misguided, idealist, Coubertin believed it was possible to get peace and brotherhood through games and did not see the fallacy in his own argument: that by promoting competition between nations you got not harmony but war, not peace and amity but strife. His French opponent, Charles Maurras, who hated Dreyfus, democracy and all foreigners, saw this well enough and supported international sports meetings on the grounds that he felt the more the French competed against barbarians the more the French would come to hate foreigners. Coubertin's idealism was finally prostituted by the Nazis in the 1936 Olympics. He was too ill to go and his recorded voice spoke of 'the most important thing at the Olympic Games is not to win, but to take part, just as the most important thing in life is not to conquer but to struggle well'. Even as he spoke Hitler and his cohorts were staging a Games which were, in effect, a celebration of Nazism and Hitler was perfecting his plans for world conquest.

James, the Marxist, should have been expected to see all this. Instead he burnished the myth of an English sporting Eden as one where the whole world was welcome. Where did James get such a view of English sports? It is clear what his inspiration was. He refers to it again and again – it is his belief in the English public-school code: 'I learnt and obeyed and taught a code, the English public-school code, Britain and her colonies and the colonial people. What do the British people know of what they have done there? Precious little. The colonial peoples, particularly West Indians, scarcely know themselves as yet.'

It was not that James was unaware of the racial situation in the West Indies or of what he calls the national question, the question of West Indian self-government and the formation of a federation of the islands. But in school these things did not matter and James, in any case, was much taken by individual Englishmen, men who may have been politically reactionary or even chauvinistic but were personally kind and tolerant. All this made James think that they were following the right policy even if at times they could not help being partial to the white boy in the class in preference to James. And just as James saw the school as a bulwark against the world where he was to receive hard knocks, he saw the English world of sports as a bulwark against the reality of life.

Interestingly Naipaul, reviewing James's *Beyond a Boundary*, was one of the few to pick up James's references to the code of the English public school and commented, 'twenty years ago the colonial who wrote those words might have been judged to be angling for an OBE or MBE'.

How very different James is from the Indian writer Nirad Chaudhuri. Chaudhuri was born in India at about the same time that James was born in Trinidad – the closing years of the last century. Both are colonial products, yet their writings about India and the West Indies could not provide a greater contrast, not least in the way they have been received.

Chaudhuri, who has written extensively about the Indo-British interaction, is generally seen in India as an apologist for the Raj and often abused quite virulently. The poet Nissim Ezekiel described one of his books, *Passage to England*, as slavish in its love for England. Chaudhuri's image as the poodle of the English stemmed from the fact that he dedicated his autobiography to the memory of the British Empire, an empire which had conferred subjecthood but withheld citizenship, nevertheless 'all that was good and living within us was made, shaped and quickened by the same British rule'.

Yet now, rereading James and Chaudhuri, there can be no doubt who is both more critical and perceptive about the British impact on their colonies. It is Chaudhuri who is very severe on the British in India – at one stage he compares the British in India to Nazis whose personal behaviour towards Indians ruined the impact that British letters and British learning had made on the Indian mind, James, in contrast, has very little to say that is harsh about the English in the West Indies. In the 1950s, totally misunderstanding the situation in South Africa, he even opposed a boycott of sporting South Africa. Nevertheless, while Chaudhuri is reviled in India, James, partly because of his Marxist past, is seen as the great radical historian of the West Indies and his device of using cricket as a metaphor to explain the West Indies is both admired and copied.

The contrast in the treatment of the two writers tells us much about how these two societies, India and the West Indies, viewed sport. In the Caribbean cricket has enjoyed an intellectual prestige it has never done in India. In the Caribbean a man of letters could also be a lover of cricket – that was rarely the case in India. For men like Chaudhuri their imbibing of English learning was the culture of the 18th century, long before sports entered the English cultural equation. James came to it when the 19th-century sporting ethos had been formed.

So, unlike James, Chaudhuri has little to say about cricket, except for one brief reference in his autobiography to the discovery of a picture depicting English cricket in a school textbook. It made a profound impression, so much so that although he loved cricket and played it, he could not but compare the drab efforts of his team 'by the side of the cricket world revealed in that coloured picture. The game was transformed, it was cricket suffused with the colours of the rainbow.' This, it seemed to him, was how the game was played in England. After that he could not take the Indian efforts seriously – not even Father Prior at the Oxford Mission in Calcutta could get Chaudhuri to play any sports, even badminton. The glow cast by English cricket seemed to turn Chaudhuri away from the sport in India, instead of towards it as with James. This apart, Chaudhuri has written hardly anything at all about the effect of English sports on the colonials, so why do I say Chaudhuri rather than James who provides the greater, more insightful, observations on the contradictions of the English colonial experience? Now it could be said that I would make such a remark. Am I not, like Chaudhuri, a Bengali? Would I not stick up for him? The fact is he does not need me to stick up for him and I say this because Chaudhuri, while appreciative of the British influence in India, particularly Bengal, is, unlike James, also aware of how the British did not follow through on what they had created. He makes the point in the cultural and political context, I would echo it in the sporting context.

As we have seen, Chaudhuri argues that the British as imperialists failed to behave in the example set by the Romans who converted even former slaves to citizens of Rome as long as they accepted Roman ways. His reference to Rome is important, particularly when you compare it with how James feels about Rome. We know how he feels about ancient Greece. But in the middle of his long eulogy of Greece, there is a throwaway line about Rome. He says the heritage of imperial Rome is 'more than ever a millstone around our necks and a ball and chain on our feet'. This is the only reference to Rome in a 254-page book and it jars. Perhaps James hates Rome because the Romans did not care for organised games, certainly not in the way the Greeks did. But in so dismissing the Romans with that curt half-sentence he misses a crucial point. The point is that the British, having started their imperial adventure as expansive Romans, had become insular Greeks. A Berber from North Africa could be a Roman who helped colonise Britain but such acceptance of peoples from different cultures and colours would have been unthinkable for the Greeks. And it was as the British swung away from the jaunty, all-embracing Roman imperialism to the narrow, exclusive Greek view of the world that organised games began to emerge in this country. The result was that, taking their cue from the Greeks, just as British administrators dubbed my Bengali ancestor's attempt to speak English as 'Babu' English, so English sports reacted with horror and indifference to those non-Brits like me who did take to their sports.

James does not seem interested in all this. The result is that James has left us with a legacy which is a very heavy burden to bear. Just when people like me, lured by the promise of English sports, had realised that the games of the English did not belong to us all, that they did not transcend all boundaries of race, colour and creed, there was James stepping in to create a cosy fantasy about a mythical past which we could all cling to even when the reality suggested we were under a delusion. If modern British sports administrators did not care for us, or treated us like sporting Calibans, we could ease our worries by rereading James and looking back to that golden period of Arnold, Hughes and Grace when we would all have been accepted, when we would all have been treated as their boys. What is more, if we stretched our arms sufficiently back we could have linked up with Olympus Apollo.

It is only now, as I write this, I realise both how absurd James was and how naïve I was in not accepting that in creating my English sporting fantasy I had divorced the English sporting world from the political and historical England that gave birth to it. Worse still, I had so falsified it as to make it unrecognisable.

So when celebrated English sports journalists like Peter Ball or Mike Lewis or even my good friends Jim Pegg and David Robson – albeit half in jest – questioned my pretensions to understand football, or mocked my devotion to Tottenham, they were not being cruel but reflecting their sporting heritage and tradition. All of these good people have happily encouraged me to write on cricket, even praised my writing and insights, believing that as an Indian I must know about cricket. But they could not understand how I might know anything about football or any of the other English sports. I can hardly blame them. The fault lay with me for believing I could ever be totally part of their sporting world. However much I proclaimed my love for Tottenham, or recited the double team, I would always be the hunter boy wanting to learn archery from the Aryan guru but denied the privilege because I could never be accepted as an Aryan.

The story of the hunter boy is part of Hindu folklore and comes from *Mahabharata*, one of the two great classics of Hinduism. The story illustrates how the Aryans of India coped with non-Aryans who dared to claim to be as good as them. It goes as follows. One day princes of the royal house are hunting in the forest. One of their dogs scouring the woods returns with its mouth muzzled with a number of arrows shot with an amazing quickness and precision. The princes are astonished by this feat of archery and want to know who could be responsible.

They discover it is a hunter boy, definitely not an Aryan, and a person who should not have such knowledge of archery. But on asking him where he learned his skills they are shocked to discover that he has been taught by their own guru, the Brahmin Drona, who is only supposed to teach archery to the royal princes, or in any event not have any non-Aryan pupils. The princes rush back to Drona to ask why he has taught a non-Aryan hunter boy. Drona is surprised to hear the tale and denies he has done anything of the sort.

The boy is summoned and the truth emerges. He had sought lessons from Drona but was refused since, as a Brahmin, Drona could not teach such skills to a low-born non-Aryan – a person so completely outside the magic Hindu circle. The boy's response to this refusal was to return to the forest, set up an image of Drona, worship it and, using it as an inspiration, try and learn the skills. Through sheer devotion and hours of practice, he is successful and that is why, he says, he now regards Drona as his teacher.

Now it was, and still is, the practice amongst Hindus that a teacher can ask for a gift from his pupil. Generally he asks for land, money, cattle, but in theory he can ask for anything. Drona knows his Aryan duty. He cannot allow a non-Aryan with such skills to flourish. So he asks the hunter boy for his right thumb. The boy instantly cuts it off and presents it to Drona, sacrificing the very thing that made his skill. Cruel as the story is in Hindu mythology, it is a warning to those who presume to be what they cannot, who covet worlds which do not belong to them, cannot ever belong to them.

The English, to their credit, have never approached, even remotely, such cruelty. While I may have been like the hunter boy and have had my moments of worshipping English sporting cut-outs from afar – as, for instance, following Tottenham through *The Times of India* – they have never demanded anything like the penalty Drona did of the hunter boy. They may have mocked my loyalty to Tottenham but they have tolerated it. And when I did end up working for *The Times* group in London, the paper from which *The Times of India* derives its name, nobody came up to me and said they wanted my right thumb or, what I suppose would be its modern equivalent, my mouse.

It is not like the English to be quite so cruel. Unlike my Hindu ancestors they are not a cruel race. Their image of a tolerant, fair-minded people is no myth. Indeed, the English, contrary to their own myths, are not even a true imperial people. The Romans and the Greeks were imperial people, despite the fact that they had different kinds of empires. The English have always had a problem coping with their empire. Late in the 19th century they did take to glorying about the empire but this did not come easily or naturally to the English – their fundamental national feelings are about an island race resisting aggression. The chorus of Rule Britannia about Britons never, never being slaves sums up the basic feelings of the English better than any other verse and they have never been able to resolve these contradictions. Later on in this book I hope to take up the challenge thrown down by Matthew Engel and discuss how a modern English sporting patriotism my be created, one that goes beyond the narrow definition of race. But here let me tackle what may be called the Omichand problem.

Omichand was a businessman in Calcutta who was involved in the conspiracy Robert Clive and the East India Company successfully hatched to get rid of Siraj-ud-daullah, the Nawab of Bengal. It meant forming an alliance with Siraj's general, Mir Jaffar, the ablest and best of them. In return for being made King of Bengal in place of Siraj, Mir Jaffar agreed not to help Siraj when Clive attacked him. The conspiracy worked brilliantly and with his victory at Plassey over Siraj, the English empire in India was launched. Omichand was Clive's agent in this and at one stage threatened to blow the whistle and tell Siraj unless he was paid very large sums of money. Clive and the English in Calcutta, who were convinced Omichand was a crook – but had to associate with him because everybody else was also crooked, perhaps more so – decided the only way to deal with Omichand was to be as deceitful as all around them. They produced two versions of the treaty they signed with Mir Jaffar. The true one had no clause about any payment, to Omichand, the false one with forged signatures had. Clive justified it on the grounds that Omichand was the 'greatest villain upon earth', and that it was necessary to deceive him in order to achieve the far more important objective of securing English possession in that part of the world.

Many years later, on his return to England, Clive's behaviour in India was the subject of a parliamentary enquiry and a censure motion in the House of Commons. The proposer, Colonel Burgoyne waxed lyrical about how Clive had looted Bengal for his personal gain and deceived Omichand. Clive defended himself much in the style of Napoleon justifying the shooting of Duc d'Enghein; he would if necessary deceive Omichand a hundred times. The debate showed the English at their most sanctimonious. Part of Burgoyne's resolution was accepted, that Clive had made money, but he was also praised for 'great and meritorious service to the country'.

The verdict, as Clive's biographer Nirad Chaudhuri says, meant the Commons had ducked the question: how do they 'condemn Clive without condemning the very establishment of British power in India, which by the moral standards that were at that moment being applied to Clive's conduct was naked aggression and usurpation, if not robbery . . . His misdeeds, if there were any in reality, were inconsequential and minor, compared with those of the Company. England could not retain the stolen goods if they called Clive a thief.'

The English have always struggled with this dilemma. They have wanted the glory of the empire but have recoiled from the messy, underhand, often criminal, dealings that accompany the acquisition of such power. They like to be seen as moral, upright, honest men and women – which by and large they are, probably more than any other people on earth – but when it is pointed out to them that in being an imperial power they might also have been cruel, vindictive, greedy, dishonest and evil they look away, unable to accept they could ever have been so false to their essentially good and honest nature.

In the imperial context this has led the English to have a guilty conscience about their empire and, says Chaudhuri, eventually paved the way to the abandonment of the Indian empire in 1947. The inability to reconcile the existence of the empire with an English character, which was essentially not imperial, also explains why since then English historians have struggled to come to terms with the end of the Raj. In the sporting context, as I have said, it means that the English confronted by their sporting empire – created like the political empire more by chance than by forethought – are shocked and puzzled to find that people who are not English know anything about it.

This is compounded by one other trait of the English character. The English, by their own admission, are not a philosophical people. They have a horror of the continental pedants – one reason why they found the Brahmins of India, probably the world's greatest pedants, so distasteful. As befits a people who started the industrial revolution, they are a supremely practical race and they even have in their language an expression which admirably sums it up. As George Steiner has said, in no other language will you find the expression, 'What's your game, then?' It expresses the English horror of over-elaboration, distrust of anybody trying to be too clever and anything that smacks of airy-fairy ideas that have no practical meaning.

So in sports, when confronted by the basic philosophical and historical contradiction between the promise held out by English sports and the grubby reality of its insular, racist roots, the English response is to convert the problem into a personal one. South Africa's sporting apartheid became a question of whether they would allow D'Oliveira to play for England. Yorkshire cricket's inability to integrate its Asian community into its cricket structure becomes a question: when will Yorkshire field an Asian? It is easy to see how by personalising the issue in this fashion it can be made dramatic but the implication is that the moment Yorkshire play an Asian the whole tangled problem of race and culture is magically solved.

But such solutions can only be palliatives. Worse still, by personalising it, it deflects the argument from the fundamental examination of the real problems faced by English sport. These are the questions of who is considered English, how do you become accepted in English sport, what do you have to do – more so if you do not come from what is considered a traditional background – to be treated as an equal member of the sporting community?

For some in English sports such questions can be deflected with bluster, and a certain obnoxious populist style. Brian Clough is a master of that and every time I hear him I wonder if that love affair I began with Tottenham and English sport on 8 May 1961 was not a very big mistake. Would I have been better off if I had fallen in love with the New York Yankees?

But then I know I could not have. Like millions of others besotted by English sports, I am now too old to change my loyalties. I still have a love for East Bengal football but it is no more than the distant memory one may have of one's first girlfriend. It cannot replace my love for Tottenham, or my moments of acute anxiety on match days. In any event, as Veliz says, we like in a world of sports made by England. We have no choices left. Our only hope is that maybe, someday, we can make the English appreciate their heritage and what it means both for them and us. That one day we can make then realise that we sporting niggers also count. But to do that we must understand the English sporting disease and its many manifestations.

CHAPTER FOUR

The Coon, the Baseball Bat and Enoch Powell

Some 15 years ago a train used to run on Saturday nights from Nottingham to London. It left Nottingham at 19.03 and arrived at St Pancras just after 21.30. It was an unremarkable train. The first-class coaches, which were usually in the front, consisted of cubicles set off down a corridor. This marked first-class from the second-class in a much more class-conscious manner compared to present-day trains where all compartments blend into one long corridor and what distinguishes first from second is more the quality of the furnishings. When I first encountered the train the cubicles had some of the feel of the trains in *Brief Encounter*, exuding an air of seclusion and intimacy. Over the years, and particularly on winter nights, they also conveyed some of the danger and fear of an alleyway. If they had first held out hope of adventure, they later threatened menace.

But their full significance did not become clear to me until I took a fateful trip – returning from covering a football match they made a horrifyingly indelible impression on me. By now my train travel – this was early in the '80s – took place almost wholly on Saturdays as I travelled up and down the country to report matches for *The Sunday Times*. In those pre-Murdoch days the paper provided a first-class rail coupon for the journey – a trim-looking white coupon with neat blue borders – which meant I kept away from the great mass of travelling football supporters.

By this time I was more than aware of the need for separation. Ever since my return to England in the late '70s, I had noticed how Saturdays had changed. They no longer carried the innocence of the time when I paid to go to watch football. Then I had thought nothing of going in the company of the most disparate friends, very often from other clubs and all of us happy flaunting our competing allegiances. Thus I had gone with John to see Tottenham play Stoke, a 2–0 Tottenham victory, where my only moment of distaste was when John said White Hart Lane did not have the passion of Highbury. I put that down to the fact that John was an Arsenal supporter. Later still a whole gang of us went to see Leeds destroy Tottenham and the worst I had to suffer was cruel taunts from Aspi – a committed West Ham supporter. And then when Judy had come into my life, Saturday sojourns at her Chelsea home acquired a different dimension. Come half past two we would just step out of her little one-bedroomed flat, walk down to the Bridge and watch Osgood, Cooke, Houseman, Bonetti and Hudson.

In going to these matches and many more I did not feel I needed to make any special preparation, let alone take any precautions. If I did not go to football as regularly as I went to Sainsbury, which was every Saturday morning, I went often enough. And just as my trips to Sainsbury did not require any special thought, except making sure I had enough money, so going to football was no different and a lot more carefree than going to the theatre. Indeed, John and Judy were both friends from the theatre, John playing the carpenter and Judy Mrs Sin, the widow in *The Good Woman of Setzwan*, while I played the first God, and going to football was our way of showing that we could be hearties as well as arties.

Even in the mid-'70s, as the first reports of football violence started seeping in, it did not touch me. In any case it was often presented in the media as something rather odd if not quite comical. The older journalists who spoke about it certainly saw it as a joke and the first time I heard about it I burst out laughing, although that was partly because of the way Basil Easterbrook pictured it. I was in my first year as a journalist and it was towards the end of the 1974 cricket season. We were all crowded into the small Oval press box, just below the pavilion, watching Zaheer Abbas who – despite Trueman's declarations that 'he fucking can't bat' – was scoring a double hundred against England. In a pause during play, Easterbrook pulled a face as he contemplated his winter activity. The season had already started and he said, 'I have to go to the football next Saturday.' 'Not Manchester United, I hope,' said someone. United that season had been relegated to the second division for the first time since the war and their supporters had started causing a lot of mayhem. 'Oh, well, if it is United,' said Easterbrook, 'I will have to get out my gas-mask. Haven't had it out of the cupboard since VE-Day.' The thought of Easterbrook, quite the most fastidious journalist, who always started the day's play by arranging his sharpened pencils in a neat row in front of him, having to don a gas-mask to protect himself during a football riot was so hilarious that we all burst out laughing.

Some six months after this *The Observer* noted the erection of the first barriers at the Stretford End and its report was as follows: 'The Stretford End . . . is a kind of academy of violence, where promising young fans can study the arts of intimidation. This season the club installed a metal barrier between the fans and the ground. It resembles the sort of cage, formidable and expensive, that is put up by a zoo to contain the animals it needs but slightly fears. Its effect has been to make the Stretford terraces even more exclusive and to turn the occupants into an élite.'

But now in the early '80s, football violence was not quite that fashionable and it had long since stopped being a laughing matter. Saturdays brought a sense of foreboding and going to football was no longer a simple matter of just heading for the ground. I suddenly became aware that there were a lot of hurdles to be negotiated before I got there. When I arrived at one of the London railway stations I found policemen in the forecourt complete with dogs. I had read John Moynihan's description of long train journeys in the '50s: talking football while England whistled past the train window and the waiter brought endless trays of food and wine. Let alone restaurant cars, most Saturdays I was lucky to find a buffet bar that would serve anything. Even if one was open it nearly always carried a notice saying that this train had been declared dry.

In the past I had never noticed or cared whether there were policemen on the trains; now their presence reassured me. More so when I arrived at my destination and found myself in the midst of young supporters who would suddenly break into a run or start shouting very loudly. I could hardly, if ever, make out what they were saying but their air of menace was unmistakable.

My apprehensions were eased by the presence of police, but the sight of policemen with dogs escorting the away supporters to the ground produced mixed feelings: relief that thus hemmed in they could do nothing, but sadness that such extraordinary measures should be necessary just to make sure a game was played without violence. Football violence and the steps taken to prevent it were now changing the landmarks I had traditionally associated with the game. In the past it was the pylons carrying the floodlights that from a distance indicated where the ground was. In a strange town it often acted as a sort of makeshift but unerring A to Z. Now it was the sight of police vans and dogs waiting some distance from the ground that was a much truer indicator. And I no longer needed the referee to start glancing at his watch to be aware that the match was nearing its end. A few minutes before the end the public address system would warn the away supporters to stay in their enclosure until the police had cleared the ground of home supporters. Then and only then would they be escorted back to their coaches or the railway station.

Football matches may have always been tribal affairs, but never had the warring tribes been so openly identified. Segregation had become mandatory and as supporters approached a ground they had to declare their tribal allegiance. Home or away? asked the police and the stewards to help them direct the fans to the right, safe enclosure. About this time, Gordon, a friend, told me a story which left me both bemused and worried. He lived in Bedfordshire and had taken his son to watch Luton play West Bromwich Albion. For some unaccountable reason his son was a West Bromwich supporter. Gordon thought nothing of it except when he got to the ground. The police asked him: home or away? Pardon, said Gordon, not sure what they wanted to know. Home or away? insisted the policeman, and since his son wore the West Bromwich scarf he and his son were directed to the away section where they were penned in for the duration of the match when, in many ways, they more naturally belonged to the home section.

As I heard the story I wondered what I would have done had Judy and I been asked: home or away? I could hardly declare my allegiance for Chelsea. I cannot remember ever watching Chelsea play Tottenham in Judy's company and while Judy's love for Chelsea was quite strong it did not, I think, go much beyond Alan Hudson's legs. I consoled myself with the thought that when I paid to go to football the game made no demands except the one on my wallet. Now that I was paid to watch, the game was exacting a tribute from me by making me feel physically very unsure.

By this time I was well aware that London had become a much more violent, assertive place compared to the more carefree city I first knew in the '60s. Then, I had thought nothing of walking at two in the morning from Piccadilly Circus to Brixton. Unable to get a taxi, I had just taken to the streets, unaware of any sense of danger. Indeed, for a couple of years I had lived in Brixton sharing a flat with Josey, the large florid mother-in-law of a famous television personality. Josey had been badly beaten up in Nigeria and we often spoke of her experiences there. But the idea that a similar thing might happen in Brixton never occurred to us. Josey had become friendly with a white girl whose husband was a black band leader, and we often went to the local pub savouring what we felt was a marvellous multicultural atmosphere.

Once I was stopped by a black man who looked very menacing. It was gone twelve midnight, I had just emerged from the Brixton underground station and was wearing the thick, rather elaborate, white fur coat that was then so fashionable with certain film directors. He had his eye on it and I was about to react to his demands when his partner said, 'Let him go, he is a brother.' On hearing the word brother the man immediately stepped aside and I walked away unmolested. I wasn't sure how to take 'brother' but I put it down as one of those things and it did not affect my confidence or my feeling that I had as much right as anybody else to go anywhere in London at whatever time I chose.

Then in the early '80s a couple of things happened which made me re-examine all this, culminating in my experiences on the 19.03 from Nottingham which made me question whether I should even bother to watch football any more. The first of the incidents had nothing to do with football but it set a pattern and so suddenly and viciously did it happen that it filled me with a dread that took a long time to conquer. On Friday, 30 May 1980 – I remember the date because it was the day before Ian Botham was appointed captain of England in succession to Mike Brearley – I was returning from *The Sunday Times*. My head was full of Botham. I had heard whispers he would succeed Brearley and the next day I was travelling to Taunton to see Somerset play Middlesex. If Botham's appointment was confirmed it would mean an early encounter between him and Brearley.

The Piccadilly Line train was crowded and I had to stand in the aisle between the seats holding on to the straps. Sitting in front of me were some skinheads, both boys and girls. As the tube came to Holborn they got up and I moved back giving them room to go. As one of the skinheads went past me he suddenly let fly with his fist smack in my face.

I had not spoken to him, I doubt if I had even glanced at him, and the act was so unexpected that for a few minutes I did not know what had happened. This disorientation was worsened by the fact that the force of the blow had sent my spectacles flying. I was more shocked than hurt and even more mortified that although the compartment was crowded and a lot of people saw it nobody said or did anything, even when I groped my way around the compartment to pick up my glasses. As I scrabbled about on the floor of the carriage, I saw one or two of them look at me. The rest ignored my gaze as if this was a private quarrel, something they did not want to know about.

At the next stop I staggered outside holding my face – the injury was not great – still unable to comprehend what had happened. Soon I was overcome with a range of emotions: dread that it might happen again, remorse that I had not fought back – but it was so sudden they had gone before I could react – and a dreadful sense of inadequacy about my physical frailties which did not leave me for a long time. When I got home my uncle, who was visiting from Liverpool, made matters worse by doubting the incident had ever taken place. I was late for our dinner appointment and he was not best pleased. So instead of sympathy I had a hard time even convincing him of the truth of my story. He refused to believe that anything like this could happen in a London tube. He had been living in this country since the early '50s, was one of the first Indians to become a consultant, and stories like mine were to him tales from newspapers, meant for public consumption, not necessarily true.

I kept my counsel but after that I reacted to a skinhead just as I used to react to our family doctor's Alsatians. If I saw one coming I gave him a wide berth, often crossing the road to avoid the beast.

It was some months after this, in the early summer of 1981 – and towards the end of the 1980–81 football season – that this skinhead menace acquired a football face. I was on my way to Norwich to cover their game against Arsenal. The match was unremarkable but I had persuaded John Lovesey that this would be suitable for an experiment in reporting. I had read in *Time Out* how most journalists and directors watched football from a seat in line with the centre circle rather than behind the goal as the terrace supporters did. This, said the writer, gave them a middle-class bias as opposed to the supposedly more genuine working-class view provided from behind the goalposts. I had dismissed this as the sort of pretentious rubbish *Time Out* occasionally came out with but it did strike me that depending where you watched a football match from you might have a different perspective, not in a class sense but as a way of looking at the game.

So I suggested to Lovesey that we send not one but five reporters to a match. Get one to stand with the hard-core terrace supporters, another with the manager in the dugout, a third with the chairman and the fourth with the season ticket-holder in the main stand. These four journalists would report the match through the eyes of their chosen subjects. In addition there would be the normal match reporter sitting in the press box to provide the usual match report. With a page devoted to this one match, the reader would get a feel of how different people, all of them supporters of the same team, saw the game and the whole exercise would indicate that a football match had many dimensions. It would also address the charge made against us journalists that our reporting never corresponded to the match as seen by the supporters and was more often a figment of our preconceived ideas.

Lovesey was attracted to the idea but in my view devalued the concept somewhat by allowing the match reporter 900 words or so while the four of us had no more than 250 words each, instead of the equal space I had envisaged. Lovesey's version, I felt, lessened the impact and robbed my idea of some of its purpose. Nevertheless it was a major feat to persuade a national newspaper to send five reporters, including Brian Glanville and Rob Hughes, the number one and number two football reporters of the paper, for this fairly ordinary league match with Arsenal.

So I was fairly full of myself when I travelled down to Norwich on the train. Apart from myself, the famous five consisted of Chris Lightbown, Denis Lehane, Hughes and Glanville. I had been assigned to sit in the directors' box with the then Norwich chairman, Sir Arthur South; Lehane was with a season ticket-holder; Lightbown, who was still seen as the voice from the terraces, with a young terrace supporter; and Hughes with Ken Brown, the Norwich manager. Glanville, probably the best match reporter of recent decades, was to do the match report.

Norwich was a town I always liked visiting and the train journey, which I made often, was a delight. The walk to Carrow Road took us past the canal and I chatted happily to Lehane and Lightbown as we moved along with hundreds of supporters. By this time a large crowd had gathered outside the ground and they seemed to be in good spirits. There was just one moment that jarred. As I made my way to the entrance marked 'Directors' I heard a cry: 'Get your copy of the *Bulldog*, get your colour supplement.' I turned to see a man with close-cropped hair, wearing a bomber jacket on the arm of which was the NF insignia, selling copies of a paper marked *Bulldog*. Lehane and Lightbown heard the cries as well and they seemed somewhat embarrassed. To me it was by now part of the environment round a football ground. I was, after all, aware of racism and had learned to accept such things.

I soon forgot about the incident as I tried to portray the match through Sir Arthur South's eyes. All of us had been provided with excellent crib sheets on our subjects by Rob Hughes who had already been to Norwich and done a fair bit of preliminary work. He had picked out both the season ticket-holder and the terrace supporter – Bert Horrex, a 65-year-old who sat in Block C, seat eight, and had been going to Carrow Road since 1937, and Mark House, a 13-year-old who used his pocket money to watch

81

Norwich. Hughes, who had interviewed all of them, had carefully noted down Sir Arthur's confession that he did not know anything about football but he knew men. He never interfered with the manager and did not know the team until he arrived at the ground. If Steve Walford, whom Norwich had recently bought, committed an error, then the first time it happened he would not say anything. But if he repeated the mistake he would ask Brown if he knew he had this tendency. Was that why Walford was available rather cheap, his price knocked down from the original asking price of £400,000?

Sir Arthur lived up to his advance billing and Hughes's notes made it easy for me to write Norwich versus Arsenal as seen by the knight. More interesting in some ways was the insight the whole experience provided in a world I hardly knew existed. Until that moment I had not realised how class-ridden football clubs could be. I had watched football as a supporter or from the press box. At Norwich, for the first time, I was admitted to the directors' box, the holy of holies in football. It was a world removed from the pen where away supporters were herded. Here there was no frisking, no injunction to wait until the home supporters had left. I was now the chairman's guest and immediately made aware of the almost mystical significance football clubs assign to the word chairman. From the moment the steward met me, saying, 'The chairman is expecting you', never once did I hear Sir Arthur South referred to by his name. Many people spoke to him during the course of the afternoon but it was always yes, chairman, no, chairman, chairman this and chairman that. And the style and opulence of the hospitality available to directors and their guests surprised me. As a football supporter I was aware that football grounds provided more than soggy meat pies and wretched instant coffee. The standards of press box hospitality varied from the sumptuous spread at Arsenal – provided, so the joke went, to compensate for their football – to Nottingham Forest, where a half-time cup of tea was a treat second only to getting an interview with Brian Clough. By the time I came on the scene Clough had stopped attending post-match conferences. But that afternoon at Norwich I was introduced to the comfort the real bosses of football enjoyed before, during and after a game. I had not been invited to the pre-match meal that the Norwich board, the visiting Arsenal directors and their guests had partaken of, but I was ushered into the boardroom for a pre-match drink and at half-time there was a magnificent spread supplemented by as much free drink as anyone could manage. I have since been to many boardrooms and the bigger clubs easily outdo Norwich but it was at Norwich that I first became aware of a certain kind of well-heeled woman in expensive furs, tasteful but costly jewellery and with what looked like a permanent suntan. Many years later I learned that the tan was very often acquired after hours under a sunbed rather than actual exposure to the sun, nevertheless the women there were very far removed from the sort of occasional woman of pallid complexion I had seen on the terraces or the stands. And even if Judy, or rather her well-off father, could have afforded some of the jewellery I saw on the women in that Norwich boardroom, I doubt if Judy would have been persuaded to discard her jeans and tee-shirt for a dress with a plunging neckline enclosed in a fur coat.

My mind was full of these wonders of the boardroom when after the match I met up with Lehane and Lightbown to walk, or rather run, back to the station. There was a train at five past five and we were all very keen to get it. We got to the station just as the train was about to pull out. Normally I would have walked the length of the platform to find a first-class compartment but there was no time for that and, following Lightbown's lead, I jumped in the first available compartment with Lehane just after me. As we did so the train left. It was now, as I walked down the aisles towards the first-class, that I realised what I had done and the great peril I had put not only myself but all three of us in.

We had got in at the back of the train packed with Arsenal supporters returning to London. They should have been in a good mood. The match produced the familiar 1–0 to the Arsenal scoreline – although we were some years away from it being converted into a song – but far from being happy they seemed very angry. As I walked through them they looked at me with faces like thunder. Suddenly, as I went past one large, fat supporter he looked at me and cried out, 'Coon, coon, hit the coon over the head with a baseball bat.' As he said so he got up and started following me. It was my extreme good fortune that by the time he did I had gained some distance on him and a couple of people had interposed themselves, quite unwittingly, between me and him. But this only seemed to add to his sense of urgency to hit the coon.

So, as the train sped away from Norwich, a strange procession made its way. Lightbown was in front of me, Lehane just behind me, after that a couple of others and then this fat Arsenal supporter crying out, 'Coon, coon, hit the coon over the head with a baseball bat.' I had never heard this song before and it was only later I learned it was a very popular football song. As he sang the Arsenal supporter was trying to shoulder his way past Lehane and the others to get at me. I quickened my step but I could not really make a run for it. I was going through some very crowded compartments and they were all filled with hard-faced, young men who looked angry and menacing and brought back visions of the skinhead whose fist I had encountered at Holborn station. As the cries of 'Coon, coon, hit the coon over the head with a baseball bat' grew nearer and louder, I feared the Arsenal supporters we were passing through would take up the chant and reach out for me. It was clearly an incitement to provoke such an assault on me, but fortunately for me they didn't. Then just as the man chasing me brushed past Lehane and reached for me, I stepped into the first-class carriage. And the first person both of us saw sitting there was a policeman – a black policeman.

Whatever the fat Arsenal supporter may have felt about the policeman's colour, this was one coon he could not trifle with. Now, as the policeman put himself between me and him, the situation was completely transformed. The supporter's cries died as if someone had switched off the power and as the policeman started to question him he looked more than a little confused. Beyond the policeman I could see the first-class cubicles where Brian Glanville was sitting with the rest of the football reporters amicably chatting away and totally unaware of what had happened. I have never felt such a sense of relief as I did when I saw them. At any other time their presence would hardly be a cause for celebration, now I sank amidst them with their moans of uncomprehending editors and moronic footballers and felt I had regained paradise.

This overpowering and oh-so-sweet feeling of being rescued obscured everything else. Once the policeman had apprehended the coon basher I had lost interest in him and was quite prepared to let the matter rest. But Lehane, a tough Irish-born journalist who had reported on the troubles in Ireland, was most outraged by what had happened and insisted I bring charges. I eventually agreed. Lehane, by now, was in his element. It was he who rang the office – in those days before cellular telephones we had to wait until we got to Liverpool Street – and then decided that we ought to recover in a fish restaurant in Soho that Lehane knew well. There, over champagne and oysters, the man hunting coons was put behind us and the night ended with Lehane's recounting his experiences as a journalist.

It was winter by the time the case came to court and Lehane and I returned to Norwich to provide evidence. I had doubts about the journey. Would the coon basher be on the train; would he have with him his mates who might complete the job he was so keen on the previous spring? But I need not have feared. This midweek journey in the pale winter sunshine could not have been more different to the one that spring evening. If he was on the train we did not see him. At Norwich we were met by a very friendly policeman who epitomised all the best in English police work.

When I finally saw the Arsenal supporter he could not have looked more different to the frightening vision I had carried of him since that train ride. Now instead of jeans and tee-shirt he wore a suit, his disorderly hair was slicked down – he had washed it but had not blow-dried it – and he looked an unremarkable if rather overweight young man. It turned out he was a chef who was not always in work and his story, as told to the Norwich court, was a sad one, made all the more pitiable by his extreme contrition. He had got into bad company, now he had straightened himself out and such behaviour would not happen again. His plea of guilty meant we did not have to give evidence and he was fined £20 for using abusive language and threatening behaviour.

Before I had arrived at the courtroom I had been apprehensive about how I would feel when confronting him again. In that crowded train full of Arsenal supporters, and in the middle of his tribe, he had looked like an ogre with me the alien. Now he was the outsider in surroundings that to me were part of the reassuring correction systems necessary in a civilised society. On the train he had behaved as if he was the butcher and I was a mere sacrificial lamb waiting for the slaughter. Now in the courtroom he seemed to be going through such a terrifying sense of bewilderment that I actually felt sorry for him. He was clearly intimidated by the court, the judge, the lawyers in their wigs. When he apologised and promised never to stray again I almost felt like patting him on the back and saying, 'There, there.' I did not, but I felt both removed from his world and not a little contemptuous of his background and upbringing. The difference was emphasised when at the end of the hearing he slinked away unable to meet my eyes, while Lehane and I went with the policeman for a very civil lunch and then a leisurely return home to London.

Years later I was to read in Bill Buford's *Among the Thugs* his experience of football violence on a train coming back from Wales. A drunken supporter got into a first-class carriage and tried to set alight a well-dressed man whose clothes and manner indicated his wealth. Buford pictured it as 'a telling image: one of the disenfranchised, flouting the codes of civilised conduct, casually setting a member of the more privileged class alight'. Lehane saw my battle with the Arsenal supporter in similar terms and since I had only pressed charges on his insistence the punishment meted out and, even more, the supporter's contrition were for him a victory for civilisation. On the train back from Norwich, Lehane, pressing endless drinks from the bar on me, began to dwell on this and other matters and grew increasingly expansive. He was now with *The Daily Express* and long before we reached Liverpool Street he promised me the job as cricket correspondent once he had got his feet under the table there.

All this made that midweek evening train ride a marvellous contrast to the journey back from the Arsenal match. Just as almost everything surrounding that train ride was a nightmare, now everything was reassuring. The gathering autumnal mist which allowed us fleeting glimpses of the passing East Anglican countryside, the elegantly dressed businessmen and women, so perfectly behaved, not only polite and thoughtful to each other but also to strangers, and Lehane's visions of the journalistic worlds we could conquer all made me feel that this was just the England I had always imagined. By the time the train came back to Liverpool Street the sometime employed chef was like a Victorian cartoon villain, little connected with my everyday world. I may have glimpsed Caliban on the train back from the Norwich versus Arsenal match but now, six months later, Camelot had re-emerged and everything was all right with the world.

Three weeks later I was on the 19.03 train from Nottingham and these cosy images were shattered, like so much brittle glass. The Arsenal supporter may have reformed but there were many others from different clubs who shared the same tribal instincts, and they all seemed to be waiting to hit the coon. None of them were waving baseball bats but they might as well have been for all the ill-will they exuded towards me.

I was in Nottingham to cover Forest's game with Leeds and my main concern about the match was that it was unlikely to be used in the London edition of *The Sunday Times*. In those days, long before separate sports supplements and with only four pages devoted to sports, *The Sunday Times* covered at best four or five football fixtures. Generally the matches favoured were north-south matches, Arsenal versus Everton, Tottenham versus Manchester United. The reasoning was that such matches were of interest both to the reader down south and up north and could be carried in all editions. Matches such as Forest versus Leeds were held to be of limited interest: at best Midlands and the north and of no interest for southern readers. I knew that the London edition that would drop through my letter-box the next day would have no match report by me, my match being replaced by one featuring a London club. I consoled myself with the thought that I would soon be in India covering India versus England.

The game in any case did not deserve wide circulation. Although it was early November, Leeds already looked doomed – they duly went down at the end of the season. The match turned out to be poor, redeemed by the weather which my notes say was brilliant. Forest scored first through Ward in the 22nd minute, Butterworth equalised for Leeds in the 43rd and the

Forest winner came in the 53rd minute when Robertson scored from the penalty box after Graham was adjudged to have handled.

I had hoped to catch the train that left Nottingham at about five-twenty but I knew this was going to be a struggle and when I got to the station I found I would have to wait for the 19.03. With the station dark, dank and uninviting, I found a Chinese restaurant nearby where I had a meal. By the time I returned the London train was waiting and I headed for the first-class cubicles at the front.

The cubicles – there were six of them – were completely deserted but this did not worry me. I quite liked the solitude. I had Arthur Schlesinger's biography of Robert Kennedy, which had been my book on my football travels that season, and there were newspapers including the sporting pink. I settled down to read, quite happy to be on my own. There was no reason for me to be anxious about the trip: the football fans and the police had gone and it seemed very peaceful. It was some time after the train had left Nottingham that I became aware that I had every reason to be very worried – this would be no usual trip.

The first sign was shouts and cries in the corridor leading to the cubicles. Soon I found a boy – he could not have been more than 12 – pressing his face against the door of the cubicle and flattening his nose against the glass in racial ridicule. He was joined by a second who shouted 'Seig Heil', and then started marching up and down the corridor.

A few minutes later there were more boys – four of them in all – and they slid open the door of my cubicle and entered. They introduced themselves as trainspotters. One of them, a chubby boy who wore plimsolls, resembled, apart from his colour, my own features at that age. He did most of the talking.

Who was I, what did I do, he asked?

When I told him I was a sports reporter he turned to his friends and they looked at me as if they could not believe me.

'How do you know anything about football?' he asked. 'Pakis don't know anything about football, do they?'

I let that pass.

Then the chubby boy asked again, 'Who do you work for?'

'*Sunday Times*,' I said. This seemed to throw them and I got the impression that *The Sunday Times* was not a paper they were familiar with.

'What's your name?' asked the chubby boy. When I told him he said, 'What? Not Patel? All you Pakis are called Patel. That is what the Paki who owns the corner shop is called.'

I could have said that Pakis, meaning Muslims from Pakistan, could hardly be Patels who were Hindus from India or East Africa, but felt silence was the best part of valour. However, my silences or occasional monosyllabic responses, far from deterring them, only seemed to encourage them.

Soon the chubby boy asked, 'What do you think of the National Front?' When I made no response he asked, 'What do you think of Enoch Powell?'

'I understand he is a very fine Greek scholar.' This reply seemed to throw them and for a few minutes silence reigned.

Then they started again. The chubby boy noticed I had a sporting pink and asked whether I knew the Manchester United score. He was, he said, a United supporter. I extended the paper to him. He looked at it: '2–1 to United.' But then his face contorted into a scowl. 'That wog Moses scored again.'

By now the boys were getting really tiresome and, with hindsight, I should have asked them to leave. But I felt they posed no physical danger and, believing the less I did the better it would be, I kept quiet.

For a time they left me in peace and even left the compartment. But soon they had returned and now there was a different mood. They no longer wanted to chat, they were acting as my well-wishers out to warn me of the dangers ahead. The chubby boy came in and said, 'There are a bunch of hooligans in the next compartment. Chelsea supporters. They are not in a happy mood.' Chelsea were then in the second division and that day they had lost 6–0 to Rotherham. I was aware of the reputation of Chelsea fans and the news that they were on the train threw me into utter confusion. When I had boarded the train I was reassured by the thought that there could not possibly be football fans on it. The Leeds fans would be heading north, the vast bulk of Nottingham Forest fans would hardly be travelling to London and the few that might be must have got an earlier train. I had not anticipated that a journey back from Nottingham could take in Chelsea fans returning from Rotherham. I was not aware that Chelsea fans were anywhere near me and the news the boys brought was like being told the Indians were about to ambush the stagecoach.

The boys seemed to sense this and began to play on my fear. For what seemed like ages, but was probably no more than 15 minutes, they would come in and out of my cubicle warning me of the hooligans in the next compartment and the dangers that lay in store for me. The train was now passing stations so familiar to me from university days at Loughborough. Then, as the train thundered through such stations, I had seen them as reassuring landmarks and hoped the journey would be prolonged. Now I desperately peered through the darkness hoping against hope that I would see signs for St Pancras.

Just before Wellingborough the boys returned and the chubby one said, 'They are going to get you before St Pancras. We are getting off at Wellingborough.' Then with a smile which suggested he had tried to play the good Samaritan but could do no more to help me, he and his friends were off. As the train left Wellingborough I decided to take what precaution I could and put on my coat and muffler. I opened and reopened the Kennedy book, shuffled the pages of the newspaper, but could not concentrate on the words. I dared not look in the corridor, aware that that was where my nemesis was supposed to come from.

Just as the train left Luton the lights went off, plunging my compartment in utter darkness. I thought this was an accident. I later learned that there were switches in the train which determined people could get at and use to plunge the train into darkness. The Chelsea hooligans had undoubtedly done that. I flicked on my lighter and checked my watch, praying for the minute hand to move faster and St Pancras to come. Just then the lights came back on and as they did so the long-threatening Chelsea mob finally arrived. There were about ten of them, their blue and white scarves flaunted across their persons. The leader was a man dressed in a woolly red jumper. He theatrically flung open the door of the cubicle and, dancing a jig in front of me, seized me by my lapels. 'He's mine,' he cried. Then, pressing his face close to me, he said, 'OK, mate, this is a mugging.'

As if on cue the lights on the train began flicking on and off and as the train plunged in and out of tunnels there would be brief spasms of light followed by utter darkness. By now the mates of the man who had claimed me had crowded into the compartment, some of them dancing up and down on the seats in front of me. One stood in front of me and started to shadow box silently, another pushed me about. They all disputed the right to work over what they called 'the wog'.

The man in the jumper released me, or rather pushed me away, and as I sank back to my seat he grabbed my briefcase and scattered the contents round the compartment with a triumphant shout. Another one snatched the lighter from my hand and smashed it against one of the walls, while another grabbed my cigars and yet another asked for my wallet but then seemed to lose interest and started jumping up and down in front of me. All the while they talked amongst themselves: who did the wog belong to, who would have him? Who would make the kill? I was now surrounded on all sides by the Chelsea army and felt like a missionary tied before the fire while the natives danced around me. I could feel the flames licking me and it seemed it was only only a matter of time before I was tossed in.

I did feel genuinely that I might not live through it and my mind seemed to dwell on curious irrational things. I had changed the way I took notes for the match, particularly the precious team formation of which *The Sunday Times* was so fond. Had this, I wondered quite stupidly, disturbed the traditional pattern, altered the cosmic waves around me and brought about this unexpected retribution? I also thought of the pair of gloves I had left in the driving compartment of my car at St Pancras, a natty pair that I had recently bought and which I usually carried in the outer pocket of my overcoat. Now I had this vision that after they found me, they would go to my car and unearth the gloves. The story would be headlined: The Man Who Left His Gloves Behind.

Then, suddenly, just when it seemed the Chelsea mob had made up its mind and was ready to roast me, a cry went up: 'Old Bill's coming.' The train was slowing down in its approach to St Pancras. A lookout had noticed that the Transport Police had boarded the train and as if by magic the Chelsea mob forgot about me and vanished. I feared it might be a false hope but to my great relief I saw the train was pulling into the platform. I slowly gathered myself and my things and made my way out. As I did so I could see a fire burning in a toilet behind me.

I was shocked, but angry as well, and my first port of call was the Transport Police followed by the stationmaster's office. By the time I got there I was quite worked up, my fury increased by the fact that throughout the two-and-a-half-hour journey I had not seen a single British Rail official. The stationmaster looked at me steadily and said, with a mixture of sympathy and helplessness, 'I am sorry, Mr Bose, but the guard is a human being too, he doesn't like walking up and down the train.'

In those days *The Sunday Times* offices were at Gray's Inn Road, very near St Pancras, and I got into my car and headed there. The Saturday ritual of Gray's Inn Road meant that the sports department had decamped to a bigger room on another floor and I arrived to find the usual sports room empty. I was glad. I had gone there to tell Lovesey that I did not want to report football any more, it was not worth the hassle. But finding nobody there I sat at a typewriter – one of those heavy typewriters so common in newspaper offices then – and wrote a little note to John Lovesey which, without giving any details, mentioned I had had a bad experience on the train back. I felt curiously better after that.

Lovesey responded very sympathetically and decided that this was a story *The Sunday Times* should feature. He assigned Dudley Doust, the sports feature writer, to it. Dudley, an American, was famous for the way in which he teased details from the person he was writing about – often trivial details which other writers might have thought were inconsequential but which Dudley used to paint a fly-on-the-wall picture of what had happened. He had collaborated with Mike Brearley to produce two excellent books, one of which had a marvellous recreation of Derek Randall's epic innings against Australia during the 1978–79 series. Dudley had spent hours with Randall extracting all the details and the joke in *The Sunday Times* was that whatever I had suffered at the hands of the Chelsea mob was nothing compared to what Dudley was going to put me through. Sure enough, over the next few days Dudley rang me at least a dozen times, possibly more. No fact was too unimportant, no detail too inconsequential. But the article he produced – 'Journey into Terror on the 19.03 from Nottingham' – was a masterpiece of recreation. Lovesey ran it as the lead item on the sports feature page, although one *Sunday Times* editor thought it ought to have been on the front page of the paper.

The article created an incredible reaction. It was picked up by newspapers in this country and in India, where I even made the front pages. My own writings had never given me prominence, now something written about me had suddenly made me famous. In the odd way these things can work out some people even thought I had written it and complimented me on it. There were anxious calls from parents and friends and I was inundated with letters both deploring the incident and expressing outrage and sympathy. One person, who had experienced abusive chanting from Manchester United supporters in a game with Spurs, sent me copies of letters he had written to Martin Edwards while others expressed their dismay and sympathy. Eddie Norfolk, writing on behalf of the Association of Provincial Football Supporters in London, commiserated and Monica Hartland invited me to a dinner of the association. In the press boxes my colleagues saw me in a different light, and while their sympathy was welcome I did not like the sensation of being singled out in this fashion.

For a time I thought of giving up football reporting. Was it worth it? But then I decided that to do that would be to give in to the people who had tormented me. The face of the chubby boy and his mates always came back to haunt me and I did not want to become another Paki Patel who was not supposed to know about football. I was also helped in the decision by the fact that after another match – when I drove to Ipswich to report their game against Swansea City – I spent some weeks in India covering the England tour. Within days of my return I was back on football – the FA

Cup match between Swansea and Liverpool, which saw Liverpool win 5–0 – and I did take the train to Wales. But, fortunately for me, I had the vast, comforting bulk of Ken Montgomery, to whom I stuck like glue, both on the way up and back to protect me.

But the incident on the Nottingham train had marked me. After that I grew reluctant to take trains and did not take one for almost five years until the beginning of the 1985 season when I travelled to Manchester City to see Tottenham play. Whatever match I was assigned to, I drove, even if it meant driving up and back to Swansea in a day. At times, towards the end of these 400- and 500-mile return trips, I was in danger of falling asleep on the motorway and once or twice I even nodded off – but nothing could make me return to the train. For me they carried a dread and a menace that was almost unspeakable.

I also now planned my football trips as if I was a general preparing for battle. The more I analysed the incident the more it was evident that I had fallen victim to the remnants of the Chelsea army that had travelled that day to Rotherham. The police had escorted the main army safely back to London but that still left scattered bands to terrorise the countryside and it was one of these bands I had encountered. They were like a guerrilla army and since I was clearly their natural target my objective on Saturdays was to avoid the sort of ambush I had suffered on the 19.03 from Nottingham.

Whatever match I was covering I always checked where teams like Chelsea, West Ham and Leeds were playing and took detours to avoid their possible paths. I always went very early, often arriving at the town some three hours before the match. And after browsing through yet another small town bookshop I would drive up to the ground, at times even before the stewards had arrived. Sometimes I had to wait until they unlocked the gates. But I knew by getting in so early I could park my car as near to the ground as possible. My objective was to cut down the distance I had to travel from the ground to my car after the match. My experiences of both the train journeys from Norwich and Nottingham had convinced me that the greatest danger I faced on a Saturday was not when travelling from London during the day, but on the return journey at night. It was then that I was likely to fall prey to a mob like the Chelsea one and next time I might not be so lucky.

CHAPTER FIVE

The Sporting Calibans

In his book on John Barnes, Dave Hill discussed with Paul, a black Liverpudlian, questions of race, football in Liverpool and the reaction of white Liverpudlians to blacks. Paul said, 'And white people retort by saying that black people are racist . . . Black people can be prejudiced but they can't be racist. And when there is prejudice, it is born out of years and years of suffering. And denial. Which makes them feel inferior.'

I think I know what Paul is trying to say but I reject the idea that only whites can be racist. If by racism we mean that people of a certain colour feel that they are superior to people of a certain other colour, then all people are capable of being racist. Even slavery has not been a white monopoly, having been part of all societies, and long before the white man inflicted it on the blacks of Africa there was a flourishing slave trade which took blacks to serve in the Muslim world. This is one aspect of slavery that has not received much study and only passing comment.

I have certainly heard more openly racist views in India than anything said on the subject in England. Indians can be very unfeeling about a person's colour. Of my two sisters one is fair by Indian standards, the other dark. My mother always said quite openly to her face, 'Pity about her complexion. But she has good features.' So often did she and others say it that I came to believe that because she was dark she was not really beautiful. Only after I came to this country and an English friend told me my sister was beautiful did I realise that she was and that beauty had nothing to do with skin colour. Growing up in India skin colour was

always important. The good Mr Khandalgoakar, who on my father's orders took me to so many cricket matches, would stand outside my father's office in busy Flora Fountain and, pointing to a dark-skinned Indian passing by, say, 'Look at that blackie.' He, like some Indians, had very fair skin which he took care never to expose to strong light. And, of course, I was well aware that my Bose ancestors had long practised a form of eugenics: always making sure the brides they selected were fair.

I was often told that my real grandmother, who had died young, was very fair, an observation that acquired pointed significance because my step-grandmother, the only one I knew, was very dark. On that account she was shunned by the family and my memory is of her sitting in a corner, ignored by everyone. It was this, plus Hans Christian Andersen stories, that made me elicit a pledge from my father that should anything happen to my mother I would not have a stepmother. I assumed all stepmothers would be dark, ugly and somehow evil. Interestingly, all the instances of colour prejudice I heard about as a child were of people of a lighter skin disparaging those of a darker skin.

But if Paul means that while all people are racist, what makes white racism different is that we all live in a white world, a world made and shaped by whites, then he would have been on surer ground. At the start of the 16th century, when the European nations seeking trade started colonising the world, the idea that Europe would emerge as the dominant continent would have been laughable: the Mings in China, the Mughals in India, the Ottomans in Turkey – who for another century would expand their powers in Europe and nearly capture Vienna – were all more powerful and better organised in terms of civilisation, scientific ideas, mathematics, even culture. Indeed, Europe was beholden to these countries for keeping the flame of civilisation alive through the European dark ages and had borrowed extensively from the Islamic world. But it was Europe, and its seemingly disparate countries, that prevailed. For various reasons Europe emerged dominant and in the 19th Europe began to gain mastery, European thought and actions, words and deeds reshaped the world. There had been civilisations and empires before: Asian and European, white, brown and black, but they had not succeeded in remaking the world in its image as Europe has done in the last 100 or so years. The Roman Empire may have been the greatest empire in recorded history but it had no impact on India or China, if anything it was Indian pepper that saved Rome from the wrath of the Goths.

What was remarkable about the European expansion, surprising and unexpected as it was, was that it reached out to all parts of the world, obliterating some civilisations, changing others, but leaving nothing unaltered. So much so that of today's major powers only Japan has completely escaped European colonialism – parts of China were colonised – and even Japan was occupied, albeit for only a couple of years, after the Second World War. This European armlock on the world has so revolutionised it that in the last century while Asians and Africans have had their moments, they have generally been reacting to Europe and the actions of European peoples, whether in Europe or elsewhere. What is more, the ways of thinking and speaking, the ideas articulated, even the languages used, are either European or created under European influence.

To illustrate, I cannot read or write Bengali, though I can speak the language of my ancestors. I can only communicate fluently in English. But even if I could write Bengali, the Bengali language itself resulted from the interaction between the Bengalis and English. The language may be based on Sanskrit – the ancient Indian language now, like Latin, a dead language, not used by anyone except priests during prayers – but its inspiration has been England. One of the greatest names in Bengali literature is Michael Madhushudhan Dutta. He introduced blank verse to the language but he did so after trying to become a poet in English and being told by his English friends that he would perform a far greater task for his people if he went back to Calcutta to become a Bengali poet.

It is this that makes white racism different. All people may be capable of racism but white racism is often institutional: prejudice combined with a power structure to enforce it in all walks of life. This was the case in the Deep South of America until well into the 1970s and, of course, in apartheid South Africa. To say this is not to complain, merely to state the obvious, although it is strange how often even the most astute English mind can fail to appreciate the fact. It intrigued me to note how rarely did rational, otherwise reasonable, even well-meaning people, understand that what made apartheid South Africa abominable was not prejudice but institutional racism from which people of the wrong colour had no escape. The argument against it was not that one group of people did not like another because of their colour, but that racism was part of the constitution.

Whenever I debated South Africa I would always be asked about the untouchables of India. My argument would go as follows. Yes, untouchability was, and is, a terrible system and there can be no justification for it. But it is not enshrined in law, far from it. Under the Indian constitution the untouchables benefit from positive discrimination with educational places and jobs reserved for them. So much so that now some Indian higher castes, the traditional oppressors of the untouchables, try and claim they are untouchable in order to gain the reserved college places and jobs. What is more, when India framed its constitution the man who wrote it was Dr Ambedkar, an untouchable who had managed to escape the wretched caste system and become a distinguished lawyer. If, I concluded, there came a time when a black man framed the South African constitution then at that moment the argument would be over. I would have thought anybody could understand this argument, this difference between apartheid and prejudice, but it was amazing to find how few did.

I was made vividly aware of this some years ago when, at the end of a day's play in the Old Trafford Test between England and India, I dined with David Frith and Qamar Ahmed. Ahmed had some of his Pakistani friends who took us to a restaurant in an Asian part of the city. Sometime between pappadums and the nans the talk turned to South Africa. Gatting had just come from his disastrous rebel tour, Mandela had been released but the picture was far from clear. Frith was gushing about the township cricket programme of Ali Bacher and wanted resumption of cricket links. I said while all of it was interesting, nothing would or could change until apartheid went. Frith looked at me stonily and said, 'What is wrong with you people? Why can't you give the whites any credit, they have done so much to change things in sport.' I began to explain that with apartheid being a totalitarian system based on race there could be no effective changes at the margins, the system would have to go, a position that Bacher understood well enough and has long since endorsed. But as Frith got agitated, Qamar tapped me on the arm and said in Urdu, 'There is no use arguing apartheid with whites, they do not understand.'

It led me to conclude that many whites, never having lived for any length of time under non-European rule – let alone having to accept a non-European system of thought and ideas – find it difficult to see the connection between prejudice and power and how this translates into racism. It is something the Jews, who regained their political power only after 2,000 years of alien rule, have always understood. But even here it required the advent of Nazism and its horrific ideas to convince some German Jews that their hopes of assimilation with German society were futile.

I had, of course, been aware of racism long before I became a sports reporter. I had arrived in this country just after Enoch Powell had made his infamous Rivers of Blood speech. The speech had been the subject of not only very many Letters from London in *The Times of India* but also anguished editorials and I had read and reread descriptions of the dockers marching to the House of Commons in support of Powell with a sense of utter disbelief.

The week before I arrived, David Frost had interviewed Powell and the confident assumption was that he would do to Powell what he had done to Emil Savundra, whose television exposure by Frost led to his disgrace. Frost's failure to destroy Powell – some felt Powell had emerged enhanced after the television interview – was the subject of animated conversations both in the university common room and the Students' Union.

But much as my university dons denounced Powell, his speech had made immigration, before then very much an underground subject in this country, both fashionable and controversial. I was made immediately aware that I was part of an English problem: the dark-skinned foreigner in their midst. A stranger in a foreign land always had a heightened sense of awareness but wherever I looked in those days the spotlight seemed to be on my colour. That autumn BBC 1 had started screening *Till Death Do Us Part* with Alf Garnett articulating what a lot of people had thought but until then could not, so I was told, summon up the courage to declare. (It has always struck me as odd that to declare racial prejudice openly can be seen as a sign of honesty and courage. Many years later, when I suggested to a caller on a radio programme, during a discussion on sporting apartheid, that by that measure the Nazi extermination campaign against Jews was the most honest programme ever undertaken by man, he spluttered and fell very silent.) Over the years a multitude of incidents would emphasise that my skin colour made me different and not always very welcome but in those early years the most irritating thing was landladies who sounded ever so pleasant and welcoming over the telephone, but who, the moment they opened the door and saw me, would say very curtly, 'Sorry, the room has gone', before slamming the door shut.

So in London, the great metropolitan centre of the imagined world that I had created in Bombay, where I had hoped to stand out for what I thought and wrote, I was more often singled out for the colour of my skin. Not long after I came down from Loughborough to London I took up residence in a hotel in Paddington. One night I sat in the TV room watching a new sitcom featuring Spike Milligan playing an Indian and speaking with what is known as the Peter Sellers Indian accent. Before the programme started I was just one of the many hotel guests in that room. By the time it had finished and Milligan had repeatedly said 'Goodness gracious me', I was acutely aware that everyone was looking at me, almost wishing that I would open my mouth and confirm that that was how a real-life Indian spoke. Among my fellow guests were a young white South African couple and as they passed I could hear the boy mimic the Indian accent: the minced South African accent overladen with the supposed Indian one sounded quite hideous but his blonde female companion found it hilarious.

At the same time there were other people who, as if to balance this, emphasised that they set me apart from the great mass of immigrants whose concentration was so worrying the English nation. Some of them while expressing their anxiety in terms of the overcrowding of this tiny island, would then say that, of course, they did not mean me. They would say, 'If only all immigrants were like you, we would have no problems', and one or two would say, 'But you are more English than we are'.

Within days of my arrival in this country I had been told, 'But you speak English so well', and the lady in question refused to believe that I had not been born in this country. When I tried to explain my Jesuit schooling in Bombay, I could see I was compounding the confusion for what had started as a discussion on racial prejudice was now being transformed into one about England's much older prejudice about those in the grip of Catholicism.

And soon I, too, shared their belief that I was different. Within weeks of arriving at Loughborough I was asked to help with some Bangladeshi workers who, despite living here for many years, did not speak English and were not following management instructions. I spoke to them in Bengali but when the workers invited me home for dinner I shrank from the invitation and was glad to leave the factory, thinking how little I had in common with them.

Despite my colour, or perhaps because of it, I conveyed respectability, even reassurance. Two months after my arrival in Loughborough I was voted president of the Students Union. The result was a surprise, as much to me as to most other people in the university, and one of the girl students, when asked why she had voted for me, said, 'He doesn't look like he'll run away with the Students Union money.' This may have had overtones of the trustworthy Patel shopkeeper but I took it as a great compliment. Later still, when I finally reached Fleet Street, the fact that I worked for *The Sunday Times*, and not one of the increasingly distrusted tabloids, gave me a cloak of respectability, even authority, which I quite relished.

To sum up: I was an immigrant, but treated as several cuts above the stereotype of the 'Paki' from Bradford or Southall. I was a journalist, but not of the dirty mackintosh, foot-in-the-door tabloid brigade who grubbed around for tittle-tattle from players and managers. I was a gentleman from *The Times* who supposedly wrote elegant essays in the style of Geoffrey Green or Neville Cardus. It required those three train experiences to strip me of all these illusions. Faced with the football hooligan at his most elemental, neither my supposed middle-class English upbringing or accent, nor my press card from *The Sunday Times*, was any defence: I was as vulnerable and naked as any other common or garden Paki caught in the frenzy of the mob.

Of course, my experiences, however terrifying they were at the time and whatever psychological scars they may have left on me, were nothing compared to what the English football hooligan has inflicted and continues to inflict on others. The nadir was reached on 29 May 1985 when, just before the European Cup final between Juventus and Liverpool at the Heysel Stadium in Brussels, 39 people died and 600 were injured following a charge by Liverpool fans into the section packed with Juventus supporters. For more than a decade English football had been journeying down this path, inflicting carnage and violence, often on bystanders, almost always in a foreign city or stadium. If since Heysel it has been comforting to believe that such hooliganism has been eliminated, the riots in Dublin in February 1995 put paid to such complacent thinking. Dublin was like Heysel, if in a different way, a first: the first time an England international had to be abandoned because of crowd violence. In a sense, although not in the way Brian Clough means it, the 96 deaths at Hillsborough must also be seen as part of the hooliganism problem. The Liverpool fans who died that day were not rioting, but they died because they were crushed at the Leppings Lane terraces against barriers that had been put up to curb hooligans.

Yet through all this there has been one constant refrain – do not blame English football. The excuses are many and varied: it's only a minority and an unrepresentative minority that causes problems; in any case it's society's problem, it's not a football problem, and even if it is, it is not confined to England. Football hooliganism, so the apologists say, affects the whole world. And then the last alibi: it has all been got up by the press seeking to sell newspapers.

Bill Buford, in *Among the Thugs*, has summed it up well: 'The crowd is not us. It never is.' Drawing on some of the greatest Western thinkers – Sigmund Freud, Edmund Burke, Edward Gibbon, Thomas Carlyle, Gabriel Tardi, Hippolyte Taine, Plato and Socrates – Buford examines how theories of crowd behaviour have been built up. The philosophers and thinkers have pictured the crowd in various ways, all of which are uncomplimentary: troublemakers, riff-raff, vagrants, criminals, morbidly nervous, excitable and half-deranged, scum that boils up to the surface in the cauldron of the city, barbarians, the vulgar working class, people driven by the impulses of the spinal cord and not the brain, unable to think for themselves, vulnerable to agitators, outside influences, infiltrators, communists, fascists, racists, nationalists, phalangists and spies. But, above all, a crowd is not us. English football has specialised in this act of denial, this supreme tendency never to accept responsibility, always to blame the troubles that take place on and around its football grounds as the work of others.

One of the letters I received after my experiences on the 19.03 from Nottingham, written the day after Dudley Doust's article had appeared, was from Ian Todd, of the National Federation of Football Supporters Clubs.

The letter was kindly meant, and I appreciated it greatly. Rereading it now it is interesting to see how Todd employs almost all the classical 'the crowd is not us' phrases. Not only is violence caused by a minority of travelling supporters but British Rail is held responsible for providing concessionary travel cards and special offers – I particularly liked the bit about BR's 'commercial desperation' which enables this minority to travel. The press is not without blame, of course, and there is a tug at the sympathy cords for the vast majority of well-behaved supporters not getting any credit. If we are to accept his argument it means that when football fans behave monstrously, they should first be tagged as an unrepresentative minority and then the people who transport them and the press who report their deeds should be held responsible for their actions.

Football never encourages them, football has nothing to do with them, football does not create the conditions where these people can grow and prosper. Nobody in English football ever explains how come a minority always cling to football and since, in this view, they clearly do not belong to the game, the game seems to feel no responsibility to even look at itself and ask if there is anything it has done or not done to encourage such behaviour.

Two very different incidences illustrate this English football refrain perfectly. Heysel and Dublin. Ten years and a great deal separate these two acts of football hooliganism. Unlike Heysel, nobody was killed in Dublin or even seriously injured – in many ways the worst injury was that suffered by a *Daily Mirror* photographer whose nose was bitten by Vinny Jones in a Dublin hotel. Yet not only were both Heysel and Dublin wretchedly vivid exhibitions of English football hooliganism at work on foreign fields, but both provoked almost identical responses: general expressions of outrage, shock, then after a time the whole episode was forgotten.

Both incidents took place against a similar background. As television showed pictures of mayhem and violence, confused studio guests – in the main ex-footballing greats who had been gathered to commentate on the game – tried to make sense of it and ended up expressing inarticulate shock, horror, outrage that the fair name of England had been once again besmirched by an unrepresentative minority. This was followed in the next day's papers by a sense of guilt. In the *Sun*, the day after Dublin, Martin Samuel, their chief soccer writer, said: 'Do not talk to me about being English today. I do not want to be English. I want to be a citizen of another country, any country. Tin-pot African dictatorships, South American dictators, tiny European Republics where the President goes to work on a bicycle. I want to hand in my passport, renounce my nationality, hang my head in shame. Just do not ask me to associate with this scum. Do not ask me to share a flag or a common bond with the low life who have shamed the nation at Dublin's Lansdowne Road. These bastards – I will not call them men, or anything normally associated with the merest scrap of dignity or self-respect – have left me sick to the stomach. As I sit here, I'm angry and confused and uncertain as to whether I want to watch another England international again . . . As Lansdowne Road cleared, a voice from the tannoy thanked the Irish fans for their impeccable behaviour and the English around me applauded. How we wanted to swop nationalities, how we wanted to switch our passports and cite Dublin as a city of our birth. But there was no escape from the English last night. For the first time I'm ashamed of my accent. I do not want to open my mouth and reveal my guilty secret, but I will do for one last phrase: may those bastards rot in hell.'

This was in the great tradition of English polemical writing: clear, direct, powerful. But readers barely had time to take it in before the sense of shame was replaced my another more enduring emotion: anger at the failure of the foreign authorities to properly police these events. Such anger surfaced within 24 hours of the Dublin riots. With Heysel it took a bit longer, but in both instances it was articulated with energy and conviction and provides a more reliable and ultimately terrifying insight into a certain kind of the English sporting mind. Here Heysel is the more revealing example.

In the immediate aftermath of Heysel, it seemed that the English game would be completely revolutionised. Mrs Thatcher called the soccer writers who had been at Heysel to Downing Street and it was soon clear that the Government would impose ID cards which everybody going to football would have to carry. Despite many objections – from within and without the game – Mrs Thatcher persisted and it was only the carnage of Hillsborough and Justice Taylor's report that finally slew this Thatcherite dragon.

Nevertheless there was one immediate consequence of Heysel which remains with us to this day. The Liverpool fans in Heysel had been extraordinarily drunk – on this everyone I agreed – and drink was considered the main cause of hooliganism. So drink was banned from English football grounds, or rather more accurately nobody could drink in sight of the pitch. This led to some rather comical arrangements for those who had executive boxes. In the Thatcherite yuppie '80s these had emerged in our football grounds with the intention of providing their occupants an opportunity to eat and drink in great comfort – and in great quantity – whilst watching a football match. The box-holders could hardly go without their gin and tonic and the ban meant they had to be served in an ante-room – a place from where they could not see the pitch. The result was that in football grounds with boxes a new phenomenon emerged post-Heysel: a crush in the allotted ante-room before the start of the match and a near stampede to get to the room and the drinks during half-time and at the end of the match.

Although ID cards were vigorously opposed, nobody questioned this particular Thatcher edict and football seemed to accept it was an evident answer to hooliganism. Yet while drink may have played a part in Heysel, I have never in 20 years of reporting seen football crowds drink like the crowds during the Varsity match between Oxford and Cambridge at Twickenham. That is the nearest to a sporting midwinter Bacchanalia I have ever experienced. On the only occasion I have been to the Varsity rugby match I arrived an hour before the kick-off to see the carpark at Twickenham awash with wine, champagne and all kinds of spirits and drinks. Car boots seemed to have been stuffed full of bottles which kept being produced throughout the match. I had long been accustomed to seeing foaming pints of bitter at cricket or football, but a cricket or football supporter has never given me the impression that he goes to the match with the object of getting drunk. That afternoon at Twickenham rugby supporters did. Bottles of wine were openly taken into the stand and drunk with an unrestrained enthusiasm I have never seen in any sporting ground. The Varsity match has since become so famous, or notorious, for drinking that the police have been known to set up breathalyser testing units outside the carpark at Twickenham, confident that a rich haul can be expected. Yet, despite the incredible amount of drink, I did not see any suggestion of hooliganism and there never has been any hint of trouble at these matches.

There are many explanations for this. The Tuesday in December when the Varsity match is played – and it's always a Tuesday – is the occasion for the brokers and other people in the City of London to travel down to

Twickenham and use the excuse of a rather poor rugby match to relive their university days. There is also a big class factor: rugby supporters are middle class, drink wine instead of beer, can handle their drink better and know how to behave at sporting occasions. Most football supporters, not having had the privileges of a public school education, cannot handle drink – or so the theory goes. Possibly so. But the eagerness with which drink has always been blamed for football's troubles shows how quickly football clutches at straws. And the way that foreigners and their inadequacies were blamed for Heysel and Dublin indicates the inevitable crutch English football grabs when yet another bout of hooliganism makes for unwelcome headlines.

A perfect example of this English habit is provided in the only book on Heysel that was written – but never published. Its title, *Heysel – A Case of Impossible Justice*, might suggest that we are in for a heavy dose of difficult jurisprudence. But you don't have to read very far, indeed the first page of the preface, to realise the main thrust of the author's message. The preface is entitled 'The Buck Stops Here' and it is very quickly clear where the authors believe the buck should stop. 'The fact remains that on the night of 29 May 1985, at Heysel, the Belgian authorities were guilty of criminal neglect. They simply did not know what to do. Faced with a situation of explosive proportions they panicked and were not swift in dealing with it effectively. Had they taken the situation in hand immediately, there may well have still been some fighting, a few bruises and black eyes maybe – to be deplored, but nothing more – and the Belgians would have earned our praise and gratitude as they did in the wake of the Zeebrugge tragedy, during which they showed great courage and bravery. Britons will always remember with gratitude the Belgian response to the capsizing of the *Herald of Free Enterprise*. But it is clear that at Heysel the Belgians blundered.'

It is understandable that the Liverpool-based authors – one of whom is now dead – should see the city and its football clubs in a special, kindly light. But when that light illuminates a subject in such a fashion and when Juventus, most of whose fans were among the 39 killed (nobody from Liverpool was killed), are held as much to blame as Liverpool, then we need to look more closely at the storyline that has changed from one where both Liverpool and English football have reason to be ashamed to where almost everyone is to blame but Liverpool.

To do that we need to look at this unpublished book in some detail. Let us start with an early chapter, entitled 'When in Rome'. This describes how the previous year, on 30 May 1984, Liverpool went to Rome to win the

European Cup, beating local club Roma, and incurred the wrath of the Roman supporters. Some of them ambushed the Liverpool fans which led to a comical aftermath where two of English football's finest journalists, Colin Mallam and Hugh McIlvanney, were rounded up by the Roman police for their own protection along with two thoroughly bemused American homosexuals.

The authors of the book argue that the Liverpool fans' experience in Rome created a burning hatred for Italians amongst them and shaped their attitude towards them. It is an interesting point in a book which seeks to put Heysel in a proper historical context.

But what are we to make of this? The authors are describing how European fans have a history of trying to upset the visiting team: gathering in the team hotel at four in the morning to disturb players who are asleep, turning the central heating full blast in the dressing-room and instructing ball-boys to deliberately fumble the match ball when it goes out of play in order to put players off their rhythm. That is not all. There is another even more reprehensible dirty trick played by foreigners: 'Presenting bouquets to players as they run on to the pitch. What in the name of diplomacy does the average football player do with a bunch of flowers on a football pitch?' ask the authors.

When I asked one of the authors, David Stuckey, as to how presenting flowers could be seen as a dirty trick, he tried to excuse himself by saying, 'That's what one of the Liverpool players said.' Not that Liverpool would stoop to any such underhand tactic: 'Liverpool, however, were not known for resorting to dirty tricks. So far they had found honesty to be the best policy and it had worked for them every time.' Evidently in this view honesty and giving flowers to an opponent on a football field were mutually incompatible.

Authors who see the presenting of flowers as a dirty trick must be credited with singular insight and a perception not gifted to ordinary mortals. So it is hardly surprising to find their summary of Liverpool's history reads as follows: 'Liverpool has always been a city of extremes, an exciting city, its past giving it a glamour and mystery akin to Marseilles or Casablanca. Its cosmopolitan mix of races, its glorious past as a major passenger and freight port, and more recently its explosion of artistic talent in music and other fields, gave it a mystique that was irresistible.'

You do not have to know much about the history of Liverpool to realise that there is one thing missing in this almost lyrical summary: its association with slavery. Liverpool throughout the slave trade was the port from which the slaves were shipped to the New World, a trade which brought Liverpool great prosperity. Thomas Jefferson, the founding father of Liverpool, was a slave trader and the profits made from the slave trade – Liverpool being ideally placed between Africa and the Americas – helped nourish the banks and the textile industries and made many a family rich. Memories of the slave trade have always made Liverpudlians uncomfortable and Ferdinand Dennis in *Behind the Front Lines* noted how George Frederick Cooke, an 18th-century tragedian, was once booed and hissed by a Liverpool theatre audience. He responded: 'I've not come here to be insulted by a set of wretches, of which every brick in your infernal town is cemented with an African's blood.' Dennis writes: 'Cooke's dissatisfied audience fell silent. And it is a silence which still seems to pervade Liverpool today. The past is not only another country, but it is one too far away to be seen.' Since Dennis's book was written, Liverpool has taken steps to acknowledge the part the city played in slavery with an exhibition in the refurbished docks. But when I asked Stuckey why he had not alluded to slavery he said. 'Oh, I was just doing a quick summary of Liverpool. The book was written a long time ago and I can't remember what was written.'

Denial of the uncomfortable bits of one's past is not an exclusive Liverpudlian trait, many people in many countries exhibit it. We could not live with ourselves if we accepted every wart that we had, let alone every wart on the faces of our ancestors. But when denial becomes a weapon to obscure uncomfortable facts then it is easy, as Ian Jack was to write after Heysel, for Liverpool to sentimentalise itself and its football. However, for Liverpool to do that it has had to produce a picture of the city and its football that omits some very important parts of the landscape.

To judge this let us first travel with Stuckey and his co-authors down the city's football road which, next to the Beatles, is the great love and glory of the city: 'Liverpool is a soccer-mad city, where neat terraced homes in the Coronation Street-style rows which crowd in around the football grounds of Liverpool FC and Everton FC have the bricks surrounding their doors and windows painted red and white, or blue and white, depending on whether the faithful "worship at Anfield or Goodison Park" – according to the lyrics of the Scouse anthem *In My Liverpool Home*, made famous by The Spinners.

'And worship is not too strong a word in a city where football is a religion, and highly paid soccer stars idolised for their skills. Worship, in fact, had a lot to do with the formation of Liverpool's twin football teams. Everton began life as the boys team from the quaintly named St Domingo's Chapel . . . If rivalries existed in the early days they tended to spring up on sectarian grounds – Everton was always the Catholic team, and Liverpool the Protestant. These divisions tended to blur in the years after the war, and recede gradually into folklore, but certainly it is true that at one time Everton had a strong Irish contingent of players, and strong links with Glasgow Celtic, another staunch Catholic side. Yet it was said that not until Kenny Dalglish followed Joe Fagan that a Catholic had managed Liverpool, just as Graeme Souness became the first Catholic manager of Glasgow Rangers [sic].

'In any event it was not surprising that Christian influences and traditional values of good sportsmanship and fair play were always a leading factor in the clubs' make-up. Goodison is still unique in that it is the only first division ground to have a church in the corner of its ground – the Victorian bulk of St Luke the Evangelist separates the corner of the main stand from the Gwladys Street terraces. However, when Billy Graham came to the UK to conduct Mission England in the mid-1980s, he chose Anfield as one of his venues.

'Take this together with the Scousers natural sense of humour and general lack of malice and you should have a friendly atmosphere in which to enjoy good football and family fun.'

Some of the facts in this lyrical potted 'history' are absurd – neither Dalglish nor Souness are Catholics, it was Souness's first wife who is Catholic – but what is really interesting is again what the authors leave out. Like the absence of any reference to slavery in Liverpool's history books, there is a whole section of Liverpool's population who have been completely ignored, as if they did not exist.

Here is an observer who is prepared to provide the missing bits and suggest that there might be another side to the Liverpool football story, one that contradicts the picture of Scousers without malice or hate, always singing wonderful lyrics. It is 29 October 1987, almost two and a half years after Heysel, and Liverpool are playing Everton in the third round of the Littlewoods Cup. It is John Barnes's first season for Liverpool, and Liverpool are unbeaten in all competitions since the start of the season. Although the television pictures do not dwell on this the observer notices what happens when the action involves Barnes: 'Every time the Liverpool winger got the ball he was loudly and vehemently booed. Every time he advanced towards the corner flags at the Anfield Road end he was showered with abuse. Photographers stationed along the goal line were astonished by the violence of the language directed at him, clearly audible to the players at the edges of the field. Barnes took corner kicks in a hail of spit. Meanwhile, a substantial section of Everton's fans assailed Liverpool's new hero with chants, prepared especially for the occasion. One, based on the popular campaign anthem *Here We Go*, was changed to contain just a relentless repetition of a distortion of the home team's name, " Niggerpool, Niggerpool Niggerpool". The other, based upon the lament *What a Load of Rubbish*, goadingly proclaimed "Everton are White! Everton are White!".'

The observer is Dave Hill, whose study about John Barnes and the affect his arrival would have both on Liverpool the football club and the city is chronicled in *Out Of His Skin*. He writes: 'The crowd at Anfield and Goodison celebrate their sense of being Liverpudlian, an identity bound up with decade upon decade of heels dug in against the odds, of perennial survival that is not quaint or glorious at all. It is a matter of profound tragedy that running through those Saturday afternoon exhibitions of solidarity there is a disorienting streak of brutality which confuses working-class Liverpudlian staying power with ignorant, lumpen white power, It is the definition of whiteness that underpins the isolation of black Liverpool from the humour, the poetry, the music, the football.' It is here that Hill quotes Paul, who says that as a boy he would go to Anfield on Saturday afternoons and find not humour and poetry but fists: 'I don't think there was an occasion when I did not have to defend myself – physically defend myself.'

We only see what we want to see and that Stuckey and Co should not see the blacks, despite the fact that they can comment on the Catholic-Protestant divide, is not surprising. Steve Coppell grew up in Liverpool, played with the first tide of black players to make an impact on the English game and at Crystal Palace managed some of the most high-profile ones, but in the Liverpool of his youth he never met any blacks – the only non-whites he remembers were Chinese.

What makes Stuckey and Co's omission truly significant is that the book was being written in 1989, two years after Barnes's arrival had alerted the world to the colour issue in the city's football. Yet from the moment Heysel occurred Liverpool and its officials were keen to emphasise that the club and its supporters were not responsible but that National Front supporters, hailing from London, had created a lot of trouble.

Immediately after the game, even as the dead bodies lay littered around the Heysel stadium, John Smith, the then Liverpool chairman, claimed to have evidence of such infiltration. He claimed that he and Bob Paisley, the former Liverpool manager, had been confronted in the VIP area of the stadium by right-wing elements from England. Six members of the Chelsea National Front had boasted to him of their part in provoking the violence.

Bob Paisley said that he was forced to leave the directors' box at the start of the game as dozens of fans poured over the dividing wall and that the person next to him claimed he was a Chelsea supporter and was wearing a National Front badge. A number of banners decorated with swastikas were recovered after the match, including one marked 'Liverpool Edgehill . . .', a banner with 'England for the English' and 'Europe for the English' was observed and a contingent of the National Front were clearly seen in blocks X and Y. One party leaving Brussels main station consisted of Londoners wearing Liverpool colours, carrying Union flags and sporting National Front swastika tattoos.

Malcolm McDonald, a BBC producer and also a Liverpool fan, who was there, recalls how he arrived at Heysel Stadium to find the approaches littered with hundreds of posters from the National Front, making a very straightforward racist appeal to the Liverpool fans and blaming blacks for causing white unemployment.

The fact that there were National Front agitators at Heysel should come as no surprise. The NF has long targeted football and Liverpool fans, coming from an area of high unemployment, would be an obvious choice. The climate was right for the National Front to operate but the intriguing question is: did the city or the club do anything to discourage this climate or in any way change it? And even if we accept that the entire trouble at Heysel was caused by the NF – Justice Opplewell, who examined this evidence, did not conclude that the National Front was responsible for the disaster – it is difficult to resist the conclusion that Liverpool, the club and the city, with its inability to look its history in the face, its desire to suppress its own slave past, its denial of people of colour who have been part of the city for more than a century, created just the conditions for the NF to prosper.

A book on Heysel which seeks to be a historical record may be expected to address such issues. But for Stuckey and his co-author such issues are of no interest. As far as they are concerned the culprits of Heysel are well known and they are not from Liverpool: 'The authorities in Brussels should have taken due notice and been warned by what took place in Rome in 1984. 'The stadium was hopelessly inadequate as we have already stated and was the responsibility of the Brussels municipality who owned the ground. The organisation of the Belgian FA was hopeless as he have clearly indicated. The supervision by the various police forces was pathetic. And last, but by no means least, a great deal of responsibility lies with UEFA whose representatives cleared the ground as fit for this European Cup final. It is perfectly true, as the Belgian Public Prosecutor said in his submission to the court, that if the defendants had not been on the terraces, no disaster might have occurred, but that is begging the question. If all the authorities had done their job properly and the match been organised on a proper basis, it might not have prevented some fighting – which we hasten to say we would deplore in any event – but it would not have resulted in disaster.'

A more emphatic and depressing example of the denial by English football of its responsibility could not have been written. Such is that state of the Liverpool denial of Heysel that while Hillsborough is mourned, and rightly mourned at Anfield, with a memorial to the 96 who died there, there is no memorial to the Juventus fans at Turin. Liverpool had planned to hold a mass for them on the tenth anniversary but quietly decided against it because it was not sure if very many people would turn up.

Liverpool's denial of any involvement by its fans for Heysel goes so far that even independent observers seeking objective explanations for the event hesitate to say that Liverpool fans were involved. On the tenth anniversary of Heysel, *The Sunday Telegraph's* two-page retrospective – one of the few papers to devote decent space to the tragedy – was dominated by a picture showing the Juventus fans being crushed against the wall as the Liverpool fans charged across them. The caption under the picture said: 'Awful images . . . panic-stricken supporters, the majority of them Italian, tried to scramble to safety from Heysel's Z block after a charge by Liverpool "fans". Thirty-nine were crushed to death.' The inverted commas round fans could not have been more eloquent, suggesting that they were perhaps not fans at all, but, who knows, alien beings from outer space? After all, how could we believe that the Scouse football fans could ever have behaved like this? Are they not known the world over for their warmth, love and kindness, even if they do find the presentation of flowers in a football match as something of a dirty trick?

There is one other aspect of the Liverpool reaction to Heysel which is very interesting. Almost a third of this unpublished book is devoted to examining how 26 Liverpool fans were extradited to Belgium and put on trial. The defendants not only pleaded innocence but were outraged that they had to face trial in Belgium and not in England. David Mellor, then a Home Office Minister, responding to fears by relatives and friends that the Belgians would put on a show trial, had said, 'It is long-standing policy that the appropriate place for prosecution in these cases is the country in which the offence takes place.'

Stuckey and Co dismiss the Mellor argument and not only share the defendants' outrage but their description of the whole trial has a feel of the

Roman senate denouncing the wicked ways of the barbarians. 'Procedures under Belgian law are very different to procedures in British courts of law. In Belgium there is no prosecution case and no defence case. The defendants are called first and, after they've been called along with the witnesses, the public prosecutor sums up and makes submissions – after the defence has given evidence. There is no cross-examination of witnesses as we understand it. The President of the Court questions each defendant in detail, and if his lawyer wants to ask any questions he must, in effect, put the question through the President of the Court, or with his permission. In this country the prosecution gives its evidence. British courts are used to almost old-fashioned courtesy. British prosecutors are in the habit of saying, perhaps: "My Lord, in regard to prisoner A the prosecution feels it cannot proceed against this man. But of course it is a matter for your lordship's discretion. Subject to your lordship's permission, we would like to withdraw the case against him." The judge, having satisfied himself that the prosecution have reasonable grounds for its [sic] views in this matter, will order the prisoner to be discharged. In Belgium, the fact that the public prosecutor is allowed to suggest that certain defendants should be acquitted does not mean they will be acquitted. The court still has the absolute right to pay no attention to this suggestion if it does not agree with the public prosecutor's conclusions . . . To British journalists, accustomed to dignity in court proceedings, the Belgian system seemed to contain more than a little element of farce. Anything could happen in the archaic atmosphere of the Belgian Palais de Justice – and frequently did. British pressmen were highly amused at the antics of the Belgian media timidly filming the arrival of the English defendants. Jittery cameramen, believing their own hype that these were monster roaming free, went as near as they dared, always ready to beat a hasty retreat should their quarry round on them. Then there was the metal detector through which everyone had to pass before entering the courtroom. It was so efficient, one defence lawyer had all but undressed by the time it was discovered that it was his tooth fillings which were settling the alarm bells off.'

Such distrust of foreign justice is not confined to football. In recent times two cases, both involving Britons in America, have highlighted the mistrust that American justice can provoke amongst the English. And the idea that the English cannot receive justice abroad is, of course, an old one. To read Stuckey and Co lampoon the Belgian judicial system is to revisit the world of Ilbert Bill in the days when Gladstone was Prime Minister, the good Lord Ripon was the Viceroy of Indian and Calcutta the capital of the Raj. The Ilbert Bill concerned the sensitive question of who could try the

English in India. Could they be tried by an Indian magistrate or an Indian Sessions judge? In 1873 it had been enacted that a British-European subject could only be tried by a European magistrate or a Sessions Judge. In the Ilbert Bill Ripon tried to build a measure which would allow Indian Sessions judges to try Europeans but this raised such a storm of protest from the English in India, who were horrified that their Indian subjects should sit in judgement over them, that Ripon had to withdraw and agree that the Europeans might claim a jury half of whom would be Europeans. It is a sobering thought that more than a century after Ilbert, and despite the fact that in Belgium we are dealing with Europeans, all part of a single market and soon, probably, a single currency, the mind-set that outraged the Raj in India still exists as far as football is concerned.

Such an attitude figures even more strongly when English football supporters are at the receiving end of what is always presented as the excesses of the foreign police. Then, as during Chelsea's match with Real Zaragoza in the 1994–95 Cup Winners' Cup, the foreign police are accused of overreacting and assaulting innocent English fans.

Here the details of what is alleged to have happened are particularly illuminating. In the first leg, played in Spain, Chelsea lost three-nil. Christopher Davies, who reported the match for *The Daily Telegraph*, recalls: 'Soon after the third goal was scored some of the Chelsea supporters started throwing things. The Spanish police waded in and they were quite undiscriminating in who they dealt with: both the good and the bad Chelsea fans were assaulted.'

One of the good fans was Steven Frankham, who is a prominent Chelsea supporter, being a director of the Chelsea Pitch Owners, the company set up to buy Stamford Bridge. Mr Frankham was later to write long and detailed letters to Ken Bates, the chairman of Chelsea, denouncing what he called 'the disgraceful behaviour of the Spanish police in Zaragoza'.

According to Frankham, and this is backed up by the observations of a Chelsea steward, a detailed plan had been worked out to make sure there was no trouble during the match. The preparations had some of the hallmarks of a military campaign. Soon after the Chelsea fans arrived at the airport they were escorted to waiting coaches, surrounded by the Spanish police. After they had boarded the relevant coach the stewards told them they would be dropped off in the town, about five to ten minutes from the stadium, and they were to report back to the coach at six-thirty Spanish time. Once they were back and seated in the coach, their match tickets would be handed out.

However, things did not work out according to plan. They were not dropped at the originally agreed point but outside the stadium where there were other football coaches as well. As if this was not bad enough, what happened next was even more worrying. 'On leaving the coaches, the majority of fans were directed to an area surrounded by police where they could not eat or drink for approximately three hours prior to collecting their tickets for the game.' The way Frankham puts it, it would appear that to allow a football fan three hours to eat and drink before a match is an invitation to a riot.

Fortunately, Frankham and his friends took taxis and went to the town for lunch. Frankham does not elaborate whether this meant they did not eat or drink; we must assume they did but presumably not for three hours, or perhaps they are fans who can cope with eating and drinking for three hours without feeling riotous. but when they returned at six-thirty to collect their tickets the coaches were no longer there, there were no Chelsea Football Club officials and 'after three hours of standing around and drinking, people were getting very concerned that they had not received their tickets. As you can imagine, there were numerous people waking aimlessly around and looking for information and advice which, unfortunately, was not available. Nearly three-quarters of an hour later, the tickets finally turned up. The whole situation became chaotic because no one was sitting in their respective coach as they had been parked elsewhere and fans were just, once again, walking around and trying to find out who was distributing the tickets. Meanwhile, the police presence had increased and they had started to push people around while the fans were attempting to obtain their tickets.'

All this was a prelude to the Spanish brutality play as witnessed by Frankham: 'At about 7.45 p.m. the police told everybody to move to the stadium immediately – despite whether you had just purchased food or drinks or not – you had to go then. In fact, the police attacked the fans indiscriminately. On arrival at the gate of the stadium, everybody queued sensibly waiting to be searched one by one. The police discarded anything they thought could represent a missile – even small batteries out of cameras – and threw them to the floor in a big heap with little regard whatsoever for people's personal belongings. Many supporters had bought pennants prior to the game which have a very fine steel bar to support the pennant when hanging. These the police ripped out, damaging the pennants and, again, through [sic] them on the pile. The irony of this was that inside the stadium, a guy was selling pennants, complete with steel bars, in front of the police! My friend's son, who is approximately nine years old, had his

CFC backpack deliberately ripped whilst the police were searching it. The child was in tears and, as you can imagine, his father was furious – again, showing the total disregard by the police of personal belongings. Inside the stadium, there were no stewards either English or Spanish directing the fans to their seats. It was a free for all and, in fact, many had to sit in the gangways. I, also, had to sit between two seats!

'It is important to realise that because the gangways were not clear and, for one reason or another, the eating inadequate, people were standing in a gangway that the police insisted was kept free. A young man in front of us had just returned with a packet of crisps and as he was attempting to make his way to sit on the steps, along with many others, he was forcibly pushed by the police, dropped his packet of crisps into the gangway and as he bent down to pick them up, was brutally attacked, being constantly hit over the head and around his body by the police. One of my friends in the front row of the upper tier was so incensed by the situation and was complaining to the police. For his efforts, he too was attacked and sustained at one point what we thought was a broken arm. His brother was assisting him to the medical centre when the police started to push him. Understandably, being outraged by what he saw happening to his brother, he started shouting at the police complaining of their actions. They then did no more than drag him outside into a police van where three police officers beat him senseless. When travelling home, he was suffering with concussion and had lumps the size of golf balls all over his head. This incident was not uncommon. The police were laying into the official trip supporters for no reason whatsoever. At half-time, the medical room was full of injured – I had never seen anything like it.'

There can be little doubt that the Spanish police overreacted. Also, as Davies observed, contrary to Chelsea's wishes, the Spanish sold tickets not merely through the official Chelsea Travellers Club but to anybody who wanted a ticket. Their philosophy was: 'This is a football game, if somebody wants to come and watch it, why shouldn't they?' For Frankham this was clearly outrageous behaviour and contributed to what happened.

But even if we share Frankham's outrage at the way the Spanish police behaved, the letter tells us more about Frankham and the brutalisation that football fans have accepted in this country over the last 20 years than about the Spanish police. It would be easy to satirise Frankham as the insular Englishman abroad, complaining about the lack of English police and the absence of sufficient interpreters, but more significant are the restrictions which many others may consider an infringement of civil liberties but which Frankham readily accepts as the price for watching his beloved

Chelsea. So for Frankham it is quite normal that to see a football match you must have proper segregation of crowds, fans cannot be allowed to eat and drink for three hours before the match, a journey abroad to watch a sporting event must be a military-style operation with precise times for every move. Any deviation must be seen as a conspiracy and cause of acute anxiety.

Frankham is hardly alone in this. All English fans are prepared to put up with such restraints, so much so that if one of the element is missing, like proper segregation, irate fans ring up radio programmes complaining. One that sticks in mind is a female Southampton supporter complaining that she and her friends were made to sit next to Manchester United supporters, the outrage in her voice as she described it suggested that segregation, which was brought in to curb hooliganism, was the norm and anything else was contrary to nature, or at least English football nature. Not for the first time English football had confused the symptoms with the cause, the short-term palliatives with proper, long-term solutions.

. Twenty years ago when hooliganism in its modern form emerged, English football, instead of examining the game and its development – its unwillingness to break free from its insular traditions, the inability to realise that passion was turning to hate and was creating the conditions for the monster to prosper – preferred to deal with the outward symptoms. The game hoped that better policing both inside and outside the stadiums would contain the problem. And since then, whenever it has been confronted by the hooligan problem, it has only been able to offer the explanation that it must be the work of forces beyond its control. It has failed to realise that this amounts to trying to explain the problem away rather than solve it.

In this process any evidence that runs contrary to the image of a warm-hearted English game, full of passion on the field and wit on the terraces, has not so much been obscured as suppressed. The censorship of Stalinist Russia or Nazi Germany pales in comparison to the efforts made by the English game to deny the existence of the enemy within football and the filth it produces every time a match is played. The rising crescendo of 'You are . . . a fucking shit', as the opposing 'keeper takes a goal kick, is never mentioned, although it is a constant refrain heard in every ground in the land, and even outside. Instead, television cameras and commentators lovingly focus on endless repeats of *You'll Never Walk Alone*.

And while the wit of the fans is rightly honoured – the Arsenal North Bank singing 'Shilton, does your wife know where you are?', after reports of his philandering in that day's paper – the more cruel jests are ignored.

For instance, shouts by West Ham fans at Gary Mabbutt and Teddy Sheringham just after they had come back from eye and knee operations, 'He has only got one knee', 'He has only got one eye'.

All great wit wounds, and the ability to strike the right balance between wit that is funny without being cruel is always difficult. There are moments when football can produce wit that sparkles without wounding. It is the time when the *fatwa* against Salman Rushdie is much in the news. The Celtic-Rangers match has just ended and the Rangers fans are being escorted from Hampden Park. They see a lone Asian Celtic supporter and start chanting, 'Salman Rushdie, Salman Rushdie'. Even the Celtic fans appreciate the wit.

However, if in the name of wit a game consistently allows the scum to rise to the top and then pretends it does not exist, then the game is saying something about itself. Ian Jack, writing after Heysel, noted how the Liverpool fans charging at Heysel shouted, 'Wops-Wops-Wops-Wops': 'A joke, of course. Surely even Croxteth and Toxteth have a broader image of Italians than that of ice-cream sellers who surrendered, too promptly and sensibly, in the western desert. Or do they, or we? During the recent royal progress through Italy *The Mirror* carried a front-page story about the Princess of Wales's dress sense: "Italian designers say Frumpy Di! Our advice to them SHUTTA YA FACE!" Another joke, of course, a harmless line from a popular song. Robert Maxwell, *The Mirror*'s proprietor, has already opened a relief fund for the Italian victims of Brussels. Jokes do not lead to savagery. But they are, perhaps, part of the dull-witted chauvinism that helps promote it.'

And it is a chauvinism that requires an enemy to hate and pillory.

Here is a memory. It is the 1984–85 season. Stoke has a pleasing team with Mark Chamberlain, young, bold, attractive, on the wing. Stoke are playing Liverpool. The Stoke press box is oversubscribed and I am given a seat just outside alongside season ticket-holders. I find myself next to a man in his '60s who looks like he saw Matthews play. Whenever Chamberlain gets the ball he urges him with, 'come on, Mark', as if he was his son or probably grandson. So do the ladies around him. Some of them look old enough to be Chamberlain's grandmother but their body language suggests their feelings are less maternal and much more intimate.

Liverpool are all white, so who will be their hate figure? The Stoke crowd do not take long to decide. They select Graeme Souness and no sooner does he get the ball than the tenderness the elderly man has been exhibiting – the gentle, almost paternal cooing of Chamberlain, issuing from softly pursed lips – is replaced by a sound that seems to come from the pit of his stomach. His round, wrinkled face is now a snarling, hard knot of flesh, the mouth drawn tightly, eyes no longer watery but seemingly blazing and the words that issue, urgently and ferociously, repeatedly question Souness' parentage. The referee is warned to watch out for his tricks and the world at large told how devilish Souness is. As the match progresses Liverpool come more into their own and Souness has more of the ball. I look at the faces around me and observe the change. They had looked so ordinary, even welcoming, when Chamberlain had the ball but now they are filled with hate and contorted with a rage that seems inhuman.

It is all part of the game, say football's great and good. Perhaps so, but here is another snippet from my memory box. It is the post-match conference at Sheffield Wednesday. The referee has been cruelly barracked and called all sorts of names, of which 'Who is the wanker in the black?' is the most polite. There has been some bad behaviour by the players and Howard Wilkinson, the then Wednesday manager, is condemning this aspect of the game. I suggest to him that the names the crowd was calling the referee did not help and cannot be for the good of the game. I expect him to agree but he looks at me as if I am naïve and says, 'In this game the referee has always been called names. That makes no difference. In our days referees were barracked. All part of the game. That should make no difference to how players behave. They must always be professional, at all times.'

Yes, the abusive name-calling of the referee is part of the rich fabric of football. The cherished image of English football is that while the game is being played the supporters have hate for the referee, hate for the opposition, but when the final whistle is blown all this hate is forgotten and everyone goes home friends, right? But what if, as now, they don't? What if the supporters, being human, cannot make such sophisticated distinctions, cannot suddenly turn from hating to loving? In the halcyon days, so lovingly recalled, when crowds of 50,000 were common at football matches, and youngsters were passed over the heads of adults to sit in front and then after the match safely returned to their parents, good old-fashioned English barracking was part of the unique atmosphere of the English game. The supporters loved his team but did not hate the opposition. However, now that the vast post-war crowds have gone, they have taken with them their essential good nature. Now it does not take much for wit to turn to hate and barracking to be converted to animal grunts directed at a black player.

The result is an atmosphere in English football grounds that those who watch English football day in and day out see as nothing odd, but which leaves the outsiders coming fresh to English football bewildered and confused. As so often it is the foreigner's experience that is more instructive. Here is Bill Buford describing his first encounter with the uggh-uggh-uggh-uggh-uggh chant that resounds around English stadiums whenever a black player has the ball: 'The first time I head the ape grunt – the barking sound that supporters make when a black player gets the ball – it was so foreign I couldn't figure out what it was. It was a deep, low rumbling, and I had trouble placing where it was coming from; underneath the ground perhaps. That such a sound could be coming from the ground was frightening. I thought: it's an earthquake, if only because that was the only sound – that low, bass drumming – that seemed to be comparable.'

Buford eventually worked out who was making the sound. Another time he took a friend visiting him from America to a match at Queen's Park Rangers. 'The moment a black player touched the ball, the grunt started: uggh, uggh, uggh, uggh, uggh. My friend turned to me and said: "What is that curious sound?"' When Buford explained it was because a black player had the ball, 'the looks that crossed my friend's face were so genuine and so unmediated – bewilderment, outrage, disgust, but mainly incomprehension – he couldn't understand it. The grunts continued: uggh, uggh, uggh, uggh, uggh. Both of us looked round. The grunt was coming not from a few lads, but it seemed from everyone on the terrace – old, young, fathers, whole families. Everywhere we looked we saw the ugly faces of men grunting, sticking out their lower jaw in their cruel imitations of apes . . . My friend's face was still fixed in an expression of intense comprehension. I couldn't explain it. I was embarrassed to be living in this country. It's England, I said.'

Buford may be ashamed but I have heard it so often I am inured to it. However, every time I draw attention to it I am told by good English friends that I have misjudged it, I have maligned the good English crowd. Here is another memory. It is 1989. Tottenham have gone to Tranmere to play in a League Cup match. It is a dark winter's night. Gascoigne and Lineker are playing but so is Mitchell Thomas. The moment he touches the ball the Tranmere crowd, as if on cue, start grunting: uggh, uggh, uggh, uggh, uggh. I am taken aback but only for a moment. Thomas is the only black player on the park and it is clear the grunts are directed at him. However, this is soon accepted as background noise, inevitable in the game, and we are all taken by the ebb and flow of the match. Gascoigne scores, Tranmere score twice, then right at the end Tottenham draw level through what we think is a Lineker goal but turns out to be an own goal.

117

I am reminded of the Thomas booing when a journalist mentions it in his copy but explains that it started after he had committed a foul on a Tranmere player. I know the booing started long before that, the moment he touched the ball for the first time in the first minute, some minutes before the foul. After the game, as Paddy Barclay, then with *The Independent*, drives me back to my hotel in Liverpool I mention it. He seems very sceptical of what I have said. Then he tells me a story. In another match he had written that a black player had been booed because of his colour and received shoals of letters denying that and saying it was because he had fouled their favourite player and played a dirty game. I argue with Barclay, perhaps one of our most perceptive writers on the game, but not too forcefully. I, too, know of letters, letters which always deny that there is anything wrong with the English game, which see any attempt to portray the enemy within as an act of betrayal, or worse. Over the years, whenever I have written about racism in football, I have met with abuse. I have never received a single letter which accepts that there may be a problem, let alone that I may be making any worthwhile points.

Here is another memory. It is the spring of 1987. Tottenham, under David Pleat, playing some of the most blissful football seen for 20 years, have advanced to the FA Cup semi-final. In those days Cup semi-finals were still played on Saturdays, although as it happened, and largely on police advice, the other semi-final between Leeds and Coventry was played on a Sunday.

Tottenham's match is at Villa Park and I have arranged with Hyman Wolanski and his two sons to travel to the match. Hyman is a late convert to Tottenham. He inherited his season ticket from his father-in-law but by 1987 he has been enslaved by the magic of Hoddle and Ardiles. Hyman and his two sons cannot be more ideal companions. The journey up the M1 is slow – so tortuous that the start is delayed to allow supporters to arrive – but the sun is shining, it is a lovely spring day, and I am thrilled to be reliving my days as a supporter. For almost the first time since I took to journalism I am going to a match merely to spectate and support, rather than to report. The communal spirit, fun and laughter such occasions produce is infectious. The only time laughter stops is when I mention that I am about to buy an Audi car. 'I would never own a German car,' says Hyman. He does not have to explain: his family, originally from Poland, are one of the many who perished in Auschwitz.

As we are about to park our car outside the Granada Social Club, next door to the main entrance at Villa Park, I became aware of the ugly face that always lurks in English football. A group of Watford supporters are passing the car. I have every reason to feel relaxed about such supporters. The club has done so much to promote the family image of the game and its two greatest stars are John Barnes and Luther Blissett. but immediately they see my face the chant goes up, 'Paki, Paki', followed by, 'I'd rather be a dog than a Paki'. I am still trying to take in all this when a Watford supporter – he cannot have been more than 12 years of age – shakes his fist in my face and says, 'Where do you think you are – Bangladesh?'

I think: such a lovely day, such unprovoked anger and what an odd question. The supporter has only to look around him and realise that if any ground can look like it is in Bangladesh then it is Villa Park, completely surrounded as it is by Asian homes whose children quickly gather round cars promising to 'mind' them in the hope of picking up tips. Perhaps the supporter is confused. He knows all about Tottenham being a Jewish club – shouts of 'Yiddos' are soon to engulf us as we approach the stadium – but he must be thinking, what is a Paki doing amidst Jews?

Soon I have other things to think about and much to savour. Watford have in goal – a last-minute choice – a man called Plumpley who has been plucked from a wine bar in Wales. Just before the match a supporter, reflecting the eternal fears of supporters, worries he may have a blinder. 'Bet you he plays a blinder. I have known it to happen.' Instead he plays like a wine bar manager. After 11 minutes he fails to hold an Allen shot and Hodge scores; two minutes later Allen himself scores and we neither know nor care that it has taken a deflection. In half an hour our cup is full as Spurs are 3–0 up. We sing, in a heady mixture of joy and cruelty that partisanship produces, 'You should have stayed in the wine bar.'

Thoughts of Bangladesh and dogs being better than Pakis are far away as I hear a supporter say, 'Bombard him, Spurs. He couldn't catch AIDS.' And there is always Arsenal to mock and humiliate. The defeat, a few weeks earlier, in the League Cup semi-final – and this after leading three times – has been mortifying. As Spurs score their fourth goal and win 4–1, I join in the singing, 'Are you watching, Arsenal, this is the real cup.' As the match ends Waddle, just in front of us, sinks to his knees in thanks – it is his first Wembley final – and I cannot care less if *some Watford supporters* want to repatriate me to Bangladesh – a country I have never even visited.

The next day I wrote about my experiences in the *London Daily News*. A few days later a postcard arrived. Written in spidery handwriting, with no address and an obviously fictitious name, it read as follows:

Mihir Bose And Friend Hyman,

Your remarks in today's L.D. News re your visit to Villa Park is a bit claptrap. Have you ever realised Asian and Jewish remarks you make is breeding Nazism all over again. Because we Jews and Asians have taken over again. Remember Germany 1936–1945. Wish you schmocks would shut up. I'm scared for my kids in NW8 and others in NW4, NW11 and other areas.

L. Cohen

A crank? Possibly. And anybody writing about racism, whether in sports or other walks of life, is bound to get such letters. Some years later, at the height of the row about allowing people from Hong Kong to settle in this country, I wrote an article on immigration criticising the policies of successive Labour and Conservative Governments and suggesting it should be related to economic needs and the competence of the immigrant rather than his or her colour. Since it was the summer of 1989 and England were getting beaten by Australia I suggested the great immigrant need of the summer was for top-order batsmen and probably a high-class spinner. It led to an unsigned letter from Bexhill in Sussex, 'from a group of indigenous ladies who love their country and would like it back'. And their way of 'getting it back' was to urge me to leave. They said they would happily wave me 'a speedy farewell'. Nor are such cranky letters always about race. Write on any controversial subject and you are bound to get some illiterate replies from cowards unable to even give their names.

There is one exception to this and that happened when I wrote about football racism in *The Daily Telegraph* at the beginning of the 1993–94 season. Then, far from wishing to hide their racist views in such anonymous fashion, some were quite happy to parade it. Days before the season was due to start the Commission for Racial Equality joined the Professional Football Association in launching a campaign called 'Let's Kick Racism Out Of Football'. Their aim was to put more black people in the stands, and in the boardrooms.

I wrote a think-piece on this in the next day's *Telegraph*, briefly mentioning my own problems at football and highlighting the fact that before blacks began to be targeted by football crowds, Jews had been the target. One of the experiences I narrated was of the night two years earlier when Tottenham played Chelsea in a League Cup quarter-final at Stamford Bridge. It also turned out to be the night the Gulf War began.

I had been invited there as a guest of one of the pools companies but due to some mix-up, or negligence, I found myself not in one of the chic executive boxes – as I had hoped and anticipated – but in the West Stand. The result was that the three of us, a PR man, a PR woman and myself, sat amidst the great mass of Chelsea supporters for whom Tottenham and its supporters were not only the enemy but, worse still, the Yiddish enemy. The match would have been bad enough for me, Chelsea so completely dominated Tottenham that Spurs were lucky to escape with a nil-nil draw. But it was made much worse by the fact that every time a Tottenham player managed to get to the ball – which was not very often – the whole mass of Chelsea supporters bayed, 'Kill the Yids'.

The only Tottenham player who looked remotely 'Yiddish' was Vinny Samways – he is actually of Italian stock – and there was nothing rational about the murderous shots. But as the entire stand and the adjoining shed reverberated, and with the floodlights that dark, cold January night giving Stamford Bridge the sort eerie quality to be seen in 1950s grainy movies, I began to think of Brian Glanville's remark that on such occasions Stamford Bridge can be the footballing equivalent of Nuremburg. I prayed that Spurs would not score for I could not guarantee my reaction and the thought of what might happen should I suddenly jump with joy did not bear thinking about.

Thoughts about my own safety, though, were overshadowed by the reaction of the PR lady who had clearly never experienced anything like it. She was so frightened and bewildered that she could not be consoled – not until we hurried away from Stamford Bridge at the end of the match and retreated to a restaurant, some three miles away, and she was on her third glass of Chardonnay.

My *Telegraph* piece was meant to raise questions about how effective the campaign of let's kick racism out of sport might prove but the mere fact that I had narrated some of my experiences proved too much for some *Telegraph* readers. However, unlike the cranky postcards and anonymous letters, this time I received letters where the writers clearly identified themselves – providing addresses and telephone numbers – but whose racism and hatred for people who were not white was so palpable that it was, in some ways, even more disturbing.

In many ways the response I got from one Robert Henderson was the most disturbing. It was not so much a letter as a racist thesis: a thick envelope containing a two-page typed letter that ended up quoting Milton in support of his views. This was accompanied by numerous other essays seeking to prove that racism, and in particular sporting racism, was justified. Henderson submitted an 11-page essay on 'The Liberal Bigot'; a 17-page one on 'Men, Morality and International Order', which called for mass repatriation of immigrants from Europe and apart from citing Trollope and the Younger Pitt in support also brought in Wellington; a one-page note entitled 'Koranic Quotations' and, perhaps the most interesting, a ten-page essay on 'The Trouble with England' which attempted to analyse the performance of cricketers born outside England but playing for England. It came complete with a chart listing cricketers batting and bowling averages by the colour of their skin. Robert Henderson had a problem here since six of the players in what he called his 'England Qualified Interlopers Test Record' were whites who were originally of a different nationality: New Zealand and South Africa. But he got round this by saying that since they were white they would easily assimilate into English society but the others, like Roland Butcher of West Indian stock, and Hussain of Indian stock, could not. His clinching argument was a supposedly cricketing one. That the 'white interlopers', like the white South Africans Lamb, Robin Smith and Tony Greig, had better batting and bowling averages than the 'coloured interlopers'. So in essence while playing anybody non-English was wrong, it was quite all right as long as they were white, since in any case they did better.

Henderson is something of a special case and three years sfter he wrote to me he found an outlet for his views which told us a great deal about racism in cricket. But here let us concentrate on football and ask why that article in *The Daily Telegraph* resulted in so many letters from people willing to be so openly identified as racist. The simple, knee-jerk reaction that *The Telegraph* is right-wing will not wash. *The Telegraph* may be politically right but it is a far more humane, tolerant paper than some supposedly liberal papers I have worked for.

The more pertinent reason could be that when it comes to football and racism a nerve is touched among some English followers of the game, more so as my article was trying to show the historical connections of football prejudice going back to anti-Jewish feelings. The Jewish subject in English football is all the more important because this is a subject little discussed in English sport, even by Jews.

Not long before I wrote *The Daily Telegraph* article I had ghosted Irving Scholar's book on his years as Tottenham chairman. The Jewish support for Tottenham is well known, including the practice of waving the Star of David after Spurs have scored a goal. However, Scholar and his associates were the first Jews to get on the board. Before this there was something like an unofficial apartheid: the supporters were mainly Jewish, the board was always Gentile. I felt we should discuss how he dealt with this sporting manifestation of anti-semitism in the White Hart Lane boardroom but try as I might I could not get him to talk about it. It was with much effort that I could even drag out of him the occasion when he had been subjected to horrific anti-semitic comments at Luton.

It had come in the wake of the nastiness that had crept between the clubs following David Pleat's move from Luton to Tottenham in the summer of 1987. Scholar held David Evans, Luton's then chairman, responsible. He had agreed to Pleat's move, negotiated a £100,000 transfer fee, then tried to prevent Pleat going by whipping up a press campaign against Tottenham. Pleat. in Luton's eyes, compounded matters by going back to the club and luring some players and coaches, something all managers do but which never fails to infuriate supporters. The result was that season Spurs-Luton matches had an edge and were not pleasant. It reached a nadir when Spurs played at Luton. A supporter walked past the directors' box and, looking Scholar in the eye, sang:

The yids are on their way to Auschwitz
Hitler is going to gas them again
No one can stop them
The yids are on the way to Auschwitz.

The song was a cruel anti-semitic twist to the one Spurs had sung in the early '80s when they twice won the Cup. Scholar finally told me the story but refused to let me use the words in the book. For him these things were not discussed in polite company.

However, even his desires to ignore the Spurs-Jewish links are not quite as deep-seated as that of Pleat himself. If Scholar was the first Jew in the Tottenham boardroom, then Pleat was the first Jew in the Tottenham dug-out, the first to be appointed its manager. But while Scholar was worried by anti-semitism, Pleat was horrified by exuberant displays of Jewishness by supporters. When Spurs supporters waved the Star of David after a goal – and Tottenham's performances that season meant they had plenty of opportunity – he complained to Scholar. As Pleat tells the story, 'I suppose Irving is middle class, therefore does not mind. I found it disturbing.'

In their different ways both Scholar and Pleat were trying to do the same, they just wished that any talk of Jews and how football reacts to them would go away. The problem with that approach is that if you do not discuss race openly it can lead to absurd conclusions like pretending that Eric Cantona's kung-fu kick was a reaction to racist abuse. The myth about this being a racist incident was so easily accepted that within weeks Nike had a new advertisement featuring Cantona and Les Ferdinand protesting against racist abuse. The impact, using black and white film, evoking '50s newsreel pictures, was powerful and further burnished the myth that Cantona had indeed been subject to racist abuse. What nonsense. Of course he had not. He had been abused as a Frenchman and abusing the French has long been an English pastime. The words hurled at Cantona were not very different to what De Daussure heard in the streets of London back in 1726. In a letter to his family he recorded that the worst insult the English could hurl at anyone was, 'French dog . . . this name is the most common, and evidently, according to popular idea, the greatest and most forcible insult that can be given to any man'.

This is not in any way to excuse the Palace supporter, whose background stands little scrutiny, or ignore the fact that he deliberately set out to bait and provoke Cantona. However, to label what he told Cantona as racist is, in some ways, to devalue the debate on racism and prevent a proper examination of it. The abuse Cantona and Ferdinand get are not identical and cannot be equated. But such an equation comes all too easily to English football. Not willing to look at the enemy within it, is always seeking to explain inconvenient events by linking them to wider social issues in the hope that the problem will go away. The process may be simple but it leads to tremendous distortion.

It requires a perspective from outside to see how curious this has made English football. So curious indeed that I had to go to the United States for the World Cup to restore my faith in the game England had given the world.

I had gone to America warned by friends that while the football would be lousy and the Americans disinterested, at least the phones would work. In fact, the arrangements for the press proved to be a nightmare. Nearly all the people manning the press centres were volunteers, white, middle-class volunteers – these being the ones attracted by soccer in America, where it shows no sign of being taken up by the working class, white or black – whose knowledge of the world was so incomplete that they often confused *The Sunday Times*, London, with *The Sunday Times*, Johannesburg. All this led to tremendous problems with tickets and the journalistic headaches I had in trying to cover the World Cup were immense.

However, all this was more than made up for by the wonder of the crowds – crowds whose behaviour proved that sports, and above all football, can rise above nationalism, racism and almost any kind of divisive 'ism' to produce something universal and beautiful. So much so that after a month in America I was ready to believe again that it was possible to go to a game without fearing for one's safety. I was even ready to discard the defences I had painfully acquired in almost 20 years of reporting football, the idea that the price of being paid to watch football is eternal vigilance: watch out for the drunken hordes of supporters, or the sudden riot that may erupt, accept the fact that fans have to be segregated, the Tottenham supporter can never sit with the Arsenal one, and that policemen with dogs and horses will escort fans to the ground and patrol stadiums as if they are theatres of war, not the places for fantasy and dreams. I did see police dogs and armed police before a match but that was because the Colombian President was coming to that match and it was feared the drug barons might want to assassinate him.

So in one of the great paradoxes of modern sport, in America, the land where policemen never take to the streets without guns and the right to bear arms is a constitutional one, not once did I see a policeman even admonish anyone at a game. I never heard anyone swear let alone scream the sort of abuse common in English grounds. After years of walking up Wembley's Olympic Way through boarded-up shopfronts and smells that suggested public thoroughfares were being used as urinals, Orange Grove Boulevard, which leads to the Rose Bowl in Pasadena where the finals were staged, was disorientating because it was so normal, so suburban, so unaware that just because a football match was being played at the end of its road it didn't mean the residents had to prepare as if they were anticipating an enemy air raid.

As I walked down for a match involving Colombia I was welcomed with home owners holding up cards saying, 'Parking here, $10. Rose Bowl, five minutes.' One large black lady pleaded with me, 'I have cleared out my backyard, there is even a man helping out. Your car will be very safe, sir, very safe.' And in the carparks surrounding the stadium the atmosphere was a combination of the Varsity match at Twickenham and Tunbridge Wells during the lunch or tea interval of a Kent match. Families unpacked hampers from their car boots and had a picnic, young kids played an impromptu game of soccer, seeking to reproduce the skills of their heroes. Not even in the USA versus Colombia match, where in a stadium packed with Colombians the USA played like the away side to win, did even a single Colombian once think of avenging the defeat of his national team by territorial conquests in the stands.

This was the match where Escobar scored the own goal that was to prove such a tragedy for him. I can still remember him rushing back to clear and deflecting the ball off the toe of his boot past his 'keeper but while it stunned the Colombians it produced neither the hostility nor anger an English crowd might have exhibited, just sadness. We all know what that single mistake meant for Escobar, but let us stay with that match and its immediate aftermath. The result, a second successive defeat, meant Colombia _ who had come as favourites in the group – could not qualify. Had England been in such a position I cannot say how their supporters would have reacted. The Colombians seemed to take it in their stride. That night, returning from the match, I did require police assistance but it was not out of fear of vengeful Colombians. It was because in the dark I could not find my hired car. Three days later, when I came face to face with Colombian fans, my experience of English football made me fear for the worst, but it provided me with the most memorable image of the tournament, at once telling and poignant.

I was in the media shuttle bus taking us to Colombia's last match against Switzerland. The couple from Essex had just displayed their tee-shirt bearing the legend, 'Mexico 1970, Brazil 4, Italy 1' and had failed the Norman Tebbitt cricket test. 'Even if England were here,' they said, 'we would support Brazil,' when suddenly we were invaded by a bunch of Colombian supporters. The English journalists in the bus stiffened, fearing the worst. However, instead of anger from the Colombians there was sorrow, and instead of shouts of 'Out, out, Maturana out' (Maturana being the coach) we had a lilting song that nearly moved us to tears. As the bus headed for the hills of Pao Alto the Colombians sang:

> I go to the consul in Bogota and he asks me, what are you taking
> to the USA?
> I say my wallet and a big bag
> He says what is the bag for
> I say the bag is to bring the Cup home
> But now the bag is empty and filled only with our tears.

As the chorus died down a Colombian who lived in Miami and had been translating the song for us said, 'You know we sing that song to show that Colombia is not all about drugs and guns, it is about football, beautiful football.'

A week later, on the team's return to Colombia, Escobar was gunned down outside a Medicin restaurant, severely denting that image created in the hills outside San Francisco and staining the World Cup. It provoked much editorial moralising about the evil power of modern sport and it was horrific that a man should die for making a mistake in a ball game. It also put to shame sportswriters who use phrases like 'tragic' when describing an own goal. It could be argued that Escobar's killing showed the true evil in

Colombian society and sport and that the act was far worse than anything perpetrated by English football hooligans. Far better for a few English fans to riot after a defeat than a footballer to die a few days later because of a stupid mistake. Yet this would be to miss the point.

True, Escobar was gunned down because he scored an own goal, but in many ways it was not related to the World Cup but to the sad state of Colombia and the cruel nature of its drugs-infected society. Escobar's death, while nominally linked to football, was more a reflection of the culture of Colombia. His death could not dim the passion and the warmth Colombians brought to their watching of football and the memory of the bus swaying gently over the hills of San Francisco while his countrymen sang their beautiful, sad song showed people who could love their football and did not always translate their sadness to senseless anger as an English crowd would undoubtedly have done.

Indeed, the angriest moment I saw in the World Cup was not from the fans but from a journalist, just after Brazil had drawn with Sweden in the qualifying group. There in that incredible indoor stadium in Pontiac, as the face of the Brazilian coach, Carlos Alberto Parriera, appeared on the screen, holding his post-match press conference, the Brazilians started shouting and you required no interpreters to understand. Not even the emergence of Pele, who had been commentating for Brazilian television and whose appearance immediately attracted the entire staff to him, could stop the flow of the Brazilians' invective. It was the rage of men who could not understand why Brazil could not always produce the magic of 1970, the futile rage against the dying of the light.

That match produced two of the most striking pictures I was to see during the tournament. Some time after Brazil equalised the first toilet rolls of the tournament were hurled down from the upper tier. As they rolled past the Swedish goal one American turned to me and asked, 'What was that for?' I resisted the temptation to say it was the trademark of European football, what crowds in Europe throw in frustration and rage – for just before the match I had seen how well European and Brazilian football could co-exist. As a group of Swedes rushed up to a contingent of Brazilian fans I, reacting as I would in England, readied myself for violence. But it turned out that they merely wanted to have their pictures taken with the Brazilians. They were even more enthralled a few minutes later when they passed a small knot of supporters who carried a banner reading 'Bengal for Brazil' and turned out to be Bangladeshi immigrants living in New York.

Quixotic as the Bengalis may have appeared, their presence in Pontiac illustrated the enormous drawing power of Brazil – an appeal that can encompass Essex and Dhaka must be some appeal – and their presence summed up the crowds we saw in this World Cup. They were passionate, volatile, exuberant, but never hostile. Never once amidst the many different nationalities attracted by the World Cup did I feel a sense of menace, yet such feelings never leave when I go to football in England. The World Cup crowds did not have the wit that comes naturally to the English but when English wit can so easily turn to hate is that wit worth celebrating?

Here is another memory from Stamford Bridge, again it is Chelsea versus Tottenham but this is a match of more than ordinary importance. It comes three days after Chelsea's defeat by Millwall in early February 1995, one that ended with a riot. It means more police presence and attracts journalists expecting trouble but contrary to their fears, or hopes, during and after the match little of the trouble we anticipate surfaces. More significant is how easily wit is a cue for hate. Dennis Wise has just been charged with assaulting a taxi driver – his conviction was later overturned on appeal – and the moment he emerges for the pre-match warm-up, the Tottenham fans start shouting, 'Taxi, taxi'. This makes even the Chelsea fans smile. But the smiles freeze into a snarl almost as soon as Tottenham score. Spurs are on a roll – they have in recent seasons rarely done well against Chelsea – and their fans make the most of the goal and taunt and bait the Chelsea supporters. To lead at a ground they have not won at in years makes the Spurs supporters strut. The Chelsea fans bide their moment and it comes in the last few minutes. Then to cap everything for them Wise gets the equaliser.

It means Tottenham have not beaten Chelsea for five years and, punching the air with clenched fists, the Chelsea fans shout, 'Five years, five years'. Now there is none of the bonhomie and even good humour that had marked the game at the start. Tottenham fans' sorrow is tinged with anger that their team has failed to win, while had the Chelsea fans added the word 'Gipper' after 'Five years' then it would have had all the hallmarks of the sort of triumphalism that used to be part of Reagan's political rallies in America.

The World Cup produced none of the wit or the punchlines so common every Saturday afternoon on English grounds but then it had also none of the anger or menace so prevalent at these venues. If boring chants is the price for passion without hate then the choice is simple. The American crowds did represent the other America, the ones who are still trying to become part of the American melting-pot – Hispanics, Koreans, Brazilians, Indians, Arabs, even the Italians who regularly watch Series 'A' matches on a special Italian channel – but they all proved that it was possible to watch nation states play football without hating one's opponent. Football, their behaviour proclaimed, was a universal culture which everyone could share, an inclusive one, not an exclusive one privy only to the initiated from the right race and cultural background.

Before America, and after 20 years of reporting English football, I would not have believed it was possible to go to a World Cup and come back with such a conclusion. Nothing in the English game had prepared me for such an unexpectedly sweet experience.

CHAPTER SIX

I Don't Know Where You Would Go to Pray, Pal

That was the comment Laurie McMenemy made to me on the evening of 22 October 1983. That morning McMenemy had taken his Southampton team to Luton with Southampton thinking of winning championships rather than just avoiding relegation, more often their concern in recent years. Southampton were fourth in the then first division, two points behind leaders Manchester United, and McMenemy could field more than a useful team, including Shilton, Wright, Williams, Moran and Danny Wallace.

However, by the time McMenemy came to the post-match conference he was far from happy. The walk to the corner of the large Hatters Bar, partitioned off for the press conference, must have made him feel he was literally being made to walk the plank – he had had to go along a little iron gangway at the back of the stand to get there – and this was reinforced by the result. A Southampton side that had conceded just one goal in eight league games since the start of the season that afternoon let in three for a fairly demoralising 3–1 defeat.

McMenemy always has an imposing air about him – not surprising in a man whose six-foot-four-inch height made him such a natural as a Coldstream Guard during his National Service that he stood guard outside both Buckingham Palace and the Bank of England – but that afternoon, as he was ushered in along with David Pleat, the Luton manager, it was Pleat, much the smaller man, who loomed larger. Pleat had the smile of a man who had just slaughtered the world, McMenemy the distracted, subdued air of one who has an unpleasant job to do and wants to do it as quickly as he can and get away.

I felt for him and thought I would do my best to cheer him. It was to prove a tragic mistake. I knew of course that such football post-match conferences were not like other press conferences. In the normal one that I attended, most often given by businessmen or financial gurus of various kinds, but occasionally politicians, I, in common with other journalists, walked in feeling like a predator who would prise the truth out of people you suspected had something to hide. Some time before this I had attended the launch of Henry Kissinger's memoirs and had tried to get the good doctor to admit to CIA misdeeds in South Asia. I hadn't quite succeeded but was much chuffed when an expert on the region complimented me on getting Kissinger rattled.

But the very first football press conference I had attended made me realise that any attempt to glean real information, let alone Kissinger-style verbal jousting, would not only be a waste of time but more than likely make me the object of ridicule in the eyes of my fellow journalists. It had also brought home to me the extremely odd nature of the football press in this country.

The post-match football press conference, certainly the one held every Saturday after a match, is aimed at three distinct audiences. It is mainly for the benefit of the Sunday tabloids who are desperate to get a quote, any quote, from the two managers about the game. English journalistic legend has it that such post-match quotes became fashionable after 1966 and England's victory in the World Cup, although television and the need for soundbites must also have played a part. The result is that for the tabloids a match report is not complete without some quote from the manager, however banal.

As a reporter for *The Sunday Times* I was aware that I was under no obligation to take any notice of what the managers said. Indeed, some of my colleagues did not even attend the press conference and adopted an almost Brahminical distaste for the post-match conference, treating the tabloid journalists far worse than my mother treated the sweeper woman. At least my mother gave the sweeper woman a cup of tea, albeit in a special cup from which nobody else was allowed to drink. Some of the Sunday heavies disdained showing even such arm's length courtesy to the tabloid writers.

Also, working for *The Sunday Times*, I had been brought up on the tales of Brian Glanville and knew of his contempt for such post-match press conferences. I had once asked him which ground he most enjoyed going to and his reply was, 'Any ground where I can leave it sufficiently quickly to catch the four-fifty train back to London.' Like nearly all Sunday reporters Glanville did a runner – meaning dictated part of the match report even as the match was being played. But while most of us waited until the end to 'top and tail' it, trade terms for the final opening and closing paragraphs, so that the reader next morning would be under the illusion that it was a properly considered report written in one take, Glanville so timed his reports that even as the referee blew his whistle he was ready with his final words. Indeed, he often put the phone down seconds after the referee blew and was ready to leave the ground moments after the players left the field.

In his *Sunday Times* days Glanville rarely attended post-match press conferences and then only if it was a midweek match. Such occasions were ideal for him. With no reporting deadlines for himself he would often assume – and still assumes – the task of being the spoiler at the party, asking such complicated questions that some of his daily colleagues, who were merely looking for a few quotes before their deadlines, despaired. This desperation was particularly acute on the occasions in the early '80s when Charlton Athletic called a midweek conference to announce the arrival of the Danish player Simonsen. Such foreign transfers were unheard of, but before the Charlton manager had much chance to explain the novel transfer Glanville interposed: 'I suppose this is in line with Charlton's historic policy of importing Danish players?' – a reference to the fact that Charlton had had a Danish player in the late '40s. The Charlton manager did not recover and neither, some Charlton fans might say, did Simonsen, who neither lasted long nor made much of an impact on the English game.

Without quite having Glanville's insouciance, I shared his instincts towards the post-match football press conference and they chimed in well wit my belief that a sportswriter was no different to a theatre critic. This is how Cardus saw cricket writing and I could not imagine him going to the dressing-rooms afterwards to check on a player's or a manager's views. I did attend post-match conferences on Saturday, if only because managers often said something which quite unwittingly provided me with a theme for my considered piece. Sometimes the managers sounded as if they were trying to prove that Ron Knee of Neasden FC, *Private Eye's* celebrated fictional football manager, was not as much of a parody as we had all been led to believe. It was as a result of attending one such post-match conference, after a dreadfully boring match between Ipswich and Southampton, that the journey to Ipswich was made unexpectedly memorable by Ian Branfoot, one of McMenemy's successors. He claimed that far from Southampton being boring, mighty AC Milan were now emulating

Southampton and playing the 'pressing' game. But despite the lure of such gems I hated, and still hate, these press conferences, largely because they are so predictable and unutterably dull.

The format has rarely changed in my 20 years of sports reporting. After the match the journalists gather usually in some dingy room although the bigger clubs do provide some decent facilities. There is never any certainty the manager will appear and the longer the wait for the manager, the more the journalists fret. Some of them wander outside into tunnels and corridors hoping to discover if not the manager then a player or two. If the away team has suffered a bad defeat, the away manager is more than likely to scoot away and this is the cue for the tabloid boys to dash for the team coach. The home manager usually turns up even after a bad defeat but this might mean waiting an hour or more after the match. The usual explanation for the delay is that the manager has locked the team in the dressing-room and in such situations by the time he appears not only has the 16.50 to London gone but nearly all other trains as well. When a manager does appear, nervous glances at watches and worry about whether the journey to the station can be made in time to catch the last London train, take priority over any searching questions at the press conference.

Not that at the best of times too many searching questions are asked. The football press conference is a wonderful advertisement for an anti-information campaign. The ritual, once the manager arrives, is well choreographed and could not be more formalised. The press room steward, fancying himself as master of ceremonies, loudly announces his name and club, then more quietly asks, 'Would you like a drink?' Meanwhile, journalists rush forward to place their pocket dictating machines on the table nearest to where the manager is sitting or standing. But there is no similar rush to ask the first question, indeed, managers often play a game of dare, striking a pose which suggests: 'I challenge you to ask the first question.' And if it is not a Bill or Harry they know, they stare hard at the questioner as if unable to believe that anybody apart from a person known to them has the right to ask questions.

On more than one occasion, usually after a bad defeat, a manager can say: 'You saw it, you write it.' Generally the silence is broken by the local man, keen not to upset his source of news, asking about injuries or if he is very daring, 'Well, you must be satisfied you got the points?' or 'A bit unlucky that'. This is the cue for the manager to trot out all the old clichés: what matters is three points, taking each game as it comes, you make your own luck etc. But few have reached the heights of intellectual sophistication or artful micky taking – as his friend Alan Hansen would have us believe – that Kenny Dalglish attained. In his days as Liverpool manager he would invariably be asked how the result affected the title race and invariably reply: 'Whoever has the highest points at the end of the season wins the league.'

It was Dalglish who had also made me very aware that one subject managers hated being quizzed on was tactics: why did you play the right-sided midfield player on the left side, or play Saunders, the striker, behind the back four? Some years after McMenemy brought religion into the press conference I am about to describe, I was to see Dalglish very nearly come to blows with a journalist – who, as it happens, was black – when he asked why Liverpool, who had got beaten that day at Watford, had ended the game with Gillespie playing centre forward. Dalglish's response was to approach the man and ask, in a voice and a body language that carried a fair degree of menace: 'So you think you know more about football than me?'

Of course there are managers who can be most pleasant and make a press conference like a tutorial. David Pleat has always been a joy with his lucid erudition, and Graham Taylor, before he became a turnip man, could provide gems, even if he did at times find it difficult to stop talking. Indeed, it was after Dalglish had vented his anger that Saturday at Vicarage Road that Taylor, then managing Watford, emerged and made the immortal comment about Blisset's bowel movements. Asked why the home crowds had booed his substitution of Luther Blissett he said, 'They love Luther. If he goes to the centre circle and craps they will applaud that.'

Needless to say no paper used the word crap and that was another lesson I learned quite early from football press conferences: 90 per cent of what the manager said could not be printed, certainly not in a family paper. They uttered so many four-lettered words, so many non-sequiturs, sentences that railed away in ether that very often a simple transcript of the press conference would be the sort of awful stream of consciousness disowned even by the most slavish William Burroughs clone. This has resulted in the most curious phenomenon: the manager's press conference followed by a journalist's one. After many a press conference journalists, led by the eager tabloid boys, go into a huddle and hold their own conference to agree on what they call the 'quotes', in other words the most acceptable form of words that everyone will use. This means that the report of what a manager said is a virtual rewrite of his true words and what is attributed to the manager is more often the gist of what he said or even meant to say rather than his actual words.

How alien such press conferences were to what the rest of the sporting world was used to was brought home to me one afternoon in Toronto while watching my first baseball match. I was struck by the wealth of information available during the game. For a start this meant that match reporting no longer involved trying to be a Hercule Poirot and ten minutes after the match the journalists were allowed into the dressing-rooms with the coach happily discussing tactics and the players, some of them with towels draped round their bodies, giving intelligent, revealing comments. Standing right in the middle of the dressing-room was a female journalist and the only one surprised by her presence was me.

The manager might say that it is not easy to satisfy the British football press which certainly makes unique demands. In no other game, and no other country, is the same match reported on two successive days as it is here. Yet this happens every Saturday during the season. The Monday papers also report matches played on Saturdays despite the fact that the match has already had a few thousand words devoted to it in the Sunday papers. The result is that on Saturdays two sets of reporters are present – the Sunday boys and the Monday boys – even from newspaper groups where the weekday paper and the Sunday paper is not only jointly owned but also share joint services. The explanation given is that the weekend and weekday papers serve different constituencies and often the two readerships do not overlap. The Sunday report is more of a description of the game, the Monday one a commentary focusing on an issue or taking in wider things. This makes the Monday reporter, particularly the tabloid one, all the more eager to talk to managers to get a special angle. But since it would ruin their story if the Sundays got hold of it, it is common for a manager who has just finished distributing his pearls of wisdom to be asked, 'That was for the Sundays, what about the Mondays now?'

However, that October Saturday in 1983 such concerns were far from my mind. I had done my runner for *The Sunday Times* and was looking for something more for my considered piece. In the past Luton press conferences had provided me with some very good material. The first time I had ever covered Luton, back in 1981, when they had played Newcastle with a young Chris Waddle in the side, Pleat, seeking to bring Luton back into the first division, had mentioned in the programme that he would like to 'slip in by the back door'. When I quizzed him about it he replied that he wanted to avoid the razzmatazz that fellow promotion rivals Watford were attracting. I was so struck by this and other measured, thoughtful answers that I devoted the first of many pieces singing his praises.

Now seizing on the fact that the 3–1 scoreline against Southampton was a trifle misleading – had a couple of things gone right for them Southampton might even have won – I asked McMenemy if he took comfort from the fact that in patches Southampton had played quite well. The question certainly perked him up, although not in the way I had hoped.

'We played well? What match were you at, pal? Are you sure you are not at the wrong type of game? This is football, pal.' The implication was clear. Only someone with my lack of knowledge of football could have asked such a daft question – perhaps I should have been at hockey? My fellow journalists, who at that stage had been struggling to ask McMenemy anything, were quick to laugh at my expense but McMenemy was not finished. The following week Luton were due to visit Liverpool – then in their pomp and glory. Southampton had got a 1–1 draw there and McMenemy was asked what advice he had for Luton. 'Go to church and pray before the match,' Then, turning to me, he said, 'I don't know where you would go to pray, pal.'

This was the cue for my fellow journalists to fall about in merriment and McMenemy, his spirits now fully restored, strode out of the press conference looking every inch the giant Coldstream Guardsman who had just quashed the attempt of a midget to get into Buckingham Palace.

As it happens, McMenemy's prediction that Luton would require something divine at Liverpool was a good one. Luton lost 6–0, with Rush scoring five and Dalglish one. McMenemy could say I was being sensitive if I took his remarks in any racial sense. After all did he not, in his diary of a season published way back in 1979, have a photograph showing the four apprentices he had signed that season at the Dell? On one side of McMenemy was Reuben Agboola, who had played that day at Luton and hailed from Trinidad, and on the other, Johnny Pang, son of a Chinese restaurant proprietor. If two out of four apprentices were non-white, what more could be asked for? In any case, his crack at me could be seen as the perfect illustration of the Hyde Park Corner orator who takes on a man asking difficult questions and makes him or her the subject of his barbs, so much so that soon the rest of the audience are laughing at the intruder instead of the speaker.

But that evening, as I emerged into the darkness of Kenilworth Road and hurried to my car, I could not help feel how ironic McMenemy's comments were given what the streets around Kenilworth Road had to offer. If this was not quite like emerging out of Bombay's Cooperage and walking past the Band Stand – once the home of British military bands, now of vendors selling nuts, coconuts and various snacks – there was more than a feel of the sub-continent. My route to the car down roads with such impeccable names as Oak and Beech took me past houses and shops that clearly spelled out the shape and the feel of the new England out of Pakistan or, more accurately, Kashmir and Bangladesh. My car had been parked next to a shop called the Kashmir stores where the man with russet-coloured hair and a mullah's beard might have stocked Yorkies but looked more at home with the basket of pistachios. On either side of the road I could see women with their heads covered in shawls in the company of little boys slowly making their way home. They could have been in Mirpur or Sylhet for all the notice they took of Luton or football.

If McMenemy had asked these people 'Where do you pray, pal?', they would have thought he was an imbecile. Even in the gathering gloom I could see the minarets of three mosques surrounding the ground. But, I suppose, given the legendary singlemindedness football managers are said to bring to their business, McMenemy had not even glanced out of the team coach as it swung into the Kenilworth Road carpark.

But why single out McMenemy? His unawareness of how Luton, or for that matter most English football grounds, had changed hardly makes him unique. It is something common to almost everybody in the English game. Much is written of the enormous changes that have come to the English game – the money, the greed, the commercialism, the sleaze, the way television dictates to the game even to the extent that a football weekend is a three-day event stretching from Saturday through to Monday evening. Yet in many ways the most important, the most radical change, is hardly commented upon. This is the amazing contrast a football match now presents in this country. English football continues to stress that it is a sport for the people, arises from the community, is still rooted in the very fabric of the working-class milieu that nurtured the game. Hunter Davies's magisterial indictment of the rampant commercialism of Manchester United may have been slightly overstated – I must confess I participated in the programme but only to stress the point that I feel football clubs are inappropriate as stock market companies – but few can quarrel with his central complaint that, in contrast to Barcelona, Manchester United has divorced itself from its local community. Fans were now coming to United from as far away as Dorset and even Ireland in what is like a tourist trip.

Yet in his eloquent demolition of United, Davies missed one salient point. It is not merely United who tempt supporters from long distances, all clubs do, and it is not so much a case of the football club having left the community but the community, which nurtured football, having left the physical surrounds of the club. The bricks and mortar that housed the community which gave birth to football remain, but the people have fled. It is as if a giant UFO arrived one day and just lifted the population to another location far away, while filling the empty houses, schools, shops and parks they left behind with a very different kind of people, some of them from many thousands of miles away.

That is so radical a change that it flies in the face of everything English football has stood for. As conceived in this country the game was designed as an integral part of the community with the ground often bang in the middle of town, a few minutes walk from the railway station, next to shops and buses and surrounded on all sides by terraced houses. In the days when football was young this fitted very neatly with the life of the community. Long before television, let alone televised matches, all football matches were played on Saturday afternoons and there being no floodlights the occasional midweek matches were also played in the afternoon. Going to football chimed neatly with the very fixed contour of what was the Saturday ritual for most working-class men.

In the morning the usual factory grind, knock off at one o'clock, then a quick walk to the pub, then about two-thirty, even later depending on how close the pub was, a walk to the ground just in time for a three o'clock start. Today, not only has the tradition of Saturday working gone but the English working class has aspired to middle-class status and fled to distant suburbia. The supporters of West Ham now drive in from Basildon, that of Tottenham and Arsenal from near Luton. The houses, shops, schools they have left behind are peopled by the so-called ethnics, mostly Asians and blacks, but also Greeks, Cypriots, Turks etc, for whom the old English tradition of factory, pub, football, then home for tea is about as familiar as jam butties.

You only have to go to a ground on a match day to discover what a peculiar world this has created. In essence it is the reverse of the American phenomenon of bussing where black kids are taken by buses to schools in better-off white neighbourhoods. But that came after a long legal battle and a US Supreme Court verdict in the famous Brown versus the Board of Education of Topeka, Kansas. In England no law was required. Quite willingly on match days the aspiring middle-class offspring of working-class white people get in their cars and drive back to areas their fathers and grandfathers fought so hard and long to leave. Once they arrive they often watch a team which is half black. Their arrival in these communities can make the preliminaries to a football match like a modern-day recreation of the sort of march Hollywood has made us believe was a prelude to war in medieval times, with the away supporters escorted to and from the ground by police and the whole area swarming with police dogs, police cars, police vans and giving a very passable imitation of a war zone.

As the descendants of the old inhabitants come back to the area, the people who have replaced them watch with a mixture of indifference and dread. Most step aside, as if to say this has nothing to do with them; some board up their shopfronts and hope this tribal war will not leave scars in their communities. At times the locals can appear very unconcerned. So, for instance, the young Asian boys near Aston Villa have yet to develop quite the predatory skills of fleecing visiting motorists that is the hallmark of the poor whites around Everton or Liverpool – along with Blackburn one of the few major football grounds where the colour of the surrounding inhabitants matches that of the crowd inside the stadium. While these Asian kids around Villa Park do cadge money for tips they still have a vacant, curious look as if not sure why the visitors have suddenly arrived amidst them. In contrast, the young whites around Everton are as sharp as a button both in fleecing money and in their knowledge of football.

The approach to some other grounds can be even more disorientating. Approach West Ham from the Upton Park tube station and in a matter of minutes you change continents. The road to the ground lies through what feels like Delhi's Khan market – the principal shopping area of the Indian capital. But as the claret and blue army, almost wholly white, march to Upton Park, the shoppers at West Ham's Khan market barely look up; the football fans' activity seems as unrelated to their lives as the passage of a distant star.

What all this means is that not only has English football become disconnected from its immediate neighbourhood but in the process it has changed. Given that football proclaims it is from the society – as much part of it as uncles and schools, to quote Hopcraft – this change means that it is far, very far, from the game romantics would have us believe it still is. The disconnection from the neighbourhood has also meant it has acquired some very peculiar problems.

'So what can we do?' ask the men who run English football, wringing their hands in despair. 'We would like these people, these ethnics, who live near the ground to come to the matches. They are as welcome to football as anyone else. We put no barriers in their path, we would love them to come and watch the game. Why don't they?' Maybe they do not come, says one, because there is no Asian playing football. Give them a symbol and they will flock like sheep. If we could get one Asian player in our first team it could put 2,000 on our gates.

The man who voiced this opinion could not be more well meaning, marrying mammon to an admirable desire to reconnect football to the community. But can community relationships once fractured be repaired so easily? Can football, now played in stadia which are like alien transplants amidst people who do not march to its clarion call, ever be part of its immediate surroundings?

CHAPTER SEVEN

Jack and his Turban

We are in a room at the back of the main stand at Luton, yet another Luton room with a bar, except that it is many years since McMenemy, who has moved upwards and onwards, and there is no need for partitions – there is nobody at the bar and apart from me no other journalist present. There are just three of us – myself, Colwyn Rowe, the Luton community officer, and Terry Westley, then Luton youth team coach (some months after we spoke he became manager and later still got the sack). The question we are grappling with is: where are the young Asian players that should be flooding into Luton's youth team, the children from the houses where you only have to open the door to smell the jock-straps of Luton's players.

'What people don't understand,' says Terry, 'is we need one to come through the system. We would love to take a YTS Asian footballer. We are desperate to take one.'

That is when Colwyn comes in about putting 2,000 on the gate, saying, 'If we got an Asian player in the first team that would put 2,000 on our gates. We want them to come. We are not stopping them. They would get exactly the same treatment as an English person or Italian person.' Then, turning to Terry, he asks, 'Our gates would go up, wouldn't they? Must do.'

Terry provides the necessary reassurance. 'Young players would flock to see an Asian hero. Like Imran Khan in cricket. When they won the World Cup cricket, the streets round here were fanatical.' There is almost a sense of disbelief in his voice as he says, 'Fanatical, driving cars, hooting, flags out, fanatical. But first they have to break through the system.' Then turning to Colwyn, he asks, 'Has there been one in the football league system?' Colwyn looks uncertain, then Terry recalls, 'Yes, there was Bashir in Reading. Winger, wasn't he?'

'Where is he now?' I ask.

'Don't know,' says Terry, 'somewhere in non-league. [Bashir now plays for Aylesbury Town as a part-time footballer, his full-time job being window cleaning.] But you need someone to break through the system.' Terry is well aware that for Luton this is vitally necessary, if for nothing else than to re-establish football's much advertised links with the local community. 'Our club,' says Terry, almost in wonder, 'is at the moment really in the centre of the Asian community, right in the centre.'

'The club,' emphasises Colwyn, 'is at their back door.'

Despite this, Asians around Kenilworth Road open the back door and go all over the world but not into the football ground that faces them. Terry can only shake his head in bemusement that the community has so far refused to yield an Asian player: 'We at Luton run schools of excellence from nine years upwards. Once a week. In each group there are 20 players. They are boys who should have some football excellence. We do not have an Asian in our school of excellence. Obviously the highest majority are whites, a handful of African-Caribbean, a couple of Italians. This year in my youth team we have two coloured players. Some of them are from schools of excellence, 50 per cent are kids we have monitored since they were 13, 14. If we go and watch school games, Asians don't play in the school teams. The question is why don't they play in the school team? I would think there must be boys between the ages of 12 and 15 of Asian origin in the region who should be playing for Luton schools. That is where it starts.'

And even if the odd Asian does play for his school team, what worries Terry is that he has just not seen any Asians progress into the district school teams. 'I'd like to know why they don't progress into the district team. I see Asian players playing for their teams. Chorley and Hignall, these two schools produce players for the club and continue to do so. I don't see Asian players play for these teams. Can't understand why. I would have thought that from the age of 12 to 15 there must be some Asians in the region who should be playing for Luton schools. They cause problems in our carpark. Why don't they play in the park which is down the road? You will have to ask them that. That is the question to be asked.'

It is not a question of Asians not getting a chance because of whites. 'Some schools,' says Colwyn, 'are nearly all Asians, hardly any whites. Dallow Road Junior School, Denbigh High. They are predominantly Asian schools in Luton, nearly all Asian.'

Nor is there any lack of club-school co-operation. Dallow Road Junior School, which is 200 yards down from the club, has a nice grass pitch which the club uses for training. In return Terry takes sports lessons at the school on Monday. 'We do games with them – not necessarily football, all sorts of different games.' And as schools go, says Terry, 'Dallow Road is quite a well-equipped school, better equipped than some other schools one can think of. Dallow Road has a school pitch.'

But even when Luton have organised coaching, as during Easter when they distributed 40,000 leaflets promoting football as enjoyment and attracted 900 children, there were hardly any Asians. 'I would say,' says Colwyn, 'we didn't have more than a dozen Asians on it out of 900 children.' Then, as if exhausted by their own efforts to unravel this riddle, they turn to me. 'What to do you think?' Colwyn asks me. Before I can answer he says, 'We have tried. It is exactly the same opportunities as the English, Italians or whatever. If money is holding back Asians from coming to the ground then how come poor whites come to the ground to watch matches.'

Maybe, I say, with Asian shopkeepers it is difficult to get away.

Terry suggests, 'Diet, nutrition, all may play a part in why they are not footballers. There are so many little bits that add to one big bit.'

'Do you think,' asks Colwyn, 'the Asians want to be footballers or doctors?' Colwyn, who has run coaching sessions for Asians sponsored by an Indian restaurant, is beginning to think there is a cultural problem here. 'Whereas in England our hero as a child is a footballer, for the Asian it seems to be more a doctor or a professional person. So the first generation of children born here is probably pushed in that direction.'

The Jewish syndrome of my son, the doctor, I suggest.

Colwyn looks blank, the comparison with Jews has clearly thrown him. 'I don't know. Yeah, maybe.' He is convinced it is more to do with the dominance of the Asian father. 'It may have something to do with family background,' says Colwyn. 'In the first generation that father is very dominant. I had spoken to the headmasters. They say what the fathers say goes. So they will look up to a doctor or something like that whereas we will look up to someone' – here he pauses and searches for a name – then says, 'someone like Cantona.'

We are speaking three months after Cantona displayed his knowledge of kung-fu and while he is serving his community service sentence. I look at Colwyn and think no Asian father is likely to suggest to his son that he adopt Cantona as a role model in preference to becoming a doctor.

Terry is aware it will take time. 'You have to expect it will take time. The

African player took time. Lilleshall, the national football school, took time.'

Yes, hopes Colwyn, 'they will come, in time. They all say that where the Asian community is, is where the West Indians were a few years ago. Now they are coming along quite well, aren't they? Maybe the Asian situation will follow 20 years on.'

Terry feels it might change in ten years, but 'they have got to start playing for our under-tens or under-elevens, which they are not'.

'Yes,' says Colwyn, 'we would have to have an Asian player by the age of 15, 16. But he would need to be spotted much earlier.'

But perhaps like all solutions to a riddle we are barking up blind alleys. Peter Hart, acting head of Beech Hill Community School, just down the road from Kenilworth Road, has seen no parental injunction such as thou shalt not play. 'As long as it does not interfere with other things thaty considered more important, religious studies for instance.' However, he has noticed that on open days parents are less interested in how their children are doing in sporting activities than in maths, English and science.

The parents are the typical first generation immigrants that once migrated from various parts of Europe to populate America. 'They have come,' says Hart, 'from village communities. The parents may not even speak English. In the eight years I have been here I have seen communications get easier but it is still not ideal.'

The area around Kenilworth Road has always been a natural magnet for such newcomers. 'We tend,' says Hart, 'to get the new communities. The housing is cheap and there is a great community feel.' Twenty years ago, when Hart first came to Luton, the area around Kenilworth Road had no Asians. 'I suppose there must have originally been what we may call white English. But when I came it was mainly Afro-Caribbean. Then they moved out and now it is mainly Asian.' Even here there has been change. 'Asians of Indian origin have moved out as they have made more money. Now it is Asians from Kashmir in Pakistan and Sylhet in Bangladesh in this area.'

In Dallow Road School, whose facilities Terry finds so admirable, almost 80 per cent of the 289 pupils are Asians – evenly split between Bangladeshis and Kashmiris from Pakistan. At Beech Hill, which is nearly 100 per cent Asian, the Bangladeshis dominate – 65 per cent of the students are of Bangladeshi origin, which is hardly surprising, given that Luton has the second highest Bengali population in the country. All in all this is a poor community of Asians almost wholly from two of the most rural, inaccessible areas of the Indian sub-continent.

And over the years it has retained its classical image of a poor community. 'There is,' says Hart, 'a high proportion of the unemployed. In the eight years I have been here the majority of parents have been unemployed. The houses date from the 1900s, terraced housing, and it is a poor community.' So poor that most of the parents of the Asian children who go to Denbigh, another school near the ground, are unemployed.

Hart is keen to emphasise, 'They do love football. A lot show interest.' Some of this interest ought to be in the genes. Bangladesh may be unknown as a soccer power but interest in the game there is immense. When there was a united Bengal under the Raj this was the centre of soccer in the sub-continent. Back in 1911 a Bengali team, albeit a team from the western, Hindu Bengal, playing barefoot, defeated the East Yorkshire regiment in an important cup match in Calcutta and led to the creation of a form of Indian soccer nationalism. In the 1930s the creation of the Calcutta team, Mohemadan Sporting, reflected the growing political and economic power of Bengal's Muslim community and in modern Bangladesh matches in Dacca between the leading teams have led to riots. The soccer is often of poor quality but crowds come and the passion is there.

But, perhaps like so much else, this is not part of the heritage of Luton's Bangladeshis. They come not from the urban milieu of Dacca but from the isolated, rural villages of Sylhet where life has changed little, if at all, since long before the Raj and where urban sport is still a bit like hearing distant tales of a faraway land.

So in Luton, the sons of the immigrants, who should have had the Bengali love of soccer burnished by the English game, behave as if the game means nothing to them. Those who attend Beech Hill Community School play in the carpark to the intense annoyance of Terry, the only excuse being that it is their carpark which the school allows the club to use and Beech Hill does not have the sort of sports facilities that Dallow Road has. The carpark at times is about the only place the kids can play.

'Unlike Dallow we haven't got a field,' says Hart. 'We are a typical inner-town school. That is our major difficulty. So we play games on our playground but have to adapt the rules or play a different type of game.' The situation has worsened since the club tore up its plastic pitch and went back to grass. 'The school and the club,' says Hart, 'were much closer when they had a plastic pitch, we could go down there and play there. When the plastic was torn up they said we couldn't go there. They were very nice about it but it meant we had no field. Our children play in the carpark and there is not much sport at our school.'

However, neither the desire of Asian fathers for their sons to emulate doctors rather than Cantona or lack of sports facilities is quite the whole answer. There is another aspect, perhaps the most important. We can glimpse it in the problems encountered by a member of the Beech staff who runs a football club for the older boys on Friday night. His efforts come up against one factor that is the greatest constant in the lives of Luton's Asians, their religion.

When I had asked Terry whether the Asians were Muslims he had said softly, as if the question was supremely irrelevant, 'I wouldn't know.' To him, like so many in England where religion often means the initials C of E, but not much more, it seemed absurd to think that religion can play any part in determining whether a boy ended up as a footballer. However, it is the pull of Islam for the Asian boys which may help solve this puzzle of why they fail to appear in the schools and district teams. In this intensely religious community, which besides the public mosques has a number of house mosques, the need for Islamic religious instruction decides how much time a child may have for sports.

So the Beech staff member who runs the football club for older boys on Friday is aware that he must finish in time to allow the children to go for their religious education. 'All our clubs,' says Hart, 'finish at four-fifteen. With school finishing at three-thirty they can only play for half an hour. We have to finish by four-fifteen because mosque classes start at four-thirty. So, while other students who are not Muslims might play games or practise sports between five and seven, we can't. Whatever is done has to be directly after school. Then the children go for their religious instruction. This would, obviously, not apply if mosque classes were not there.'

Religion has to be taken into account by all PE teachers. Listen to Martin Wood, PE teacher at Denbigh, the secondary school where some 95 per cent of the 1,000 pupils are Asians with Pakistanis forming 65 per cent of them. 'We do have problems with some children going to the mosque. On a Friday night it would be difficult to play football. We try and usually fix our games on an evening when it is not so important to go to the mosque. We have to work round their religious beliefs.'

Not that Wood will accept that Asian footballers are not good. 'We have school teams in all ages. We play in the Luton league, we do have some who play in Luton schools. Our boys do go forward and we have had boys selected, four boys in under-16, but some of them are just not good enough.'

Not as good as the blacks?

'No, no, our Asian players are just as fast as anybody else. At Luton, whenever they have meetings at Stockwell Park, there are just as many

Asians in the 100 metres or the sprints. There is no difference in pace, skill or agility. An Asian boy, Abdul Chowdhury, of Pakistani origin, plays in the middle of the park as captain and he is as good as anybody.'

Like Hart, Wood has met many parents who have a very Asian work ethic. 'Fathers are dominant, and they say work hard. The Asian parents don't regard sport as highly, don't put emphasis into physical education. When we play football we don't get many parents coming. When we play a predominantly white school, most of the white parents are there, maybe one or two Asian parents.'

But, if as Woods admits, 'our football is not that good', how come Denbigh is good at basketball with the great majority of the players Asian? Yasmin Bevan, head of Denbigh, had said 'We are better at basketball. We are Luton and County champions at basketball.' And here we begin to glimpse a reason that has very practical resonances. 'At our school,' says Wood, 'we only have a small playing area, there can be no training at half-time. We have to walk a mile to the football pitch. By the time we have got there we have little time for training and it is time to come back. We would have more time if there was no mosque education.'

Denbigh, insists Wood, is just as good at sport as any other school in town. The problem may be that when the boys leave school the talent never emerges into the wider world. 'When they leave our school they tend not to mix with the local community. They tend to go into their own football teams – the Bangladesh XI, the Pakistan XI – rather than mixing with clubs who play in the Diadora league. They don't play in white teams. They tend to join those in their own inner circle. It is an insular thing. This means they remain hidden from scouts that go out looking for talent. When they leave school they tend to go back to their own insular ways of living. They don't mix, as well. There is hidden talent, a lot of skill. There are good Asian players out there.'

Could it be that Asians are smaller? 'Yes, there are differences in size with other children. They don't tend to grow as big as other children. Diet may be a factor. But otherwise Asian children have little difference in their ability, compared to any other child.' Sooner or later Terry had said, 'One Asian will say I want to be a footballer.' It was more a declaration than a prediction, as if an Asian would one day stand at Hyde Park Corner, push aside the medical books or the law brief his parents had given him and tell the world: 'I want to be a footballer.' Life rarely follows such a theatrical pattern but just before I went to Luton one such call, not at Hyde Park Corner but over the Luton switchboard, led to Terry inviting an Asian boy to Luton's school of excellence.

So it was that two winters ago Jack came to Luton every Thursday evening for six weeks. Jack, born in Hitchin, living in Baldock, who sounded like any of the hundreds of other boys who aspired to the school of excellence. But Jack was very different. He wore a turban and, as I soon discovered, Jack was not his real name. His proper name is Jagjeevan Dosanjh. Jagjeevan became Jack because his teachers, both at Hatfield Primary in Baldock and the Knights Templar Secondary School where he is doing nine GCSEs, could not pronounce his real name.

Jack is almost the classic second generation child. Bedfordshire is home. Jullundur in India, from where his father migrated to this country in 1975 – he now works in a factory in East Ham – is just a place to visit. His father's sport of hockey has never appealed to him. Jack says, 'Soccer is my first love.' This love has come from his father who talked about football and then a friend, Gurjeet, a fellow Sikh, who introduced him to soccer when he was about nine. Before that Jack had watched soccer on television. But, 'I had never been interested in football on television. I did not understand it then. I did not know what offside was.'

Later, prompted by Gurjeet, Jack played for an Indian side, Letchworth Khalsa, a Sikh team. 'I enjoyed it quite a bit.' Along with football there were other sports – cricket, a little squash, but never hockey, the game Sikhs are associated with in India. For Jack it was always football.

He soon started playing for his school team, first on the wing, then moving to midfield. Jack thinks he is fairly good and he likes his school which is 95 per cent white. But he concedes that he does not always play that well for his school. 'I don't play that well for them. There is one good player, everybody passes to him only, they are scared of him. So I don't often get the ball.' Despite this there has been some success for Jack in the school team, but it is uneven. 'In the third year we got into the county cup final and got beaten by Gough. I didn't play the final but I was in the semi-final when I got injured. I provided quite a few goals during the cup run.' His more regular outing is every Saturday for Khalsa Youth at the Ferne Hill Sports Centre, Letchworth, where there are three other Indian teams. It is mainly five-a-side football games, often organised in an impromptu fashion.

Jack quite enjoyed six weeks of training at Luton's school of excellence, although most of the people he played with were older and the sessions every Thursday night emphasised that the English game seeks boys of strength. 'We played in the gym, not a full-size pitch, which meant tight space and you needed strength. If you had strength you did all right.' Not easy for Jack who is five feet ten inches and confesses; 'I don't have much strength. My upper body is not that strong. I like running at players, I quite like dribbling, I have got a lot of pace. Before I used just pace, now I use skills.'

How much chance he may have to develop whatever skills he has is debatable. Even before I had spoken to Jack, Terry had told me that Jack was 'a pleasant enough lad but not up to the standard'. And then there was Jack's need to pursue his nine GCSEs. It has meant he has little time for football. His parents, unlike most Asian parents, do not mind his playing. 'My mum does not know much about football, my dad encourages me.' But they are not, he says, like 'black parents who encourage their children in sport. My parents say concentrate on work.'

Despite his academic commitments, he has ambitions to be a footballer. 'I would like to play professional football. Given the choice I would rather be a professional footballer than have a degree.' Yet it does not sound like the sort of desire that would break through ancient walls of apathy and ignorance. 'If I don't make it, it is no loss. If not I shall do my studies,' he says in a matter-of-fact, almost resigned, tone.

Is he being held back because there is no role model? 'Being the only Asian in the team does not matter. I don't mind that not too many Asians play football. A Sikh boy with long hair was nearly signed on by Sheffield Wednesday during a tournament at Derby two or three seasons ago. I don't know what his real name was. Chewy was his nickname. I have seen quite a few players who could make it. I don't think there is any prejudice on behalf of clubs. At Luton, when I went for training, there was no prejudice. Most of the other Luton players were white, one or two were black. But there were no jokes about my turban.' Terry had said, 'He has a turban but that is neither here nor there.' Then, after a pause, he had added, 'He changed with us,' the implication being that any man who drops his shorts in a communal situation, albeit that he wears a turban, must be acceptable.

Indeed, for Jack the worst moment of racism was not on the football field but on the streets of London. 'Six months ago we were going to London looking at shops. We went on the subway in London, to go to King's Cross, St Pancras. Some persons came by in a car, opened the window and shouted racist remarks.'

So why didn't Luton's Asians go to soccer? 'White people,' says Jack, 'have better jobs, they can afford to go to matches.' Jack's own family circumstances are: 'Comfortable. We have our own house and a van for dad from the company.' Jack used to watch matches on Sky, now they have discontinued Sky and 'I go to friends' houses or snooker clubs to watch it on television.'

At Wembley there is no doubting Jack's loyalty. 'I support England, I was born here,' he says in a tone which implies I had asked him a stupid question. But when it comes to cricket he does fail the Tebbitt cricket test. 'If India play England I want India to win.' However, this does not matter much. 'I don't really know much about cricket.'

It is a lack of knowledge that Tahir and Shamas could easily rectify. Unlike Jack they were not born in this country but came here, at 14 and ten. If Jack is third generation – born and brought up here – they are the second generation and have lived here long enough to be shaped by this country. But not it seems in the direction of the people's game.

Tahir Bashir, who is 36, was born near Kotli in Mirpur. He came to England when he was about 14. Football was well known in that part of Pakistan Kashmir. 'I played centre forward for my school team and my local team.' Two years schooling in Luton, far from deepening that interest took him away from football into the sports Asians are associated with in this country. 'When I came here my interest changed. My friends were more interested in cricket. There was no football, not proper matches.'

Bashir, who works as a production operator at Vauxhall Motors and played hockey for that company, now runs two cricket teams. 'On Saturdays I run St Joseph's, which is mixed Irish, English and with about four or five Asians. We play in the Herts and Beds League. I am captain, opening batsman and bowl leg spinners.' On Sunday Bashir goes ethnic and runs the Kashmir Cavaliers and Kashmir Colts, both comprising Kashmiri sides which play in the south-east league where the majority of players are Asian.

If Tahir still has some sporting contract with the local white English, then Shamas Uddin, who is two years younger than Tahir, has virtually none. Born in Kotli in Pakistan Kashmir, he came to this country when he was about ten. 'I played no games in Kotli. No organised sport was played. We played marbles, gilli danda, tug-of-war but no ball games. I played football when I came here, playing in defence, but I wasn't that speedy.' His experiences in football convinced him that 'while Asians are about the same in strength as black players, the black players are quicker than the Asians'.

Shamas now restricts his football to watching *Match of the Day*, having long been converted to cricket. 'Quite early after I arrived in Luton I took to cricket, opening batsman and medium-fast bowler.' Until he got his back injury he played for Luton Pakistanis on Sundays and Tuesday evenings. The Sunday team plays in the Luton and district midweek league. Although this league is run, says Shamas, 'by English people', the premier division of this league has no English team. 'The premier division has five Asian teams: Luton Indians, Azad Kashmir, Kashmir Cavaliers, Pakistani Crescents and the Luton Caribbeans, a West Indian combined side, the best team in the division.' As the West Indians were becoming champions, Markyat, the English team, got relegated. 'These five teams,' says Shamas, 'dominate Luton cricket. We have done so for three years. There are no white players in these teams.'

There are also no Asian teams in the Herts and Beds league where Tahir plays because, says Shamas, 'you have to have a clubhouse for that. No Asian team has a clubhouse.' The Luton Indians come nearest with their own pitch.

Even when Asians play the English at cricket there is a social problem. 'Lots of the Muslims don't drink,' says Shamas. 'When the match is finished the white team goes to the pub and has a drink, socialises. Some of our Muslims don't want to go to pubs. I do go to the pubs and have a soft drink but I don't stay long. Blacks and whites mix more easily. Blacks and whites follow the same music, go out. There is much more inter-racial mixing between whites and blacks. Asians do not like marrying whites.'

Shamas himself married a girl from Pakistan when he went back for his holidays. That was in 1982 when he was already in his mid-twenties and he has been back two or three times since. 'When Pakistan win in cricket I feel good. When Pakistan won the World Cup I celebrated – we went to the restaurant.' But he emphasises that he restrained his celebrations and feels that those who drove around Luton honking their car horns went over the top. Pakistan cricket and its problems are always close to him and the bribery allegations left him bewildered.

His only child, a boy of a year and a half, may become a sportsman, even a footballer. 'I will let him play whatever he is good at.' His own father, who was in the British army and fought on the Burma Front in 1944, didn't stop Shamas playing sport. 'He said do play sports but you must also study. Some Asian parents,' he says, 'do tell their children to study hard.'

Shamas is aware that apart from this Asian version of the Protestant work ethic, the demands of religious education also play a part. 'The children go to Madrassa from five to seven o'clock after school. They do that until they complete the Koran. It could take three or four years. They go from the age of five or six to about 13.'

Formative years for the children. Their white counterparts play football, they recite verses in Arabic. By the time the children of Shamas grow up it may well be very different but by then a lot will have to change. There might even be Asians not only playing but watching the game and, who knows, in the boardroom.

Ron Noades, chairman of Crystal Palace, knows all about trying to get blacks and Asians interested in the game. In his Channel Four interview on black footballers – which, as we shall see, made the headlines for all the wrong reasons – he said: 'We get black players that play the game but you don't get too many watching, in fact the people that are watching are usually the close friends of those players. We've not actually increased our gate by black players or you could say the Indians and Pakistanis over here and in places like Southall. I used to be chairman of Southall Football Club and there 52 per cent of the population in Southall was either from India or from Pakistan and we never had them watching a game, so we were actually existing on half the population that was living round our ground and looking for gate.'

But this did not worry Noades. 'No, not at all. It is just like being sexist, I suppose. I mean, I'm looking for women, I'm looking for kids, I'm looking for spectators whether they are black, white, yellow or whatever – not bothered. We want high gates and I want as many people to come to football as possible. I'm not interested in colour or creed.'

Noades's sentiments can hardly be faulted, they are even admirable. But the effect of not having blacks and Asians in the stands, let alone the boardrooms, means that football can no longer sustain the proud boast that it is part of the community, as much part of the psyche as schools or uncles. Some people's psyche, some people's schools and uncles, not everyone's. Football, in that sense, does not belong to all but becomes a sectional sport, one where a section of the population, historically brought up on it, comes to it while others, with newer or different traditions, do not.

Writers looking at racism in this country have seen this phenomenon as a sign of a damaging alienation. Dave Hill, writing in *The Guardian* series on 'Black in Britain', commented: 'Whatever their attractions, football clubs were often regarded as white institutions, from boardroom down to terrace. Black Britons remain under-represented at all levels bar the field of play and many black professionals still discourage their families from attending games for fear of what they might have to bear from white supporters.'

To change this would involve breaking down many taboos, some shared even by well-meaning men, as Jas is discovering.

It was Terry who had mentioned Jas's project to me. Terry was going to a coaches' seminar at Queen's Park Rangers where, among other things, Asian footballers and their non-existence was going to be discussed. And although Terry did not know about Jas or the name of his project, it turned out to be Jas Bains's long search for Asian soccer in this country – Asians

Can't Play Football, the title being very ironic since Jas's message is that Asians can play, want to play and are only seeking a chance to prove that they can do as well as the blacks and the whites.

Jas turned out to be the sort of man who could have been Jack's uncle. Both are Sikhs but Jas, at 32, is now part of the greying second generation whereas Jack is very much the third. Born in Wolverhampton, Jas, who is reaching the twilight of his soccer career, can recall the start of Asian soccer. 'Early Asian football originated with Sikh temples, with Sikh boys wanting to play but white teams not having them. The Sikhs started their own league round the Sikh Gurdwaras.' From there Asian teams have grown, some of whom play in integrated district leagues, others in their own little all-Asian leagues, one of which, the London Asian League, is probably the most prominent and is sponsored by Lawrentian Life Insurance Company.

Jas's project, Asians Can't Play Football, has had the support of the great and the good of football – the FA, the PFA. There is Carling money but this has come after persuasion and much tugging from the PFA whose initiative it is. Jas's research has confirmed what many of us suspected – that few Asians come to watch soccer. In Leicester, where one in four persons is Asian, only 250 attended a Premier League match. Even given that the match surveyed was Leicester versus Wimbledon, not the greatest of draws, that is a surprisingly small number.

But perhaps the biggest problem was revealed the day Jas talked to the coaches, including Terry, who had gathered at QPR. 'It was one of several regional meetings organised by the PFA,' says Jas, 'and I wanted to raise awareness of the cultural issues involved in Asians playing football. I dealt with the Asian stereotypes that they are physically deficient, parental pressure, employed in non-traditional areas of employment. I was raising issues trying demonstrate that if the Asians do not play football some of the reasons lay at the door of the clubs. It is not that Asians do not want to play or do not play, there are a whole host of issues.'

But halfway through his presentation he found 'the audience had switched off. There were some who started chatting away even as I was speaking, chatting amongst themselves. I realise there are cultural factors such as the religious factor. The schools for excellence are from five till seven and they can conflict with the hours of Islamic studies but this is not an insurmountable problem. As long as studies can be absorbed into any other day it need not conflict with football. I was trying to raise issues rather than blame football but I had clearly put them on the defensive.'

Jas's own experience at Wolverhampton shows how difficult it is to get recognised. Wolves are surrounded by Asians, Muslims live next door to their Molineux ground and in adjacent Whitmore Road there is a large Sikh community. When Jas and his friends first started going to Wolves they were the only Asians; now there is quite a following. But, says Jas, 'the management of the club have no concept of Asians or how to channel it or even give a monkey about it. Ultimately we need to take ownership and our case has to be made more powerfully.'

Since Jas started the project Asians have actually managed to put together a team. Last September, at the start of the season, an Asian XI, selected by the Bradford solicitor Aurangzeb Igbal, took the field against a Bradford City team. Aurangzeb could not be more complimentary about Bradford and how the club had helped him, first with an official Asian supporters club and then the match.

He saw it as reconnecting football to its roots. This was a match which would see English football recreate with Asian help its historic image. His hope was that on match day Bradford's Asians, who live around Valley Parade – whose fathers and mothers came from Bangladesh and Mirpur and colonised Cornwall Road and Cornwall Terrace – would pour out from these Victorian terraced houses and into the ground. Advance publicity suggested upwards of 10,000 Asians might gather. On the day fewer than 2,000 turned up and hard as Aurangzeb had worked he was at a loss to explain. Perhaps, he said, the Asians realised their team was not really good – they lost quite easily – and being hard-headed Yorkshire people did not fancy spending good money watching a match that could not be really competitive. It sounded lame and it was.

The fact is that Asian or for that matter black participation in sport cannot be reduced to simple images. And the danger always is that if you get rid of one stereotype, it is replaced by another. So a generation after black players made the breakthrough the stereotypes and set images about them continue. It was Colwyn, again well meaning and quite unwittingly, who revealed this. Almost at the end of our conversation, and after we had been speaking for some time about the speed and the pace of the black footballers and the difference they had made to English football, he said, 'But they don't swim, do they? You don't see a black swimmer, do you?'

O.J. Simpson, then still with Nicole and still the hero of both white and black America, had often joked about blacks not swimming but when Colwyn asked the question he did not mean it as a joke. It was deadly serious.

CHAPTER EIGHT

Blacks Don't Swim, Do They?

I had read about such sentiments regarding blacks but that was in faded old newspaper cuttings and they came from what looked like the prehistory of sports. In 1968 when white apartheid South Africa was still looking to hold on to its position in international sport, Frank Braun, then head of the white-only South African Boxing Association, told *Sports Illustrated*, 'Some sports the African is not suited for. In swimming, water closes their pores and they cannot get rid of carbon dioxide, so they tire quickly.'

Now in 1995 two men in Luton told me their feelings about blacks in sport which, in essence, was not all that different to what Braun had said. Yet they were a million miles from the white supremacy ideas that prompted Braun. The Luton men's sentiments were expressed in the context of an effort to understand why certain races play certain sports rather than to justify the exclusion of a race from sporting activity. They were hardly alone in harbouring such thoughts. Sir Roger Bannister has made similar comments and some time after I spoke to the Luton pair, Peter Hart, the Luton schoolmaster, speaking about why Asians did not play football, said, 'I am told Afro-Caribbeans do not float easily. Whether it is true or not, it is much more difficult for them to learn to swim than it is for Asians and others.'

What Colwyn Rowe and Trevor Westley said was, 'Blacks don't swim, do they? You don't hear about black swimmers.' Put like that it sounds damning, but it is important to state the context of these remarks. It came as I discussed with Rowe and Westley the contribution black players had made to the English game. Long years ago, before black players emerged, there had been an English dream that when English blacks started playing they would bring some of the exotic overseas styles of play: the mazy dribbles, the intricate passing, the delightful ball control, the unexpected that we had always admired in the Brazilians or the Hungarians and the Dutch. Sons of the black immigrants would bring the dash of fantasy to the traditional English game of strength and power. The men who made such predictions were good, honourable men. They had welcomed the presence of different races in this country. Their attempt to look ahead to a special black contribution in sports was part of a wider attempt by the decent, liberal people of the country to stem the tide of those who questioned the very presence of blacks and browns in this land. These well-intentioned people pictured the transformation the blacks might engineer on the sporting field as an argument for and vindication of building a multi-racial country.

Such a fusion has been possible in other countries. One has only to see Jonah Lomu and his amazing impact on the Rugby World Cup. At the height of Lomu's World Cup fame, Stuart Barnes wrote that it was evidence of New Zealand's ability to graft the flair of Lomu and his Polynesian friends to traditional New Zealand strengths of precision and discipline. In the 1970s, as England lost the World Cup and then failed to qualify for two successive ones, in 1974 and 1978, many an English romantic dreamed of an English Lomu, son of West Indian parents, who would add flair to an English game built around work rate and discipline.

But more than a decade after Viv Anderson became the first black player to play football for England, Wembley has not become the Maracana, if anything the English game of speed, strength and pace has become even stronger and even faster. David Pleat had told me this was the major effect of black players coming to the game and now in my conversation with Rowe and Westley I had confirmation. Westley said, 'Power, pace and strength, that is what the majority of coloured players have brought.'

'Black players are explosive,' nodded Colwyn. 'Ron Atkinson has a lot of coloured players and they are very fast. They have great power. It is just their athleticism. Are they an asset because of their pace? I would say they are.' So black players, in contrast to what the romantics thought, had not added fantasy – they had made a fast game even faster.

Just before my conversation with Rowe and Westley I had been asking Dwight Marshall, a black player who plays for Luton, why most of the blacks in football play as forwards. Now Westley took up the argument.

'You asked Dwight why most coloured players play up front. Their nature is very explosive, a powerful type of player. That is the front player. That is an asset for forward players, exceptional power. Gilkes at Reading is quick. I can't name any white player that quick. Why? How do black players become that quick?'

Rowe provided the answer. 'They have this fast twitch muscle that gives them speed. And they are bulky, aren't they?'

'So naturally,' said Westley, 'you start to mould that player as a front player. We have one coming through next year in my youth team. Afro-Caribbean. Luton boy. He is very, very quick. We are trying to mould him into a wide player. He has real pace. Like Ferdinand. Real powerful lad. He will bench youth team players next year because he is so powerful. That is his make-up. He isn't a midfield-type, neat, tidy, little passer like David Preece. I think generally they are powerful players and that is why they play up front.'

This was the voice of the coach looking at a player and looking for a particular asset. 'I look for a player to have an outstanding asset, any asset. One asset – maybe pace. Trevor Peek, he has reliability, week in week out. You must channel a player in a particular way. But that is not just a coloured player, you would do that with a white player.'

And if this is the way coaches think, that blacks with their fast twitch muscle must be quick and therefore play up front, would the fact that Asians have no history of soccer in this country lead them to believe they cannot play? 'I think lower down,' said Westley, 'there may be. But if you are a professional coach you look at somebody and if he is good enough he is good enough. You are going to take him. But there may be prejudice at school level. I think if boys turned up for football and there were some Asians playing, then the white boys and coloured boys might subconsciously think they can't play because they had never seen them kick a ball before. If you are not professional enough because you have never heard of Asians playing football it would come into it.'

In the end, said Westley, it was all down to performance. 'If the black players are doing very well, the other players will respect their performance. They would socially be part of the group, white players will say we want him because he is doing very well for us. If Asian players were on the scene then it will be exactly the same. If you have a black player in the youth team and he does well in the youth team the players want him in the team. Socially he is one of them. Then they socialise together. Our youth team, which is 50 per cent from our school of excellence, 50 per cent from outside, does that. They live in digs, visit each other and colour does not come into it.'

But in a way it does, although not quite in straight black and white terms. We had discussed the cultural differences between whites and Asians, how young blacks and whites could share a musical heritage – rock and roll and much of the music that has followed has been indebted to American blues and soul music. Rowe had said, 'Yes, I listen to black music. I can listen to black music. Asian music? I wouldn't listen to that, I don't know what it is.'

Of course, players can develop and develop in ways that can surprise coaches, upset perceived notions. The day I spoke to Rowe and Westley the papers were full of the reputation John Harston was making at Highbury, having been transferred there from Luton for £2.5 million. Yet the previous season, during Luton's epic semi-final run, he had played little or no part. Pleat, looking back on the semi-final with Chelsea, which Luton lost, felt he should have played Harston, not Dixon, whose heart was too much with Chelsea.

Westley was astonished how much, how quickly, Harston had developed during his two years as a YTS. 'He wasn't quite as big or as strong when he first came, he just grew. He hasn't got the pace of an Afro-Caribbean but he has marvellous touch, ambition and he fights for everything. Even in a five-a-side he will not give in.'

But for every Harston there are many who fall by the wayside and coaches trying to judge a player can only go on what they see and what potential they feel a player might have.

As Rowe and Westley put it that afternoon at Luton it all sounded very logical, even rational. They spoke as if their statements were objective, eternal truths, yet their own background conditioned how they perceived the world, one which had altered little over the years. Long years ago, long before they had come to Luton, Rowe and Westley had experienced black sporting power and formed their own opinion of how it manifested itself. They felt this gave them an insight into the collective attributes of the black athletes.

Both Rowe and Westley are from Ipswich. They arrived at Portman Road in the days when Bobby Robson was manager of a fine Ipswich side, challenging for the championship, weaving in the Dutch influence of Muhren and Thyssen with the traditional British strengths. Terry Westley, the same age as his namesake Terry Butcher, joined as an associate schoolboy player and is of a generation when there weren't black players in school, in football teams or anywhere else for that matter. Rowe says, 'Black players had not yet broken in. There was one I remember in my whole school.'

But although they knew no blacks, or had hardly ever seen them, even then tales of their power and speed had reached them. 'I had always known them as quick,' says Westley. 'I remember going to Portman Road and the quickest players in the school had to go for a 100-metre race straight down the pitch.'

'If there was a black in the race,' Rowe cut in, 'you thought he is going to win.'

'That's right,' confirmed Westley. 'I used to look up and down the line at the start of the race and if I saw a black face I thought, well, he is going to win it. They are the quickest players, aren't they?'

That is when Rowe said, 'They don't swim, do they? You don't see a black swimmer, do you?'

I looked at Rowe and then across to Terry Westley and the two faces could not be more earnest, more eager to establish that all this was part of a genuine desire to make sense of the whole question of people of different colour in sport. It was clear Rowe had spoken about the lack of black swimmers as if he felt this balanced his praise of blacks as quick on their feet. What he seemed to be saying was that they may be quick on the ground, but in water it does not work – there the fast twitch muscle is no good.

It would be easy to satirise such views, or condemn them as racist. Both Rowe and Westley are sincere men who may be naïve but have no malice. And they were in a way reflecting views quite commonly held. The black presence in football may now be taken for granted and there are many white players and managers who play, fraternise and count blacks as their friends. But even for some of them meeting blacks is still a fairly new experience.

Steve Coppell at Crystal Palace managed a team with a strong black presence, but growing up in Liverpool he had never met any blacks, never had reason to visit Liverpool 8 and the only non-whites he had come across in Liverpool were Chinese – blacks he got to know only when he became a player and then manager.

Gareth Southgate, the former Crystal Palace skipper now making a reputation with Aston Villa and England, had not met blacks until he got to Palace and then the thing that struck him was their physical build – so different to the white people he knew and had grown up with. To record such views is not to see Coppell or Southgate as racist, that is absurd, but to emphasise that we are all products of our upbringing, we all carry certain mind-sets, a point that had been emphasised when in 1992 the storm broke over some remarks made by Ron Noades, chairman of Crystal Palace, regarding black players.

Noades had been interviewed as part of a programme meant to celebrate the advent of black players in the English game. The programme drew on the remarkable number of black players at Crystal Palace in the early 1990s – Ian Wright, Mark Bright, John Salako. As the programme-makers went about their job they felt it was going well. Wright, Bright and Coppell, the then Palace manager, had given interviews which the programme-makers thought were brilliant and highlighted the role played by blacks in football. Then, quite by chance, Noades was interviewed and was quoted on the programme as saying, 'On the other hand, when you are getting into midwinter in England, you need a few of the maybe hard white men to carry the artistic black players through.'

The programme-makers say they were shocked. Gareth Crooks, who was presenting the programme, says he could not believe his ears. Noades's words were played back to Wright and Bright who were outraged, an outrage shared by the Palace dressing-room and the press. Noades was pilloried as a racist, and there was talk it could lead to the break-up of the Palace team with some of Palace's brightest black stars, Wright and Bright, leaving. (This seems unlikely and both Coppell and his then assistant manager Alan Smith say it played no part, it was just time for the players to move.)

Noades, who tried unsuccessfully to persuade Michael Grade, head of Channel Four, to withdraw the programme, vehemently denied he was a racist and to this day feels bitter about what he sees as the way the programme and, more so, the tabloid press presented him. His comments were only part of a sentence. The rest of the sentence, which was not broadcast read, 'and again some of the white players with the strong characters need that extra ability that some of the black players have got that we haven't got'.

The non-use of this formed part of the lengthy correspondence between Channel Four and Noades, who felt this had balanced what he had said about hard white men. Channel Four's lawyers said that even had the words been used it would have made no difference. There was much else he had said in the interview which had been left on the cutting-room floor and which, in many ways, was more interesting.

The instant labelling of Noades as racist may have been expected; it certainly made good tabloid copy, but it was too glib, too much part of a process that easily attaches labels like racist and prejudice to people when we are dealing with something more complex, the mind of men brought up in one generation who are being called to question by people born in another generation and reflecting very different views, mind-sets and ways of thinking. The entire Noades interview, only a small part of which was ever broadcast, needs to be studied if we are to understand how the chairman of a club that has had strong black representation on the field of play – at times more than half the Palace team were black – really thinks on this complex issue.

According to the programme-makers the Noades comments that made the headlines were not only totally unexpected but they were, in the jargon of the trade, not even 'looking for it'. Sally Hibbins, the programme's producer, was convinced that people in the game no longer thought in such stereotypes and had commissioned two comics to mouth phrases similar to ones used by Noades as an illustration of the kind of old-fashioned views that were once held about blacks to contrast the upbeat message the programme was supposed to give. The interview with Noades was very much an afterthought, peripheral to the ones with Wright, Bright and Coppell round which the programme was being constructed, and designed to provide boardroom reinforcement for the positive messages coming from the dressing-room and the dug-out. The initial questions to Noades centred around the fact that despite the presence of black players on the pitch, there were few in the stands and none in the boardroom.

Noades, having highlighted how football for some blacks was a way of getting out of the ghetto, with youngsters attracted by the ability of stars to have the trappings of success – nice cars, suits, gold bracelets – gave an eminently sensible reason for their absence from the boardroom. You only he said, get people on boards of football clubs when they are successful. He could not think of one successful black businessman whom he had seen come to watch football. 'I've got a Senator from Nigeria on our board here. He is successful in business and was in the West End when I met him so I suppose we're probably the exception. I don't know if we are the only one in the country.'

Noades then explained that he was well aware of racism, particularly when his Palace team travelled up north. He knew they would have problems from the crowd but to him this was from 'the riffraff in the crowd'. And although there were such elements, even at Selhurst Park, he did not mind that. 'It gives the players a resolve. They know what to expect, in fact. Invariably they play better so I don't mind that.' Here we are close to what the Yorkshire players used to feel when the home crowd called Vivian Richards racist names. Their feeling was that it made Richards more determined and that he ended up by taking it out on the Yorkshire bowlers.

Hibbins then asked Noades about when we might see a black manager emerge, the next step in the ladder. Noades said, 'If you are looking to see how long it's going to take for black managers to become the norm, or for one or two in fact to be appointed, you've got to go down to the coaching courses and FA badges and see how many are actually volunteering to take a coaching course, how many are volunteering to turn up and coach the kids in the evening, because they are the ones that will be managers. You can't just be a star player then suddenly become a manager. If you are not prepared to work at the game you won't be successful, and the directors in the main, if they know anything about football, will look for their managerial appointments from those people that work hard at the game, that want to be successful.'

When Sally Hibbins pointed out that some top-class internationals like Viv Anderson and Cyril Regis had taken coaching badges, Noades replied: 'Well, I've never seen any of those watching a game and I go to a lot. I go to a lot of matches, evening games, and I don't recall seeing any top-class black players there watching the game to look at tactics, to see how other teams play. I'm not saying they don't do it, but certainly in the south I don't recall seeing any of them.'

However, persisted Hibbins, suppose there was such a player that fitted Noades's requirements, and given the trend of players moving straight from being player to coach, what would Noades be looking for? Noades said, 'You have got to read the game. That's one of the problems with the black players. I don't think too many can read the game. You get an awful lot with great pace, great athletes, love to play with the ball in front of them. When it's behind them it's chaos, so you are looking for them to understand the game. They've got to really be students of the game.'

When Hibbins asked Noades how blacks could make the break into management, Noades reiterated his view that black players had a certain way of treating the game. 'What I said before, I haven't seen many black players around looking at the games because they enjoy the game. They seem to play and then want to hang up their boots, and if they are really successful they will earn enough money to live comfortably after that. That is their target. There are not really any that I know that want to be in top management.'

It is at this point, discussing problems a black manager may face with the press, that Noades uttered his words of midwinter and hard white men carrying artistic blacks. Noades had anticipated what Hibbins was going to ask and went on to say that black players have pace: 'I mean pace. Some of the black players have got tremendous pace. We had a player here we thought was the quickest white man. That was unusual. By definition all the black players were quick, well, nearly all of them.'

If this was another dimension black players had brought to the game could they not bring something to management, asked Hibbins?

Noades replied: 'Well, I don't actually know what other dimension they could add into management we haven't got already. I mean, you don't need to be quick to be a manager, you don't need to be big and strong to be a manager. I mean, they have certainly brought strength. They are good athletes, they've got pace, some of them have got a good touch on the ball as well. They still need character to make [it]. There are a lot of black players with great abilities who haven't made it in the game – it's strength of character that is important. That is really what you are looking for. I don't believe that you can actually come to this club from non-league football, possibly with a spot of talent and you will be 12 months at this club before you are really any value to us.'

'So,' said Hibbins, 'in effect what you are saying is that you feel that none of the black players who have come through in that first generation have developed, if you like, the strength of character in the analysis of the game that would make them suitable to be managers?'

Noades replied, 'I think certainly they need the strength of character if you are talking about being managers. Very few of them would actually make good players without it, those who have good character I mean. Regis at Coventry is a perfect example really. There are not very many that play on late in their careers and he's one that has. I mean, I've never really met Cyril Regis, although he played for Hayes in non-league and progressed that way so he has come up the hard way. That is another very important [thing]. For a player who is non-league, he is being paid part time, he's working full time, he's up at 7.30 in the morning. It's not until he's done that that some of the black players really appreciate football. When you get them as apprentices and coming through they are generally laid back and lazy. They need to fail, to go out to work as a lot of other lads do as well, to see what it's like working. That is a great motivator to find out what it's like, working in the outside world, to realise just what a chance and what a good career football is for you.'

Again it would be easy to see all this as racist. But that would be quite wrong. At best we can say Noades has a certain way of looking at things, a certain mind-set, but then it could be said that we all have certain mind-sets. I am hardly free of that and programme-makers who go out to make such programmes also have a certain mind-set. The clue to the whole Noades attitude, and Noades is representative of many here, comes when he said in the interview that the whole idea is to make black players English and in the process exploit their extra pace to give an extra dimension, an edge to their teams. As Noades said, 'What we are trying is to cultivate the English attitude, not the black attitude or the white attitude to the game.'

To illustrate this Noades told a story of the Trinidad black who had impressed Palace but could not be accepted because age was against him. 'Now we had an opportunity in Trinidad to take a player there who had the ability but he was 27 years old and we felt it would take a year before we would have him right in the mind with a strength of character to participate and by that time he would have been 28 years old and you have only really got him for two years. So in fact we decided not to go with it.'

If isolated and taken out of context it may sound politically incorrect, even worse, but in the round it is the voice of the English footballing pragmatist, the man keen to get results, well aware of how long footballers can play and what they are worth. Noades represents the new breed of owners, who having grown up at a time when English football was white, had no need to think of colour and whose football memory would be of Dixie Dean being called Dixie because he was felt to have a touch of the tar – an implication that Dean resented. Today Noades happily employs black players and even has the odd non-white on his board.

It is easy to see why Noades would resent being called a racist and he is clearly not a racist in the sense that he hates people who are not of his colour or denies them opportunity. If he perceives blacks in a certain way, then to an extent he stereotypes white men as well, seeing them as hard white men who probably are not as artistic as the blacks. The full Noades interview with Channel Four reminds me of the time I wrote in *Time Out* that Dennis Lillee had rhythm and the sub-editor, a white man, said, 'We whites are not supposed to have rhythm. And you know what? Because of your colour you can say that, but I couldn't.' As he said that he laughed and I joined in.

Also, if there are contradictions in Noades then they are ones he shares with many in the English game. People in the game declare that colour does not matter but then reveal thoughts that suggest that they instinctively think that people of a certain colour can only behave in a certain way. And all this laced with that most deadly of virtues – English pragmatism dressed up as reason.

Westley had revealed this to me when we discussed how Dwight Marshall had been received in his first club, Plymouth. Marshall had been a hero there and Westley said, 'Dwight Marshall told you how well he had done in the first few games. If he had been a white player and he had got to Plymouth and not done very well in the first five games, the crowd would have been on his back. If you go there and do well it does not matter what your colour is, you will be liked. That is the way supporters are. If the black player is the best player he will be idolised.'

The implication was clear. As far as fans are concerned Marshall was no different to anyone else. He may be black, he had a fast twitch muscle which made him an ideal front player, but from Plymouth to Carlisle he would be acclaimed if he scored goals, reviled if he failed, irrespective of colour. But is that how Marshall saw himself — having some characteristic black attributes, but his blackness playing no overall part?

CHAPTER NINE

The Black View

Marshall was unique. He had come to football late – 24 when he got his first professional club – and when I had spoken to Pleat he had told me he would be an interesting study. He had also told me a story about Marshall that seemed to bring out all the contradictions.

Marshall came from London and should have been glad to move to Luton. It meant he could be near his family and since he had told Pleat he planned to marry his girlfriend, who already had two of his children, Pleat thought this would have a good, settling effect. Some time after Marshall had moved to Luton, Pleat asked about his marriage plans. Marshall said he had decided not to marry. 'Why?' asked Pleat, fearful that he may have broken up with his girlfriend. 'She is pregnant again,' replied Marshall. There was no hint of irony in his tone or awareness that as a reason for reversing a decision to marry someone it sounded crazy.

Pleat had shaken his head, just as he had shaken his head when another black player had revealed that he had never heard of Wilf Mannion. 'Not heard of Wilf Mannion,' reflected Pleat, 'I used to go to Notts County as a boy just to smell the liniments. And I can still smell the abattoir. And not know who Mannion was? These players, they go to football grounds, they do not even see where they are going. When we went to Middlesbrough for their last game at Ayresome Park, one of my black players did not even know it was the last game or that the club was moving to a new stadium. He had a ghetto-blaster stuck to his ear and he was in another world.'

Again it would be simple to see it as black versus white. But it was the lament of the educated, cultured voice of football, mourning the passing of the age of reason and knowledge. The civilised Roman railing against the approach of the barbarians, aware they would win and destroy everything he held dear.

Despite all this, I was hoping Marshall would help me explore the contrasts the black player provided in English football. Marshall, born in Jamaica, arriving here at the age of five or six, his early hero being Pele, could be expected to have a very different football apprenticeship to, say, Kerry Dixon, his then strike partner at Luton. Marshall's answer began promisingly: 'Quite a lot different.' But just as I thought he might open up on the racial and social differences I realised he was treating the question in a narrow, very narrow, footballing sense. As far as Marshall was concerned, the difference was that Dixon, although turned down by his home club Luton, had worked his way from youth teams to first-team football via clubs such as Dunstable Town, then Tottenham and Chelsea. Marshall said he was different because he had to wait until he was 24 before a club would even have him.

I had to tease out Marshall's story and only then did it begin to emerge that he had had the sort of background that Noades had felt was required if black players are to build up character, working in the outside world until his early twenties before entering football. 'I had been involved in football in junior school. I had trials when I was at school but I failed to get in anywhere. I did a couple of O-levels. I did a diploma B Tech in Public Administration, North East London College near Tottenham. From 18 onwards I was working nine to five, Monday to Friday. I could only play football midweek evenings and Saturdays.'

School football had, obviously, left no impression. When I asked did he have a sportsmaster like the one in *Kes*, his response was as if I had offered him a strange drug.

'Kes? Kes?' he looked at me blankly.

Then, suddenly, he received a call from Plymouth Argyle, but here again, as Marshall told the story, it was not so much the man of colour going to part of the world where there are few people of colour, more the city boy who had never been to the country and never taken a long train journey.

'When I was on the train I thought, "The train is never going to stop". I had never been to that part of the country before. I thought, "Where the hell are you going?" I thought, "I am never going to get to this place. I am never signing for these people." These were my thoughts: "This is so far away there is no way I am signing for these people." It felt strange because

167

I had never been that far in the country by myself. I had been on school trips, had been to Spain but not that far in England. It was not city. It was country.' As he said this he laughed loudly. 'I was there for three seasons. I was made to feel welcome. To be fair to Plymouth, it is a cosmopolitan place, people come and go, it is quite a friendly place.'

At 24 he knew Plymouth was his last chance to make the grade and, as luck would have it, his feet did the talking, broke whatever barriers there might have been. 'Luckily for me I went down there and in the pre-season I scored in every game and the crowd was behind me from then. A week before we signed there was a testimonial and Aston Villa came down. We lost 2–1 but I scored again. And the season started well for me. I scored quite a lot early on, you see, and the fans were all behind me. I had my best season there, best I have ever had. Fans will always remember me for that season.'

Noades said the task is to produce players who are English and Marshall certainly sounds like that. Less than four years into the game and he knows the patter. His reaction to the Cantona incident could have been scripted by the PFA. 'I can understand what he did but at all times we have got to be professional.' I asked, 'Does it bother you that there are no black faces in the crowd?' He replied, 'It does not bother me. I don't go out there thinking we should be getting a few more black faces into the stands. There are not enough black faces, get some more. My job is to play football, that is what I want to do. Play football, not worry about which particular faces are in the crowd. It does not really come into my mind.'

It was not far removed from what Colwyn Rowe had said: 'I have never been to a football match and thought that the black players make up 20 per cent of the teams and the crowd is white. Now that you are telling me, I am beginning to think about it.'

When it came to any racist abuse he might have suffered, Marshall could barely recall an incident. 'I have been a professional for four years now and I only actually heard very few taunts.'

'What is the worst you have ever heard?'

'They said the normal things really.'

'Like?'

'What? Just coon and nigger. Just coon and nigger. But that, as I said, very rarely happened to me. Once you get on the pitch your whole concentration is on the game. Although you can hear the crowd in the background it is very hard to hear anything specific. Unless you go right to the touchline and somebody directly abuses you. You very rarely hear anything specific.' After all this it was no surprise to hear Marshall deny that black players have brought different skills or greater power to the game. 'It is hard to say. We are all individuals really.'

By now, with Marshall sounding just the sort of black player of whom Terry Westley or Colwyn Rowe would approve, I expected him to echo that, yes, it is a twitch muscle in his thigh that explained his pace, his position as a forward. But when I asked him why blacks play mainly in the front his reason was the more prosaic: the absence of role models. Why are there not too many black players at the back, few black goalkeepers and not too many in midfield? 'Maybe one of the reasons why we like playing in the glory positions, up front, is we seek glory. You don't get much of that if you are being a 'keeper. That is one of the reasons why you don't get too many black 'keepers. There are no black 'keepers, no role models for young black kids to become 'keeper. You would want to be Wright. Shilton is not a choice black kids have.'

And while Pleat had said the problem with Marshall was that, unlike a Wright, he did not throw his shoulders out as he walked on the field, like a strutting cock, Marshall did not quite fit the sporting stereotype. True, he loved films like *Pulp Fiction, Aliens, Terminator*, Eddie Murphy and action movies, but he shunned the traditional sportsman's pursuits of golf. Instead his game was chess. 'It is a very good tactical game. It is not boring. Football and chess are two different things. Chess is a very time-consuming game. I could fit in a couple of football games in the time it takes me to play one game of chess.'

Some of Marshall's thoughts were to be echoed by Luther Blissett, who shares a birthplace with Marshall, Jamaica, and came here at about the same age. However, he could not have had a more different initiation into football. If Marshall had almost despaired of playing league football at 24, Blissett was by then a hero at Watford and beyond: 'I just liked playing football. Never saw it as a problem. Went to Willesden High, which has produced black sportsmen like Chris Lewis, De Freitas, not far away was John Kelly, where Mike Gatting, Ricky Hill and Brian Stein came from. As black players are athletic – we are a lot quicker – lots of the black players are forwards, get down the wings and cross, or get behind them. It is the pace which makes us different. When I started there was Clyde Best, Ade Coke, Brendan Batson, Laurie Cunningham. I was one of the forerunners. I did hear comments like black players are fine when the sun is out, not when it gets cold or, if you kick them you won't see them. I got abuse from the crowd. They would call me black bastard, coon, nigger. Certain people would call me names. But it never worried me.'

It helped that from the beginning with Blissett that he was different –

he was part of a group. 'In Willesden High I played in an all-black team bar one white player, John West, who was our skipper. He played in midfield but he had to earn our respect. When we played other schools there would be a hostile atmosphere. We would go to some schools and there were no black players and they would be shouting coons, black bastards, niggers, the lot. But when you are in a group together you can take it. It is you, your group, against them. You go out and you want to show them. You think, I will stick the ball in the net, that will show them. When you are in a group you are there to do a job and if you have done that you feel you have answered the people who are abusing you.'

This was the advice Graham Taylor, his manager at Watford, later gave him. 'Concentrate on your game, play your game and stick the ball into the net.' The team that Taylor brought up to the first division for the first time gave Blissett his footballing profile. In its first season in the top division it came second to Liverpool and a couple of years later got to a Cup final.

Blissett played for England 14 times and feels hard done by, but his anguish is no different to any player of whatever colour who feels he should have had more chances. 'In the England set-up unless you play in the centre of the park you don't make an impact, not wide on the wings.' And for all the success Watford gave him, including a spell in Italy, Blissett is convinced that Taylor's long-ball game alienated neutrals and made Watford and its players unpopular. As we spoke of the problems Barnes suffered at international level, Blissett said, 'Had Barnes started at Tottenham instead of Watford he wouldn't get a rough ride. A lot of people resented Watford.'

These are reflections any footballer, whatever their racial origin, might make. Blissett's tone changed only when he talked of the night at Peterborough long before he became famous, a night he would rather not remember and one that I had to draw out of him. Blissett, making his way at Watford, is playing in a reserve game. It is the 1976–77 season, an evening game. 'I was the only black player in the Watford team, the only one in the park, probably the only one in the entire stadium. There were about 1,000 people. The Peterborough players were calling me names. But name-calling had never bothered me. I was not perturbed by the atmosphere. In those days I was very single-minded. There were shouts of coon and everything else. Anyway, I was used to abuse. But it was the crowd – it was just horrendous. They were shouting everywhere, in the stands, on the terraces everywhere. But the abuse and the shouting was horrible. Monkey noises – uggh-uggh-uggh-uggh-uggh every time I got the ball – shouts of coon and everything else. They didn't throw things, it was not fashionable to throw things. Even the Peterborough players were calling me names. One of our players said take no notice. They said the best way to shut these people up is stick the ball in the net.'

Blissett did not score that night and horrendous is the adjective that always prefaces his description of the match. That game made Blissett determined to succeed. He also evolved a code: 'If people spat at me, I ignored it. Players did spit on me, in isolated instances in the league, or supporters when I was going for a corner. As long as it was not against me in the face. But if anybody spat at me and it hit me in the face I would have turned on them. Then the gloves came off.'

It took Italy, where Blissett went in the late '80s, for him to realise that the game can generate passionate support but avoid the hate so endemic in English sport. 'Italy was fanatical support. I was very well treated. In Italy it is a national pastime. Everybody will have an opinion but there is no name-calling, no spitting. In Italy fanaticism is about football, it is not about hating the other team or their supporters. I think there is hate in English football, a lot of hate. I don't know the real reason for it. But something has changed. It has become far more organised.'

So would it not help if there were black supporters in the crowd? It is a question that means nothing to Blissett. He has hardly noticed that a half-black team often plays in front of all-white crowds. 'It is only since it was made an issue that I have thought about it. I didn't find it odd that there were no black people in the crowd. Sometimes I felt a little bit uncomfortable, there should be more black people. But the number of people who are black in a crowd don't mean anything. What matters is people wearing your colours. I have never thought of being black when going into a football match. I don't think of myself as being black.'

Blissett's sentiments could be echoed by Ron Noades or Terry Westley or Marshall. To look for a different tune, listen to Brian Stein. Pleat had suggested that if I wanted to speak to an articulate black player, one aware of the political undertones, I should speak to Stein. He had been part of Pleat's Luton team of the Eighties and had been as much a hero of Kenilworth Road as Blissett had been at the same time at Vicarage Road. Both had also played for England about the same time. But although they share the same skin colour, Stein had come to this country from South Africa and the difference in outlook is immense.

'I was seven years old when I came here from South Africa. My father was politically active in South Africa – he suffered 24 hours house arrest. He was always at home, couldn't read political material. We lived in Athlone, a coloured township, and the colour bar was a bit like a caste system. By the time I left South Africa I was aware. Edwin, my brother, was very aware. In England, when I met Ricky Hill and Paul Elliott, I realised they were aware. I had played football in Cape Town and I always wanted to be a footballer. My heroes were Pele, George Best. In England we lived in Willesden and the first thing that struck me was that there were no black players. When I started playing I heard this myth about black players not having stamina. They couldn't run for 90 minutes. Even Pleat said this to me. Players lack stamina, when it is snowing they can't get it going. This was in 1977. I was only 19 then. Pleat told me the myth is: when it is snowing they are no good. Stamina-wise. They lacked stamina.'

Stein went to school in Hampstead, predominantly white but a mixed school. 'We knew the difference between black and white but as kids you can adapt to anything. Kids live from day to day. Terry Dyson, the Tottenham double hero, was the sports teacher. He didn't particularly encourage me. My brother Edwin, former assistant manager at Birmingham, pushed me more. He got me motivated more than my schoolteachers. Edwin urged me to start playing. I went to college, got my A-levels, but my parents weren't wealthy – we had eight kids – and I stopped playing football after 15. Then Sudbury Colts came in and paid me £5, Edwin having persuaded them. At Sudbury I played under Des Taylor for six or seven teams. Smith was the manager of the first team and there were no problems of colour. I played for Sudbury for half a season. A chap came from Edgware, said if you go to Edgware you can earn more money and me and Edwin went. After a month and a half we had a lot of scouts watching. One Wednesday the chairman of Edgware said Luton were interested and they signed me. Pleaty was the reserve team manager.'

Pleat took over as first team manager in 1979 and soon realised that Stein was different. The driver of the Luton coach could not be more right wing. His support for apartheid was vigorous and he often voiced his dismay over the ban imposed on white sporting South Africa. Pleat, aware Stein might get into a row with him, said, 'Whatever you do, do not argue with the coach driver. It is a waste of time.' Stein avoided any major rows but there was always the crowd: 'You would get mostly supporters shouting uggh-uggh-uggh-uggh-uggh, monkey noises whenever you had the ball, or throwing bananas. Cup game against a team from the third division. Wigan or Hartlepool. Got a lot of stick. We played a game in the '80s. Cup match. One of the players called me black something. I did not let that go. I gave him a bit of stick. In the early '80s Chelsea crowds gave a lot of stick to Paul Cannonville, terrible abuse, much more than either Ricky Hill or I received. They destroyed him.

Millwall was particularly nasty – Phil Walker and Lee had a terrible time.'

But there are two abiding, horrific memories for Stein, both from the supposedly friendly, warm north – Blackburn and Burnley. 'Early in my career, north was much worse. Past Birmingham the black explosion of players did not develop. Blackburn was one of the worst. Burnley, they spat at me. At Blackburn I was a sub and I was walking through the tunnel. It was just before the match and the crowd was throwing things. Coins, bananas. By the tunnel at Blackburn the crowd were close. I was spat at. I was very upset, like. I nearly spat back. I felt like Cantona did when he was abused but I did not react like him, although then and later I had lot more abuse.'

Then there was the night before a game at Burnley when Ricky Hill and he decided to go for a walk round the town. 'It was a Friday night. This was about six in the evening. Not very dark. Just went for a walk to stretch our legs before dinner. Ricky and I, we were sharing a room as well. As we walked we became aware of a couple of kids with their parents. The kids pointed at us and said, "Look, there is a darkie," and they were laughing as if they had never seen people like us. It was like the Dark Ages.'

Stein felt his South African experiences had equipped him to handle things. 'I could handle it better because of this awareness. I had seen a lot of it in South Africa. But there it was defined. It is not defined here, it is much worse, there is no set thing. Here you can do everything but you don't know where they will stop you.'

This heightened awareness may explain why, unlike Marshall and Blissett, Stein was intensely aware that he played in a Luton team with brilliant black players watched by all-white crowds. 'At most we would have 50 black supporters, mostly friends of players. A lot of my friends used to come to watch. A lot of my friends would end up in fights. The circumstances made even more aware. Everybody is unconsciously a racist. Some of them pretend. We had a new coach one year. We had a little chat, Ricky, myself and maybe three or four black players. He had been at Derby. He said, "Brian, nice working with you. I am not a racist." For me that remark told me everything. I just couldn't get on with the man.'

By this time Stein had learned that, 'Most footballers are not aware. Footballers are not particularly bright. Most of them felt I was from some part of the West Indies. Later on in the '80s a lot of the sports stars became more aware of the racial problem. When a rebel tour to South Africa was organised by Jimmy Hill I was approached. Pleaty asked me one year to go and coach black kids in South Africa. I did not, could not.'

In 1988 Stein, like Blissett, left England to play football on the

In 1988 Stein, like Blissett, left England to play football on the continent, his destination being Caen in France, for whom he played for three years from 1988 to 1991. 'The crowds watching us were predominantly white, but it was different. To be honest, more African players were involved. Different sort of atmosphere. I was more easily accepted. Uggh-uggh-uggh-uggh-uggh monkey chants? None of that in France. True, France being a big country, you do not get a lot of away support but whatever opposition supporters were there they did not get at me. The teams had a lot of black players and a lot of them were French black players. The French crowds did not exhibit the racism English crowds can.'

Stein had said footballers were not very aware but that charge could hardly be made against Garth Crooks, perhaps the most articulate footballer of his generation, regardless of colour, and one who turns all the stereotypes, both about footballers in general and black footballers in particular, on their heads. Here was a working-class boy for whom football had provided a way to fame but who disdained the gold bracelets and the fancy trappings thought mandatory. More, here was one able to assess himself and his contemporaries with a steely but sympathetic eye.

Crooks had always been a favourite of mine. I had admired his play at Tottenham and always held him in special regard for that moment at Anfield on 16 March 1985 when, after a Micky Hazard shot had been saved by Grobbelaar, he had put in the rebound to provide Tottenham with their first victory at Liverpool since the sinking of the *Titanic*. And we had barely settled in the café opposite BBC London radio, where Crooks presents his weekly programme, when he began to speak with the sort of disarming frankness rare amongst professional sportsmen: 'Professional sport has given me access to an entire new world. But I am very ordinary working class. My father came from Jamaica in 1956, mother from rural Jamaica in 1957, and I was born in Stoke-on-Trent in 1958. Father was a manual labourer who worked in a tyre factory for 25 years. He returned to Jamaica three years ago, mother still lives in London. I went to comprehensive schools, in reality secondary modern, and the only thing different was that teachers made me interested in English and said if I applied myself I could do very well. I graduated in political science but I knew from early on that sport was to be taken seriously.'

So, was his success in football, his position as a forward player, due to a fast twitch muscle? Crooks reacted much as Marshall had when I had asked him about *Kes* – with a blank uncomprehending stare. But there was no doubting his awareness of his colour and what it meant. 'I always felt that

I had to be 15 per cent better than the white person to get the same chance.' And he is quick to pick up anyone who seeks to categorise him. 'Whenever I go to one of the footballs do's, I gravitate towards black players. Once Ray Wilkins said, "What is it with you guys, always with the brothers?" I said, "Ray, when you come you always congregate with Bryan Robson, should I read anything into that?" Ray went quiet after that.'

While Marshall and Blissett had to be reluctantly drawn on their problems with white crowds it required little for Crooks to relive that terrible day when he made his debut for Stoke at St James Park. It was a November night in 1978. 'I was the only black player on the park. Terry Hibbitt, Jimmy Greenhoff, Alan Hudson, Peter Shilton, Denis Smith, John Mahoney, Terry Conroy were playing. I was 18 years old, and I was the butt of the most cruel racism – jokes, chanting, the whole Gallow Gate Kop in unison singing racist songs and shouts. Every time I touched the ball there would be deafening monkey noises – uggh-uggh-uggh-uggh-uggh-uggh – and just abuse. I have never felt so alone, so vulnerable, so stripped of my being. Denis Smith, John Mahoney and Terry Conroy wanted to protect me. They tried to protect me. They couldn't, the whole crowd was on me all the time. At half-time Tony Waddington, the Stoke manager, took me off. I did not want to come off. Never mind, you are coming off, he said. My purpose was to perform to the best of my ability, to show them on my debut. I couldn't. I was in tears as he took me off.'

His move to Spurs, which made his career, brought another dimension. Here was a fashionable, rich North London club whose predominant support was Jewish but whose boardroom at that time had no Jews. 'In racial terms my presence was very important. Chris Hughton was already there, very quiet, very unassuming. At Spurs I had to put up with the images of the stereotype black. I perceived certain people at Tottenham saw me as a bit of a rogue, not really capable of mixing with the middle classes very well, unable to conduct myself very well.'

In many ways some of his best duels were with his own defenders, Graham Roberts and Paul Miller, in particular Miller. 'Miller was a deep thinker. Typical Essex man. Wanted to be socially mobile. Very ambitious, always keen to maximise his attributes. He had married the daughter of Maurice Kestrel [a legendary Spurs supporter]. Paul could sound very bigoted but very funny. Some of the things he said were outrageous but they made me laugh and I could not take offence. I remember sneezing and covering my face with my hands as I did so [as he tells the story he repeats the action, cupping his hands over his nose and mouth]. Miller said, "What is it with you people? Do you only come out with a handkerchief a rough diamond.'

This baiting between team-mates is one thing but there can be an uglier side, like the one that led to Paul Davis breaking Glen Cockerill's jaw. The incident, missed by the referee, was caught by the cameras and Davis was banned, a ban that so affected his career that from being on the fringe of the England side he struggled to be on the fringe of the Arsenal side. But there is a suggestion that the elbowing had been preceded by exchanges between Davis and Cockerill in a previous Arsenal-Southampton match. 'Yes,' says Crooks, 'Paul had been provoked but the ban devastated him, his action was a reaction to what had gone before but he never talks about it.'

What Davis did was not only untypical for him but other black players might have reacted differently. I asked about Ian Wright. Would it have been different had he been involved? 'Yes,' muses Crooks, 'Ian Wright is different to Davis. He is very South London, streetwise, part of that South London black sub-culture. He is into the boogie, he is very West Indian in that sense.'

Crooks is aware that he carries a double burden, that of the articulate footballer in a game where a meaningful sentence is like a novel, and that of an articulate black footballer, but pays generous tribute to others: 'Many black players have played their part. Laurie Cunningham was a gem. He had a shyness which was mistaken for aloofness.' He reserved judgement on only one black player. Dropping his voice he said, 'Viv Anderson is the most successful black player. He has done very little to promote the cause of the black sportsman.' It is the only time in our conversation he had a bad word to say about anyone black or white. For a man who enjoyed his football and finds it 'difficult to become angry' that was very eloquent.

So far the black footballers I had spoken to all fitted the stereotype: players of pace, playing up front, dazzling with goals. But there was another player who demonstrated that you could make it to the top even if you had no pace. In fact, the position he played in was the only one where pace played no part. So I was keen to talk to Alex Williams, the former Manchester City goalkeeper.

Williams fascinated me. I had a memory of a Friday live television match on the BBC – in the days when BBC and ITV shared league soccer – and of Williams keeping goal for City against Chelsea. The memory is of the dazzle of lights and of Williams, probably the only black man on the field, being cruelly baited by Chelsea fans. The noise of uggh-uggh-uggh-uggh ever time he touched the ball reverberated in my ears.

My first sight of Williams increased my fascination. Just as at that night at Chelsea he was the lone black sentinel, so he was on the afternoon I first saw him in person. However, this was not amidst baying white hordes but an audience that presented the face of English decency, good humour, kindness and generosity that I had long ago accepted as the essence of this country. A warm, caring but robust image of English football and a million miles removed from the one shown on television during the Dublin riots. This face of soccer was displayed at the Littlewoods presentation ceremony at the Institute of Engineers in Birdcage Walk where Williams had come to accept an award on behalf of Manchester City.

Williams is tall, over six feet four inches, and he would stand out anywhere, but in that English crowd – particularly at the buffet of delicious savouries on bread and stick washed down by wine – he stood out as the only shiny black face in a sea of pale pink. A couple of weeks later I was sitting in the Manchester City reception and Williams was telling me his story. 'I was born in Mosside, born and bred there. My family are from Mosside and I've always worked in that area. I started off at a local school, Wilburn High School which is in Chorton, just around the corner. It was a school where quite a lot of black players went to. It was a good sporting school. I was attracted to football rather than any other game because it was the national sport and all the youngsters at the time used to play. I used to like Manchester City and I would come and watch them play.

'I used to be quite small and so when they used to pick the team, they would put me in goal as being the last player to be picked. It started from there really. The Platt Lane complex [City's training ground] wasn't really in operation then [the complex didn't start until the mid-'80s]. I got into the school team. Then City asked me to come down for a trial and every Tuesday and Thursday night I came to the School of Excellence. When I was 16 they decided to take me on a YTS scheme. I made my first-team debut in 1981 against West Brom, aged 19. Nineteen was quite young really, especially for a goalkeeper, and obviously it was quite unique to see a black goalkeeper. But I never, ever thought of myself as being a black goalkeeper. I just thought of myself as a goalkeeper.

'I didn't really have any problems being a black goalkeeper. When I played as a youngster it wasn't looked upon as a big thing to be a black goalkeeper. I would play schoolboy football which at the time wasn't really that serious. Obviously, when I actually joined Manchester City and I was playing in the second and third teams, then it started to become more apparent to me that it was quite a unique thing. In general, because of the reception I got at most away grounds. It wasn't particularly a race thing at all, it was really, "Oh, there's a black goalkeeper."

'I never experienced anything serious playing youth and reserve

'I never experienced anything serious playing youth and reserve football. The only time I really had a bad experience was when we played down in the Youth Cup final at Millwall in about 1979. It was actually the final and so it was played over two legs. We played the first leg here (at Maine Road) and we drew the game nil-nil. They brought quite a few supporters down here and it was actually quite bad here. The shouting consisted of black this and black that, the usual sort of things. It was bad enough here but certainly when I played down there it was much worse. I can't remember anything in particular but there were plenty of the usual monkey jibes, uggh-uggh-uggh-uggh-uggh, things like that.

'I didn't particularly feel a pioneer but certainly, if you like, I was a pioneer for goalkeepers. I think at the time I was playing a lot of black players had started to come through but the problem I had was being the only black goalkeeper. Goalkeepers have a lot of time to themselves, I think. It's the nature of the game and because you are near the supporters you can actually hear a lot as well. I tended to find when I used to play, I played reasonably well and this would win a lot of the supporters over. At the start of the game they would be barracking you in one way or another, but by the end of the game they'd come to recognise the fact you were a good goalkeeper and they could clap you off. Some grounds you are nearer to the supporters. Leeds wasn't as bad as people made out. One of the worst experiences was West Ham. I remember I played there once in particular and we actually got beaten 5–0. At the start of the game I was getting all sorts of race criticism but I actually played a brilliant game and at the end they did actually clap me off the pitch – or perhaps it was because I let five in!

'Chelsea again wasn't too bad because I think there's a large running area around the pitch. So even though the abuse you got was quite bad, the fact that they were quite some way away actually did help. I remember I always played quite well at Chelsea. I do remember one incident though where we were actually in the hotel before one of the Chelsea games, and somebody sent a parcel. When I opened it up, it turned out to be a razor blade or something inside.

'There wasn't really a "worst moment". There were isolated incidents. You always hear the odd jibe if somebody says something. I remember playing at Everton one year. I was running up to the Everton end and somebody had screwed up a programme and burnt it, reminiscent of the Ku Klux Klan thing. I found at Liverpool that the racism there was a comical racism. There are two kinds, the comical mickey-taking kind, and then there's the genuine race hate of West Ham and Millwall. Liverpool was always a mickey-taking place. They would start and everybody would start laughing and it's not meant with intent, it's more of a joke. That particular instance with the programme was more mickey-taking than race hatred. Millwall and West Ham are quite bad but you've got to expect that from the dock areas of London.

'My colleagues' reaction was pretty mixed really. Sometimes they would just say, "Oh, just get on with things", but more often than not they didn't really comment as such. On the playing side they never really commented as such about the stick I was getting.

'When I was playing they were bad places to go to but I think that now most clubs have cleaned up their act. They've got a lot better now, so I certainly wouldn't like it to be taken in the wrong context. Most places are now quite accustomed to black faces. This particular area has quite a high ethnic population so most of the players will have seen or come into contact with black people. But now with so many black players in the Premier League it has changed. Black players are more common, more accepted.'

Williams left City in 1985 with a back injury and went to Port Vale, hoping he could get fully fit and return to the glory days. 'But it never happened. I had about 18 glorious months at Port Vale but they never really saw me at my best.' He cannot shake off the feeling that he did not quite achieve what he could have. 'I made the England youth squad and I was in the Under-21 squad on numerous occasions but didn't actually play. I managed to obtain a European Youth Championship medal and an England Under-21 championship medal, and my aim was to go on to the full squad and do the same again, but it wasn't to be. I have always had a sense of not fulfilling my potential. I've played at the top and I've enjoyed it and I thoroughly enjoy the job I do now.'

The job that Williams is doing is with City's community scheme, which aims to get young people involved first and foremost with the football club, play together and play football. It is centred around the Platt Lane complex, the rebuilt City training ground and one of the few in the country which can be seen from the main stadium. It is almost like a better version of Luton. Stein had found it odd that 'in this country not more has been done to attract black supporters to the game. I have no doubt that if Luton could get Asians to come they will get a lot of feedback. The club has to go to the community and make it part of the club.'

Manchester City, like Luton, surrounded by ethnics, seem to be making an effort. Williams was well aware of the problems. 'It is a deprived area. The Mosside community is 200,000 people. The majority, 60 per cent, are ethnic-orientated: Asian, black, Caribbean, Chinese. We get a lot of children coming here to use the complex. As far as unemployment is concerned, the club actually have a policy where they will only employ people from the local area. So you walk into the main office and the receptionist went to school here, she lives down the road, and all the people on match days are actually people from the local area.'

Like the area around Kenilworth Road there are a lot of ethnics about in Mosside. 'In fact, in some of the schools, 95 per cent of the kids are ethnic-orientated. We had a school recently, Royce Primary School, and I think every child bar one was Asian.' And just as Luton parents do not flock to Kenilworth Road, so Mosside ethnic parents do not come to Maine Road – but their kids do come to Platt Lane complex.

Williams was aware of the importance of young ethnics seeing blacks not merely as users but providers of service. 'I think that is important because if a lot of inner-city kids see black culture working here they are more inclined to come along, which they are doing. We certainly get ethnic, Muslim and Asian kids on our soccer schools.'

As Williams drove me back to the ground we saw an Asian couple walking past the front entrance . The man was in salwar khameez, like the one sported by Imran Khan at his wedding, the woman covered from head to foot in a long salwar and along with them was a little child. They walked on the forecourt of Manchester City, passed the crowd that had gathered in front of the ticket office queuing for their season tickets. They were not only completely oblivious of the crowd but even of the club. They did not even look at the crowd, let alone share their knowledge or enthusiasm for City.

'You will have to attract them, won't you?' I asked Williams.

Williams looked at the couple and said, 'Yes. The younger generation will come. But it will take time.'

The optimism was genuine and touching. But within a few weeks came the reaction to Imran Khan's marriage and I wondered: will they come if they find that their current heroes are always treated as aliens?

CHAPTER TEN

Guess Who Imran is Bringing to Dinner?

On the afternoon the world celebrated VE-Day with parades and a holiday to mark 50 years since victory over Germany, ITV reran *Guess Who's Coming to Dinner?*, starring Spencer Tracy, Katharine Hepburn and Sidney Poitier. The film has a certain poignant cinematic niche: 17 days after it was completed Spencer Tracy died and Hepburn, his real life lover – they could not marry because Tracy, a devout Catholic, would not leave his wife – has never been able to watch the film despite winning an Oscar for her role.

Made in the late '60s, it can be seen as the concluding chapter of the civil rights agitation that swept across America during that decade, finally providing blacks with some of the equal rights the constitution had supposedly conferred on them almost 200 years before. The film's theme, inter-racial sex, was Hollywood's attempt to confront the hidden fears of many whites. Or to put it in the language favoured by the then English Conservative MP, Sir Gerald Nabarro, 'How would you like your blue-eyed English rose to marry a big buck nigger and produce six coffee-coloured grandchildren?'

Except that since this film was set in America Katharine Houghton, a niece of Hepburn, was very much an American rose, although no less delicious, and the nigger in question was not quite the sort Nabarro had in mind. As played by Sidney Poitier he was just the kind to take home to Mum and Dad, if only his black skin could be replaced by a pinky white one. The film was all the more interesting because it posed the problem of a black man marrying a white woman who hailed not from some red-neck family but from the most liberal and modern of Californian homes. Hepburn and Tracy played a couple that had always fought for racial justice and freedom from prejudice. Now, suddenly, they had to confront the idea of integration they had so often preached reaching their own daughter's bedroom, a bit too uncomfortable a translation of their long-held liberal beliefs.

By the time ITV screened the film on VE-Day afternoon, the issues that the film sought to highlight seemed even more dated than the ones that led to the Second World War. However, even as the holiday audience was being diverted, news was leaking which by the end of the week would make *Guess Who's Coming to Dinner?* very relevant. On Friday, when the news broke that 42-year-old Imran Khan was going to wed Jemima Goldsmith, the 21-year-old daughter of the rich financier Sir James Goldsmith, it seemed as if ITV in showing the film had been preparing us for this most extraordinary of events. The media coverage of Imran's marriage was like being instantly transported back in a time machine to that period. Even the personal details provided an uncanny match.

Jemima presented the radiance and good looks portrayed in the film by Katharine Houghton and, while Imran is several shades lighter than Poitier and of a different race, brown Asian rather than black American, he, like the character portrayed by Poitier, towered over his bride in both achievement and recognition. Just as in the film Katharine Houghton is often shown looking admiringly at the doctor character played by Poitier, more than ten years older and clearly more qualified, so there were soon innumerable photographs showing Jemima in a star-struck pose, gazing with rapt admiration at the great Khan. If in the film Poitier played a black doctor who appeared to be on the verge of winning the Nobel Prize, then Imran can claim to have won all the equivalent cricket prizes and, unlike Spencer Tracy, Poitier's screen father-in-law, Sir Jimmy Goldsmith would not have had to check out Imran's cricketing credentials.

Perhaps the most uncanny resemblance between the '60s film and real life was that just like the black and white screen parents, both Imran and Jemima's families conveyed similar feelings of bewilderment and shock that their children were planning to defy convention. Part of the reason for their confused reaction may have been the curious way the news broke. It first surfaced in a Bombay newspaper, where the city's busy gossip mills had picked up the story from comments made by Jemima's sister during her visit there. The paper, probably deliberately, heightened the mystery by attributing the story to sources from Dubai and this sense of Arabian wonder clung to the news for days afterwards, with both Imran's family and the Goldsmiths offering either contradictory stories or mystifying silence. Sir James Goldsmith did wrest some control with his PR company, Taskforce Communications eventually issuing the formal announcement that Jemima and Imran were going to get married. But even after this press statement had been carried on BBC television's *Nine O'clock News* that Friday evening, nothing seemed certain.

There were reports that Imran had already got married. Imran's father initially said that his son had got married in secret two months previously, then changed his story and it only died when Imran, on arriving in London from Pakistan, denied that he had married Jemima at Regents Park mosque two months previously. Jemima was even more angry and denied that she was pregnant. However, the events that followed these denials suggested that the couple had the script of *Guess Who's Coming to Dinner?* by their bedside and were determined to make their real-life drama match the fictional twists and turns of the Hollywood film.

In the film the character played by Katharine Houghton suddenly decides to accompany Poitier to Europe and get married there, throwing her entire family into confusion. Four days after the announcement on 12 May by Sir James's PR company that 'the marriage will take place in June', Imran and Jemima fled to Paris. It was meant to be a secret journey but was soon revealed in the press and the world watched with some amazement as a curious low-key wedding ceremony took place in a Paris mosque – made all the more curious by the actions of Sir Jimmy Goldsmith who was said to have been not overjoyed on hearing of his daughter's plan to marry a man twice her age and of a different religion. Sir James flew to Paris with his wife Annabel half an hour before the ceremony started, went back to London the same evening, did not attend the marriage dinner and left poor Imran and Jemima to drive away from the ceremony in nothing more than a taxi. Sir James seemed to be reacting even more strongly than Spencer Tracy when he first realised that Sidney Poitier was going to be his son-in-law.

It has since been explained that far from disapproval this was part of Sir James's no-nonsense approach, use of taxis being part of his cost-cutting style. Perhaps so. But Imran himself was so clearly rattled that immediately after the Paris wedding he could barely read out its announcement. The London-based journalist Shahed Sadullah, to whom Imran was dictating the announcement over the telephone line from Paris, quickly realised in the halting way he was reading that the great Khan was having difficulty with the handwritten statement. In the background, Sadullah could hear

Jemima giggling as she prompted her newly wed husband.

London and the media offered more than giggles in the month that followed this curious Paris wedding. During this period as Imran, Jemima and their families prepared for the registry wedding in London in mid-June, followed by a reception in Sir James Goldsmith's Richmond home, the media interest in the couple rose to a crescendo. Some of it was of the type celebrities the world over have to cope with – paparazzi trying to photograph Imran and Jemima's lovemaking through long-distance lenses – but more interesting was the outpouring of words trying to analyse and comment on what was widely seen as the society event of the year.

Its social status was emphasised when *The Daily Mail* devoted the whole of its page three to a list of the guests, divided between those who were Sir James's and Lady Annabel's, those who were Jemima's, and those who merely merited to be Jemima's after-dinner guests. At any time the wedding of Goldsmith's daughter would have been a major London event. What made the mixture explosive was the additional complication of Imran's religion which married the older and more historical tussle between the west and Islam to the more modern and well-established concerns about race and cultural differences.

Half a century ago, when Aly Khan married Rita Hayworth, the prospect of a man of colour – albeit Aly was half Italian through his mother – marrying the great symbol of Hollywood-defined white western womanhood aroused the atavistic racial and sexual concerns of many whites. Now, in our supposedly more liberated times, this sexual side of the alliance was alluded to rather than highlighted, and even then in a somewhat curious form. The only direct reference came when *Tatler* devoted its cover to a profile of Jemima headlined 'Heat and Lust'. The cover lines read: 'Just what does she see in him? (and no, it's not only sex)', although the article inside was quite complimentary and did not discuss sex at all.

More interesting for English papers was Imran's religion which came almost as a gift to the more imaginative tabloid headline writers with, as one would expect, *The Sun* revelling in it. Reporting the Paris wedding, it led its front page with the headline, 'Don't they Mecca a lovely couple?'. The next day, an article seeking to warn Jemima of the horrors of living in Lahore – the modest house next to a makeshift camp, the nearest store, where nobody spoke English, selling no more than cold drinks and cigarettes – was headlined, 'How Khan Jemima cope with Allah this?'.

The day after the couple had their registry wedding in London *The Sun* poked fun at the fact that Jemima's £5,000 full-length skirt was longer than the Punjabi shirt and loose trousers, almost a national dress in Pakistan, which Imran wore and which the paper felt was a 'skirt'. And having defined it as a skirt it naturally made for the headline, 'Imran gets wed in a skirt shorter than Jemima's'.

But perhaps the article that most eloquently illustrated certain media attitudes was the one in *The Daily Mail*, two weeks before the London reception. On its front page it carried a picture showing Imran and Jemima returning to their Chelsea home from late-night shopping. They were walking side by side, Jemima giggling, as she let Imran carry the shopping bags. Had any other couple been involved it would have been a normal everyday picture hardly worth commenting on, let alone worthy of display on the front page. But the *Mail* saw it as an ideal opportunity for preaching about the great divide between east and west. Under the headline 'Start as you mean to go on, Jemima', the caption read: 'When Jemima Goldsmith moves to Pakistan with new husband Imran Khan, there could be a culture shock in store for her. But while in Britain, the couple are still very much embracing western ways. After a shopping trip to their local late store, early yesterday, there was no question of her walking several paces behind him. Perish the thought. And who carried the bags? Why, Imran did.'

All of this might have sounded quite witty to the paper's readers except that the *Mail*'s caption writers had only revealed their own ignorance of how society on the sub-continent worked, or at least that part of society to which Imran belonged. The idea that in Lahore somebody entitled to Jemima's privileges would have to carry her own shopping bags, or even walk through the streets with her shopping, was absurd. Like most people of means in the Indian sub-continent, the likes of Jemima are driven to the shops in a car, sitting in air-conditioned comfort in the back seat, with the front seats occupied by servants who leap out and open the car doors. They are the ones who trail behind the mem-sahib, as Jemima would be called, carrying her shopping bags. The idea of a husband going on a shopping expedition with the wife is extremely rare and certainly not to a grocery store to buy food. Even well-off wives do not go to grocery stores, food shopping is more often than not done by servants. *The Mail* had followed the classic route: taken a western concept, imposed on the east, then added the myth about eastern women always being subservient to their men, seeking to make a witty point about cultural divides.

Now, of course, such cultural solecisms are to be accepted from the tabloid papers. However, it was quite different when even the serious papers ran articles which suggested that in marrying Imran, Jemima had chosen a fate worse than death. Such warnings came from a remarkably assorted cast of characters ranging from Annabel Heseltine, who at one stage was supposedly part of a girlie group that quite admired Imran, to Andrew Neil, who for good measure branded Imran a bore. But Imran might have considered this something of a compliment given the even unkinder things some of the other papers were saying about him.

So keen were some of the serious papers to question the alliance that there were quite comical howlers, like *The Sunday Times* talking about Wohraman as a Muslim religious festival when it clearly meant Mohurram, while *The Guardian* tried to convince its readers that the way a Western woman would impress Imran of her love for Islam was by changing her name to that of a Hindu goddess. This was perhaps the most comically revealing insight into how even the most heavyweight papers portrayed the marriage and is worth dwelling on.

It came in *The Guardian's* 'Pass Notes', the paper's attempt to impart information about people in the news through witty questions and answers. In this case *The Guardian* chose the case of Sita White, with whom Imran had been involved and whose child, Tirian Jade White Kalen, he was said to have fathered.

Sita, daughter of the late Lord White of Hanson industries, had been christened Ana-Luisa White. She had met Imran on the dance floor, the instant attraction had led to a fling and she had persuaded him to father her child. The mystery was why didn't the pair get married? This is how *The Guardian's* 'Pass Notes' posed that question and also provided the answer.

Question: 'I suppose Sita wasn't prepared to embrace Islam?'
Answer: 'You'd be surprised. Do you really think Sita's her real name?'

The Guardian went on to explain how Ana-Luisa White became Sita: 'For the sake of true love, she changed her name to that of the Asian goddess of wifely devotion and sacrifice.'

Now, had Imran been a Hindu, Ana-Luisa White changing her name to Sita would have made absolute sense. Sita, the consort of Lord Rama, is venerated by the Hindus as the ultimate symbol of womanly devotion and sacrifice, the wife who is always willing to obey her husband whatever he does. But not only is Imran a Muslim, a man who had declared his newly found love for Islam, but he comes from the part of the world, the Indian sub-continent, where the great majority of Muslims are converts from Hindus and questions such as the Hindu belief in Rama and Sita and their ancient temples being converted to mosques by conquering Muslims are subjects of explosive political and religious debate. Yet awareness of such fairly well-known facts and sensitivities was amazingly beyond *The Guardian's* supposedly learned editors who seemed to think one Asian name must be the same as another, even if they come from opposed religions.

'Pass Notes' might have been on firmer ground in speculating that Imran may have rejected Ms White precisely because she changed her name to Sita, a 'kaffir' goddess and an affront to a man of such sharply defined Muslim susceptibilities. Perhaps had Ana-Luisa, instead of taking the name Sita, become Saeeda, a more wholesome Islamic name, then who knows? Saeeda White may have been standing where Jemima now does. Interestingly, although much was made at the time of the marriage of Jemima changing her name to Haiqa, she has hardly used the name since – although Ana-Luisa is invariably referred to as Sita.

It is worth stressing such mistakes not merely because they show the astonishing lack of even basic knowledge about the sub-continent from papers expected to know but because the coverage of Imran's marriage, while it had its supporters, conveyed the impression that for this Pakistani to marry the 21-year-old blonde daughter of one of the richest men in the West was a sort of invasion, the modern version of the barbarian attacking the castle and violating the most cherished princess.

What made all this curious was that Imran could hardly be described as a barbarian. For a start he met Jemima through her mother, Annabel, at the nightclub named after Jemima's mother. Lady Annabel, it seems, had always admired Imran and that evening, spotting him amidst the throng, had taken her daughter to him and, while she may not have realised how symbolic the gesture would prove, this was hardly the script of a real-life *Guess Who's Coming to Dinner?*. But even had they not met quite in this fashion, Imran, far from being the frightening barbarian, ought to have been considered the ultimate example of this country's ability through sport to transform Kipling's heathens outside the law and bring them into the fold.

Here was a child from Lahore who became a man in Oxford, acquiring along the way the best England had to offer in education and sporting and social values, so much so that he became the most prized man in London society. Let us review the transformation, as chronicled by Imran's chosen biographer, Ivo Tennant.

He arrives with the Pakistan cricket team in 1971 as very much the spotty 18-year-old. He is shaped first by his school in Worcester and then Keble College, Oxford. The claims made on behalf of Oxbridge may sometimes be exaggerated but Oxford made Imran in a way few universities have moulded their students and surely paved the way for the fateful meeting with Jemima at Annabel's. What is more, it was done through that most English of games – cricket.

Initially, says his closest friend Guy Walker, he appeared arrogant but that was because, 'he was far less confident than he was to become and because he was shy and his English was poor when he arrived at Oxford'. However, Oxford, says Walker, totally liberated him. It was at Oxford through his cricketing talents that he made his circle of friends, like Jonathan Mermagen, who for a time acted like an agent and was almost an alter ego and they, in turn, introduced him not only to the intricacies of the English class system, but to those members of it who could provide him with a circle of influence and power that would be the envy of most people. It was through this Oxford network that he met one of the great loves of his life, Emma Sargeant, the woman he came closest to marrying before he met Jemima. The intermediary was Jonathan Orders, a Wykehamist and Oxford Blue, whose brother Imran had known at Oxford. Orders had already introduced Imran to Susie Murray-Philipson, who turned down Imran's invitation to go to Pakistan. Emma Sargeant, who came in Susie's wake, accepted the invitation and the relationship followed.

Tennant, who wrote his biography in 1994 – more than a year before Jemima was publicly revealed – described Emma as the only woman Imran ever truly loved. His friendship with her, he says, brought people like Oliver Gilmour, chief conductor of the Bulgarian State Opera, into Imran's network and made him even more part of society London. If Emma played a part in this then, Tennant feels, the privilege of making Imran truly part of this select group really belongs to Orders. But whether it was Emma or Jonathan who provided the key that unlocked the high society door for Imran, through the '80s and for much of the '90s, Imran was integral to London society.

Cricket, of course, was the rock on which his reputation was founded. His prowess had grown through the late '70s, helped by the move from Worcester to Sussex and then recruitment to the World Series sponsored by Kerry Packer. By the early '80s, as Imran was christened the 'Lion of Pakistan', he also became a social lion in London's high society. Jonathan Mermagen believes that the boom of the '80s helped, as did the fact that in England, unlike in Hollywood, there are not too many people of star quality. Imran, he believes, combined glamour with achievement.

At a time when cricketers were assuming a higher profile and also developing a sex appeal, Imran became the object of sexual fantasy for many women who did not know much about the game, or even care for it. Some of the women attracted to the game by Imran spoke openly about his fanciable bum and how they would love to sit behind the bowler's arm as he ran in to bowl. Other cricketers may have radiated sexual chemistry but Imran was always top of the list, so much so that even Pakistani government officials relied on his image as a cricketer whose appeal extended well beyond the cricket field.

Shahed Sadullah tells the story of a meeting in the summer of 1982 at the offices of the Pakistan High Commission, where he was then an official. It was the summer both India and Pakistan were touring England but, more crucially, it was the summer when the Festival of India was making all the cultural and political headlines in England. The Pakistanis, always sensitive to anything that gives their bigger, more populous, neighbour a higher profile, were alarmed and increasingly resentful of the sort of press Indian culture and arts was getting. The High Commissioner was anxious to know what should be done to counteract the Indians. Shahed Sadullah said, 'Don't worry, sir, Imran Khan will soon be here with the Pakistani cricket team. The moment he hits the television screens all the publicity about India and the Festival of India will vanish.' And that, says Sadullah, is exactly what happened. 'Imran came, the girls flocked to see him and we had nothing to worry about. The television viewership went up by almost 100 per cent, of which 90 per cent were female viewers.'

For a time it seemed that every major London event had to have Imran, even at the parties thrown by Jeffrey Archer, whose devotion to cricket is almost as great as his love for politics. It is a reflection of Imran's drawing power that, almost two years after he had stopped playing, he headed the *Evening Standard*'s list of 400 people without whom no London party could be complete. This was not mere sex appeal, there was also the fascination with a sportsman who appeared to have reinvented the sporting life of the amateur cricketer that everyone assumed had vanished with the war.

The image we have of the lifestyle of the pre-war amateur cricketer is fairly well set. He was almost always something in the City but he also had private income which left him free to attend the summer parties and balls interspersed with hunting and shooting expeditions. He played cricket for fun, mostly country house weekend cricket, but occasionally he would interrupt all this to play in an important county match and more likely than not score the match-winning hundred, putting the professionals, who played cricket six days a week for a living, in the shade.

Imran's life from midsummer 1988, when he parted company with

Sussex in less than glorious fashion, until his retirement from international cricket in 1992, almost mirrored this pre-war amateur style, except that his shooting took place in Pakistan in the English winter – and the important matches which interrupted his 'amateur life' were the internationals featuring Pakistan. In an age of dedicated professional cricketers such a lifestyle would be considered impossible but Imran, keeping fit by working out in a gym, somehow defied conventional wisdom and, although in this phase of his career between 1988 and 1992 he did not lead Pakistan to a Test series victory, except against Sri Lanka, he did bow out of cricket by winning the World Cup for Pakistan, an achievement that ensured immortality in the eyes of his countrymen. Only one other cricketer – Phil Edmonds – even attempted to follow Imran's lead but his request to Middlesex to play as an amateur while pursuing his business career was promptly shot down by the county.

Vicky Woods, then working for *Tatler*, noted the effect Imran had on women, even those who found cricket thoroughly boring. Mark Boxer, her editor at *Tatler*, was obsessed with cricket and would watch it on a tiny television right through editorial meetings. Woods writes: 'Tedious. All those BBC voices maundering on about seams and creases and batting and Gatting took a bit of the fizz out of our champagne-soaked party chatter. But then the Lion of Pakistan loped into view, 35 years old and captain of his country and still not quite at his super fast-bowling peak, lean and sinewy in a dazzle of white flannel and black curls. Next to Mark himself, Imran was the most beautiful man ever to pad up to bat, and the *Tatler* girls – mostly well-connected girls with good address books – would fan their hectic flushes and make coarse jokes about cricket boxes. Ooooh. Be still, my heart. Gently bred girls don't usually swoon over professional footballers or cricketers (and when you conjure up a mental picture of most of the lads, who can blame them?). It takes a special combination of romantic good looks and heart-stopping talent to get girls all a-quiver: George Best had it, and Ryan Giggs looked for a second as if he was going to, before he cut his hair. Imran had it in spades, he fitted very neatly into good address books and into the *Tatler* social slot. He knew how to dress and hold a knife.'

He also knew, it seemed, how to reach out to those parts of English social life that can be so mysterious to foreigners but which, for Imran, seemed to be second nature. Let Woods describe it. 'Country house cricket. Bring on your Philip Naylor-Leylands and your Marquesses of Worcester and their time-honoured nobs versus villagers Sunday afternoon matches: Imran Khan, one of the most brilliant all-rounders of the past 30 years, would shorten his bowling run-up, and rein in his batting to excitable ripples of well-brought-up applause. Lady Celestial Noel (of Jennifer's Diary) watched him go out for a duck to the village blacksmith at a house in Wales. "It was hardly fair. He couldn't bowl properly or he'd have killed everybody." Lady Liza Campbell once saw him out for a duck as well, "but they let him back in and he scored six sixes".'

So, if such a man were to wed the young, attractive daughter of a rich Englishman why should there be so much gnashing of teeth and breast beating? Surely the marriage should have been celebrated rather than execrated? Would this not be the ultimate proof that English civilisation, certainly the sporting civilisation, worked? Would this not be the realisation of Macaulay's dream of making the sub-continentals English in everything but the colour of their skin? Part of the reason this was not the reaction was that the Imran who wed Jemima was considered to be not quite the Imran who had wowed London through the '80s and early '90s. Imran, said the English, had changed and the English, clearly, did not like it.

As it happened, this change had been the subject of a great deal of press comment in the days and weeks leading up to his marriage to Jemima. The Woods article, from which I have just quoted, was part of a longer piece seeking to explain how Imran had changed, and was the cover story of *The Sunday Times* magazine published just five days before news of his wedding to Jemima emerged. It is an article that repays careful study.

Headlined 'Allah's Batsman', it was subtitled 'The Conversion of Imran Khan' and the magazine's cover showed Imran, in typical Pakistani dress (what *The Sun* would call a long 'skirt'), kneeling in prayer inside a mosque. The standfirst – the lines in bold leading into the article – read: 'The playboy player is no more. For Imran Khan has seen the light. But as political power beckons in his native Pakistan, is the cricketing demigod turning into the latest Islamic demagogue?'

Woods described how the old Imran had gone and with it his pleasure-seeking days in the West. In its place had come an Imran who was preoccupied by what she termed his 'public obsessions with Islamic fundamentalism' and his ambitions for his country. His enemies in Pakistan thought these ambitions were political, Imran claimed they were educational and Woods concluded he was rather confused.

Even here it is interesting to note that the so-called reconversion to Islam was the action of a man made by Oxford, his journey back to Islam a reaction to events in the West. His spiritual reawakening, he told Woods, had come after he was 40 when, unable to counter the attacks on Islam in the West following the publication of Salman Rushdie's *Satanic Verses*, he felt he had to know more about his religion. This had been followed by his discovery of the people of Pakistan, which had come as he tried to fulfil his vow to build a cancer hospital there in memory of his mother who had died of the disease. As the hospital project replaced cricket as his main vocation, he had barnstormed the country raising funds and begun to receive the adulation of what he called the masses.

Woods felt Imran spoke of the masses in much the same manner as the Prince of Wales, showing the same sense of destiny, the same identification with the man in the street, the same humourlessness and attachment to worthy causes. In Imran's case this was all the more necessary since he was being shunned by the Pakistani rich who had been angered by Imran denouncing them as brown sahibs, men and women who sought to imitate the English and for whom independence meant merely replacing white skin with brown. All this, argued Woods, had taken Imran a long way from the playboy cricketer, the man every society hostess in London wanted to invite to their parties, so much so that he was now being projected as the putative leader of Pakistan, striking fear even in Benazir Bhutto, the prime minister.

But how did the new Islamic hero of the Pakistani masses feel about his pleasure-seeking past? In was here, towards the end of the article, as Woods tackled Imran on his life as playboy in the West, that we had the most interesting insights into Imran's thinking. This is what Woods wrote: 'He has spent the last 20 years struggling not to get married to "a foreign wife". In Pakistan he has lived the life of Muslim bachelor, careful and discreet, in a country where much can be veiled. In the wicked West, where (especially in Britain) long lenses bring down the great and good on a twice-weekly basis, he has lived the life of a fun-loving rogue – and why not? He wasn't married and he didn't dance attendance on other men's wives. He had the best of both worlds. Didn't that make him a hypocrite? When I asked him about this, he quoted a line from the Koran, and then helpfully expanded in. "Put a veil on your sin," he said. "The whole object of this little line and the huge philosophy behind it is not that you become a hypocrite, but that if you sin, it is your problem with God alone. If you exhibit your sin, you induce other people into it and it becomes a bigger sin. So when a rock star sings about cocaine and drugs and makes innuendoes to a young and impressionable audience, he is actually destroying a lot of kids in the process by glamorising it. It is to protect that section of society that Islam says 'Put a vein on your sin'. The Islamic view is what you want to do, do – you have your own personal dealing with God. Hence, for fornication (if you're caught) or adultery, you're stoned to death. But you need four witnesses watching the penetration. Didn't you know that? That's the law! Even if you're lying naked together you cannot be sentenced to death. So what does that tell you? That whatever you want to do, do it discreetly. Anyway, whatever my life was that's all in the past, so why try and glamorise it and make them sort of emulate it?"'

Vicky Woods did not pursue the logical absurdity of Imran's gloss on the Koran requiring four witnesses for penetration meant women who had been raped stood almost no chance of getting a conviction under Islamic law. If Imran's version was valid, in such a situation the man did his thing discreetly, made his peace with his god and got away with it. Woods was more concerned to pursue his interest in Kristiane Backer, the tall, good-looking German girl who was a presenter for MTV and had been Imran's girlfriend for the last three years. Backer had spoken about the beauty of Islam but when Woods asked Imran about here he ended the interview saying, 'I don't want to reply to that. No comment on that.' Then there was a long pause and he continued, 'I never do this. I try not to say "no comment". But I'm not going to comment on this and, if you'll excuse me, I'm now going to break my fast.'

However, he appears to have spoken to Woods again, giving this view of marriage: 'I saw all my friends get divorced – all my friends without exception – and that disillusioned me. But then I realised that they didn't tackle marriage in the right way. Love and romance is not really the way to tackle it. It's not how marriage works: clearly your objectives in life must be the same as well. Most people don't know their objectives in life. Most people don't know where they're heading in life. That's why an arranged marriage works. And this year I want to get married.'

Woods ended her article with that Imran wish and the impression it created was that Imran Khan, having spent the most formative years of his life, between 18 and 40, in the West, had now returned home. Woods, who did her research in February, told me, 'He was very concerned about the timing of the article. Yes, at that time he was very much involved with Jemima but he kept it a secret. What everybody knew was that he was going to marry because he made the decision to.'

What the world did not know was that even as Imran spoke to Woods he was being drawn to the approved Western-style of marriage, very far removed from the Eastern arranged marriage system he had praised to Woods – marrying a woman not because the family ordained it but because he had fallen in love with her.

All of this may suggest that Imran was being a bit of a hypocrite when he spoke to Woods but he would probably say he was drawing a necessary veil. After all, this is what he had done in 1985 when he was interviewed in *The Sunday Observer*, a Bombay paper. Asked about Emma Sargeant, he denied he had ever considered marriage to her at any time. 'They are all cooked-up stories, just like the ones that the press back home cooks up about cricket. Often things are ascribed to me that I have never said. Then my mother would get very upset until I called her and explained the truth.' Yet as Ivo Tennant's authorised biography has since revealed, even as Imran was talking to the reporter, Emma herself was in Pakistan and there was talk of marriage. It was only in 1986 that the couple parted, painfully aware that cultural differences and the life of a modern cricketer could not be reconciled. However, in Imran's defence, it must be said that the sub-continent, while often very charitable and patient, does not often like to hear the truth about its heroes.

Take the case of Pakistan's founder Mohammed Ali Jinnah. A barrister, and one of the most brilliant of Western-educated politicians the Raj produced, his love for a drink, particularly whisky and soda in the evening, was well known. He hardly spoke Urdu, the Pakistani national language, yet he organised a brilliant political coup to create the state of Pakistan, based on the principle that the Muslims of the old Indian sub-continent needed a home of their own. Jinnah never lost his love for whisky and for a politician he was uncommonly straightforward and open about his life and his intentions. However, today in Pakistan, any public references to his whisky drinking or his so-called un-Islamic ways, are severely frowned upon. He is always presented in the Pakistani national dress, never in the Western suits he favoured. Pakistan is not alone in this. Neighbouring India is also very sensitive to portrayals of the private life of its heroes. So Jawaharlal Nehru's official three-volume biography makes no reference to his affair with Lady Mountbatten, long known in India, and since confirmed by Lady Mountbatten's biographers.

Curiously, like Imran, Jinnah, the greatest of Pakistani heroes, married out of his religion and to a woman much younger. Ruttie, the ravishing daughter of Sir Dinshaw Manockjee Petit – a Bombay textile magnate and something of the Sir James Goldsmith of pre-First World War Bombay – was 18 and Jinnah over 40 when they married, Ruttie converting to Islam three days before the marriage. Bombay society was outraged, although it could not but admire the way Jinnah had asked for Ruttie's hand. Jinnah knew her father very well socially and it was while he was his house guest that he had first met Ruttie. When he decided to marry Ruttie he had a meeting with Sir Dinshaw. Jinnah started by asking him what he thought of marriages between people of different religions. Splendid idea, said Sir Dinshaw, one way to solve India's religious problems. Then, said Jinnah, I suppose you have no objection to my marrying your daughter? For a few moments Sir Dinshaw did not realise what Jinnah was saying but once he realised Jinnah was not joking he was outraged, described it as absurd and fantastic and never spoke to Jinnah again. He even tried to get an injunction to stop the marriage. For a decade after the marriage he treated his daughter as dead. Then she divorced Jinnah and gained reacceptance.

However, unlike Imran, Jinnah never cared for what today would be called the Islamic code of dress. He never hid his drinking – his evening glass of whisky was served to him even as mullahs gathered round him – and he liked his wife to dress in the Western fashion. This would lead to a famous scene at a dinner given by Lord and Lady Willingdon at Government House in Bombay. Ruttie had worn a very low-cut gown. Lady Willingdon, her Victorian morality outraged, asked a servant to bring a wrap in case Ruttie felt cold. Jinnah stood up and said, 'When Mrs Jinnah feels cold, she will say so and ask for a wrap herself.' With that Jinnah and his wife walked out and never again stepped into Government House until the Willingdons had gone.

Imran, the cricketer, has been brave on the field, resolving the many contradictions of Pakistan cricket, but when news of his marriage broke he could not quite throw down the gauntlet like Jinnah and found himself on a very sticky wicket. He struggled to justify it and rebut the charge of hypocrisy. His initial response was to go back on the ringing declarations he had made to Vicky Woods about love and romance not working. Sounding very like a Westerner he now said that one could not legislate about falling in love. But aware that his fellow Pakistanis might not understand what love had to do with it, he clung to the fact that he had kept his oft-repeated promise only to marry a Muslim, laying much stress on the fact that Jemima had become a Muslim. And since in Islam there are no boundaries of race and nationality he used the fact that she had converted to assert that this made her as much of a Muslim as any Pakistani girl. This gave the impression that he was trying to present himself as an Islamic champion of an almost mediaeval variety.

Prompted by this Islamic line, almost from the beginning the marriage was presented as a modern version of a mediaeval battle where the conquering Muslim warrior, albeit a sporting one, captures a fair Christian princess, in this case half-Jewish, and converts her to his religion. News of the conversion dominated the early coverage with *The Sunday Telegraph* trumpeting, 'Conversion to Islam gave Imran his catch.' Jemima, like a true convert, provided additional support by describing how much more desirable her new Islamic world was.

The Sunday after the Paris wedding saw *The Sunday Telegraph* carry an article by her explaining how she converted. One photograph had her in the accepted Western style – long flowing hair, champagne glass in hand and a man looking at her with lustful eyes in the background. Another, more prominently placed, had her looking demure in traditional Pakistani Muslim dress, all but her face and a bit of her hair covered in flowing silks. The article, headlined 'Why I chose Islam by bride Jemima', made it clear that Jemima had converted from her free will, not from pressure. Jemima argued that as a person of the book – Muslims consider Jews and Christians to be such persons – she was allowed under the Koran to marry a Muslim. Incidentally, this is a debatable proposition that not all Muslim theologians necessarily accept. Jemima went on to say she had become a Muslim because of her growing belief in Islam's eternal truth. Nothing could have more gladdened the heart of a Muslim. In Muslim eyes when a Jew or a Christian converts it means that they have accepted that Islam, a religion which honours the prophets of both Judaism and Christianity, is the final version of eternal truth as revealed in the Koran.

For Imran's Pakistani followers Jemima's words were all the sweeter, for here was a woman brought up in the decadent West saying women did not live by alcohol and nightclubs alone and that the shalwar khameez was 'far more elegant and feminine than anything in my wardrobe'. There could not be a more emphatic choosing of sides in the eternal battle between the Christian West and the Islamic East.

In that sense Imran himself presented the marriage as a modern-day defection story, except that the frontier crossed was not the Berlin Wall but the one between two often warring religions. The significance of such a public conversion and marriage could not have been more dramatic, given that many in the West, now that communism is dead, see Islam as the next great enemy. The symbolism of the year also needs to be stressed – 1995 being the 1,000th anniversary of Pope Urban's call, in November 995, to liberate the Holy Lands that had fallen to warlike Islam. Urban's call led to the Crusades and in such a context it is not surprising that English newspapers reacted to Jemima marrying Imran much as they had done when they realised that Kim Philby had defected to the Russians. Certainly the attacks on Imran seemed to be laced with remorse that a man whom the West had once claimed as it own had not only defected, or more correctly redefected, but in the process carried away a glittering prize.

However, even if all this explains both the frenzy and the tone of the media coverage, there is no certainty that had Imran married Jemima in a morning coat, an attire he often donned to go to Ascot, and taken up residence in his old hunting grounds of Chelsea, the marriage would not have merited a similar Western scorn and scepticism. Even then it would have been a marriage between a Paki who could never be English and a Sloane Ranger who should have known better.

It is interesting to reflect that even the great Ranji, the one cricketer from the Indian sub-continent to truly bridge the gap between English and Indian cricket, and a prince to boot, could never find a way of marrying the English girl he loved. He felt that neither English society of the day nor his own Indian, princely Rajput clan would find it acceptable. So his love remained hidden and he died a tortured man. True, 1920 and the social attitudes about inter-racial marriages is a world removed from 1995 but, interestingly, successive biographers of Ranji, while fulsome in their praise of him as one of cricket's immortals, have not been able to summon up the courage to write about this liaison. It took Simon Wilde to finally break the taboo and even then he had to do so carefully.

Imran, of course, is no Ranji, and the reactions to his marriage shows that he can no longer be divorced from his country and the state of cricket relations between Pakistan and England. Always fragile, they have soured in recent years with Pakistanis feeling that their success in England in 1987, in the World Cup in 1992 and in the English summer that followed has not been given due credit by the English. The English, in turn, have felt the Pakistanis are a bit too chippy and have used unfair means to achieve success. Their central accusation has been that Pakistanis got the ball to reverse swing unfairly, often gouging the ball with fingernails. This led to a libel case between Sarfraz Nawaz and his former Northants team-mate Allan Lamb after Lamb in a newspaper article alleged that Pakistanis cheated at cricket by illegally doctoring the ball. The case was settled with Lamb claiming he had never accused Sarfraz personally of cheating and Sarfraz declaring his honour satisfied.

At the height of the court action, Imran declared that Pakistan would not play Test cricket with England until the next century and while this has proved an exaggeration, Imran himself was drawn into the controversy when in Tennant's biography he confessed that had once gouged the ball with a bottle top. Imran has since suggested that the confession was a bit of a joke but the way it was received only exposed the worst kept secret in cricket: that England and Pakistan, whose histories have been so intertwined in recent centuries, just cannot stand each other. Cricket was proving a mirror for some deep-seated national antagonisms with events on the field reinforcing prejudices and national stereotypes and emphasising the enormous divide between the two countries.

Pakistani cricket saw the victories in 1992, both in the World Cup and in England, as final proof that Pakistan had one of the best, if not the best, cricket teams in the world and certainly the best pair of opening bowlers in Wasim Akram and Waqar Younis. There can be little doubt that as a fast-bowling pair Akram and Younis deserve to be ranked with the great pairs in cricket: Lindwall and Miller, Trueman and Statham, Hall and Griffith, Holding and Roberts, Lillee and Thomson, Marshall and Garner. Yet England, instead of acknowledging this, kept whispering that Pakistani success was due to illegal methods – such hints being dropped by English players even on the very night Pakistan won the World Cup final. For Pakistanis such whispered accusations were a terrible blow to that most sensitive of Pakistani feelings: *izzat*, honour. Most crimes can be forgiven in Pakistan but to insult a man's *izzat*, something even the poorest will proudly hold, is worse than plunging a dagger to his heart.

In Pakistani eyes English cricket has been insulting Pakistani *izzat* almost from the first moment the two countries started playing Test cricket. On that first tour in 1954, an unknown Pakistani team with only one player of genuine English experience, their captain Abdul Hafeez Kardar, created a sensation by becoming the first country to win a Test match in England on its inaugural visit. That victory also shared the rubber but English cricket damned it with faint praise, emphasising that Pakistan had been heavily outplayed in the previous Tests, that but for rain they would have long ago lost the series, and that the English selectors had rested key players. That mealy-mouthed praise made many Pakistanis conclude that had Australia or South Africa done it – it took South Africa 46 years to win a Test in England – they would have been lauded. But the audacity of a former colony, brown at that, to achieve a Test victory was too much for the white sahibs. Ever since then Pakistanis have always felt that whatever they do they will never be able to win the unqualified approval of the English.

Things have gone downhill since then with almost every tour reinforcing national stereotypes. This mutual antipathy nearly led to cricket relations between the two countries coming to an end barely 18 months after England had started playing Pakistan. In February 1956, during the MCC tour of Pakistan, some of the players decided to douse the Pakistan umpire Idris Begh, giving him what *Wisden* later called the 'water treatment'. The incident roused such feelings that the then President of the MCC, Lord Alexander of Tunis, offered to bring the players back immediately and even compensate the Pakistanis. It did not come to that – there were only two more matches to go – but it left a scar that has never been healed.

The 'water treatment' occurred in a match where the MCC had seen four of their main batsmen give out lbw and was the start of the English feeling that they could never get any justice from Pakistan umpires. Needless to say MCC lost the match and such feelings have been reinforced over the years by tales from other visiting sides to that country.

Pakistan was not only outraged by 'water treatment' for Idris Begh but scandalised that English cricket should treat it as a jape. *Wisden*, which is as much a bible for Pakistani cricketers as it is for English, even tried to pass it off as no more than a student rag that had gone wrong. Adding the insult of condescension to injury, it said, 'Unfortunately, some of the players did not realise that the type of humour generally accepted by most people in Britain, might not be understood in other parts of the world.'

Not even *Wisden* could take refuge in such cultural differences when 30 years later, in the winter of 1987, the Shakoor Rana incident very nearly put a stop to Test cricket between the two countries. A day's play was lost as the cricketers of the two countries patched up their relationship. The incident is now part of cricket myth in both countries and is a vivid, if painful, illustration of how differently Pakistan and England see things.

As the Pakistani saw it, the incident was simple. The English cricket captain had verbally abused a Pakistani umpire during a Test match. The English could hardly deny the incident but in their eyes Mike Gatting, the England captain who had done the shouting, had been provoked beyond endurance, as had his colleagues, by wretched umpiring decisions. In any case, Rana had also shouted at Gatting. For a couple of days the two cricket boards indulged in the sort of diplomacy that would have been more suited to solving the Bosnian problem let alone a cricket one. In the end Gatting apologised; Rana, too, made a statement and the Test resumed – but after that things could never be the same. Although England have played Pakistan in both Tests and one-day cricket, there has been no England tour of Pakistan to play a Test series.

In Pakistani eyes this was yet another loss of *izzat*. The English saw it as a simple case of reaction to cheating. Indeed, Raman Subba Row and Alan Smith, chairman and chief executive of the TCCB, who flew to Pakistan to solve the problem, decided to grant the players a bonus of £1,000, described as a hardship bonus. As the Pakistanis saw it, if Gatting had insulted Rana's *izzat* the granting of the bonus was an insult to the entire Pakistani nation's *izzat*. However, as Raman Subba Row saw it, the bonus was to demonstrate that cricket is not a game of cheating. As he explained to me some years later, 'In fact, an immense amount of cheating went on during that particular tour of Pakistan. The cheating was aided and abetted by Pakistani officials – oh absolutely, absolutely, there is no doubt. It was a carefully conceived plan. And we rose to the bait. That was really our mistake.'

A few months before the Rana incident, English cricket appeared to have had conclusive proof of Pakistani cheating. This came in the Headingley Test of the 1987 summer when the Pakistani wicketkeeper, Yousuf, claimed a catch off Botham after clearly taking the ball on the first bounce. It nearly led to Botham assaulting the wicketkeeper and was yet another example of cricket dividing rather than bringing the two countries together. (Interestingly in 1996 when Graeme Hick successfully claimed a catch against the Indian opener Rathore, which on television replays was shown to have bounced, there was little comment.) In the 1996 World Cup there have been further examples of how cricket embitters relationship between the two countries. There was an attempt by the English batsmen to organise nets, offering what they thought was a tip to the groundsman, but which was seen by the Pakistanis as a bribe.

All this must come as surprise to those Raj stalwarts who during the days of empire actually favoured that part of the sub-continent. Then, as the Indian nationalists, largely a Hindu-led group, agitated for independence from Britain, the majority of the Muslim political leadership happily collaborated. And the great champions of the Raj built up a cosy picture of tall, dark, fearless men who were always true to their word and honour in comparison to the devious Hindus.

Imran himself has benefited from this image. He is intensely proud of his Pathan ancestry and the carefully cultivated image of bold, brave men who bow to no man. It is a picture of him that is immensely appealing to his English friends who constantly refer to it. For some of them this makes Imran and Pakistanis like him much more desirable that the decadent West. Yet while Imran is coveted, the word Paki is itself a term of abuse and a rallying cry of white racists. Many in this country's cricket secretly echo Botham's remark that Pakistan is a country to which you do not even send your mother-in-law.

Part of the reason is that the old cliché of familiarity breeding contempt has come true. The presence of large numbers of Pakistanis, far from helping foster relationships between the two countries, has actually further divided it. Where the old Raj had struck up a working relationship with the old Muslim élite of the sub-continent, in the new multi-cultural

England almost every Pakistani is regarded as an illiterate peasant from the hills near Pakistan Kashmir. It is galling for the educated élite, who control Pakistani cricket, to find that they are confused with their poor fellow Pakistanis.

It could be argued that Pakistanis have also not helped their cause by displaying a mixture of aggressive defensiveness and a chippiness which makes them see conspiracy when there may only be a cock-up. Pakistan is a young nation carved out of predominantly Hindu India and most of the Pakistani Muslims are converts from Hindus, who have known no other home than the sub-continent. This is a part they would rather forget. Imran, on the other hand, takes pleasure in stressing his Pathan origins and how his ancestors came to the sub-continent as conquerors.

Pakistan is a young country, barely 50 years old, and like any country it has a need to connect with history. The natural thing would be to acknowledge that it has a common past with the rest of the sub-continent. Some of the past can hardly be disowned, like the ruins of Mohenjodaro and Harappa, an ancient civilisation which has to this day remained a mystery. However, if the past has traces of Hindu influence – and given that Islam arrived as a major force affecting most of the country in only the 12th century there is bound to be much Hindu influence – then the Pakistanis go to incredible lengths to disown it, as if by even admitting any such connection the very notion of Pakistan would be defiled.

Instead Pakistanis always make strenuous efforts to connect themselves with the Arab world, the source and centre of Islam, and have created a myth where, in their eyes, the history of the sub-continent did not begin until Islam arrived there. This creates many problems for any serious student of history and explains why such a young nation with such a tortured relationship to its past has produced people who have a fierce desire to prove they are the best in the world, but also find it very difficult to accept that they can ever be beaten fairly by anyone.

This is most evident when it comes to cricketing relations with their great rival India. There can be little doubt that for more than a decade now Pakistan has had a cricket team far superior to India's. So much so that, like mediaeval Hindus resisting the Muslim invaders of the sub-continent, the Indian cricket team seems to surrender mentally to the Pakistanis even before a ball is bowled. India has hardly won a significant match against Pakistan for more than a decade now. But when once or twice the Indians have appeared to be on the point of winning the annual series of exhibition matches between India and Pakistan in this country, the largely Pakistani crowd has rioted, forcing abandonment of the match.

All this may be seen as one of the pains of growing up but here Imran himself, for all his wonderful achievements on and off the cricket field, has not quite been able to help the country's cricket followers develop the sort of mature mentality to match the abilities of its cricketers. Imran does not share the sort of prejudice common on both sides of the India/Pakistan divide, a prejudice that makes it difficult for an Indian to praise a Pakistani or a Pakistani to credit an Indian. An exception to this rule was Sunil Gavaskar. During the 1992 World Cup Gavaskar predicted and lauded Pakistan's World Cup win and instantly became a Pakistani hero – some Pakistanis even said he should be given honorary citizenship. Imran has tried hard to be fair when commenting on India and he was one of the few Pakistanis who did not ascribe Pakistan's defeat during the 1979–80 tour of India – the Indians won 2–0 – to the umpiring, a common view in Pakistan. His appraisal of Pakistan's failings on the tour was refreshingly frank and mature.

However, despite his status in Pakistan, even he cannot always challenge accepted conventions or combat the hysteria that an India-Pakistan match can generate. Thus, during a charity match at Crystal Palace in 1993 between India and Pakistan, with the Indians on the verge of victory, the largely Pakistani crowd rioted and forced its abandonment. Sunil Gavaskar played in the match and recalls: 'Imran was captain and he popped into the Indian dressing-room and sympathised. He assured the Indian players that in truth we had won the match. I suggested he make such an announcement over the tannoy. He replied, "I can't do it".' It is, perhaps, understandable that he could not do it and no blame attaches to him for that, but it suggests that perhaps some of the extravagant praise of his followers needs to be tempered.

Now, had the English press coverage of Imran's marriage debated these aspects of the man it would have been both more legitimate and instructive. Instead, by presenting it as Islam versus Christianity, with undertones of the wog marrying the blonde, it fed the Pakistani feeling that it was all a racist plot. It made Pakistanis believe that the English were racists. Even before his marriage and even before he had rediscovered Islam, Imran had felt that there was a strain of racism in English cricket, a strain that made it difficult for the English to give proper credit to cricketers who were from countries like Pakistan. Racism is probably too sweeping and unfair a charge but there is certainly a reluctance to confront racism, as the Henderson affair which blew up, coincidentally, within weeks of Imran's marriage shows. This controversy suggested that the English, aware that there might be a subterranean racist stream in their cricket, would rather keep it hidden or, if it emerged, pretend that it is something else.

CHAPTER ELEVEN

The Black Sporting Angst

Some years ago, as I finished interviewing a prominent black sportsman, I was asked: 'So why have *The Sunday Times* sent you to interview me? Because they want to play the ethnic card?'

The man who asked the question was John Fashanu. We were sitting in his Mercedes coupé. I had been interviewing him for over two hours, and he was about to drop me off at Lissom Grove. At the time he asked the question I was a bit surprised, it was the first time in my journalistic experience that anybody had suggested colour had helped determine the choice of my journalistic assignment, but the more I reflected it became clear that Fashanu, like some black sportsmen, had a shrewd use of colour.

I found myself in Fashanu's Mercedes coupé a few days after the incident at White Hart Lane in November 1993 when his elbow had met Gary Mabbutt's cheek, coming within a millimetre of blinding him. The next day's tabloids carried a story saying that late that night Fashanu had visited Mabbutt in hospital and the two men spent an hour chatting together. Mabbutt had exonerated Fashanu from any blame and said he looked forward to the return.

The story was very puzzling. By the time the match finished and Fashanu had got away from White Hart Lane it would have been near ten-thirty. The traffic would still have been heavy – I took the same route home as Fashanu did – and while Mabbutt's hospital, Princess Grace, is near to Fashanu's home in St John's Wood, he would have done well to get there within an hour. If he then spent an hour it would be well past midnight by the time he left. Reporters could only have spoken to him after that. I was impressed by the reporters' diligence and much taken by the idea of Fashanu briefing reporters at such a late hour.

Fashanu's visit to the hospital also suggested that Tottenham were considerably hyping their story about the damage suffered by Mabbutt. Tottenham's version was backed up by horrific pictures showing Mabbutt's right eye. But how could a man within a couple of hours of being so badly hurt chat amiably about the return match with Wimbledon not due for several months, and what is more, talk to the man who had inflicted the damage? Something did not quite gel.

Soon there were other stories coming out from Wimbledon which were even more intriguing. In this a pattern could be discerned. Tottenham's release of the doctor's statement which classified Mabbutt's injury as a fracture of the skull had clearly inflamed Wimbledon, as also did Tottenham's call for an FA enquiry. The Wimbledon camp began to suggest that Tottenham were upping the ante as part of a diversionary tactic to distract from unwelcome publicity about the Tottenham loans problem, then emerging into the open. This was a further, more substantial, twist to the cry Joe Kinnear had raised on the night of the incident, saying Fashanu's knee, not his elbow, had met Mabbutt's eye – which would suggest that Mabbutt was stooping low with his head rather than that Fashanu was raising his elbow too high – and that Tottenham were fussing because they had failed to win the match.

I had never met Fashanu before and apart from watching him play knew no more about him than what was already in the public domain. The picture I had of Fashanu was that not only was he a remarkable black footballer but a remarkable black sportsman: on the field a picture of strength and purpose, off it a spokesman for the rising tide of African football, soon to be appointed as an ambassador for UNICEF, and intimately involved as a presenter of the highly popular television programme *Gladiators*. His physical style of play allied to his identification with Wimbledon, where his macho, robust forward play had made him a talismanic figure, seemed to symbolise a club everyone loves to hate – as summed up in Gary Lineker's comment that he would rather watch a match on Ceefax than go and see Wimbledon.

Through his assistant, Mr Mace, I arranged to see him at his flat near Lord's. Over the next two and a half hours I spoke to Fashanu at his flat, in his car as we drove to the Wimbledon training ground at Roehampton, and then again in his car as we came back to central London. The trappings of success were clearly visible – the sumptuous penthouse flat filled with desirable objects but not much sign of living; people hovering around him; and Fashanu himself giving the air and manner of a man who was clearly several cuts above the average footballer, if anything more a successful entrepreneur than a ball player. He would later tell a sympathetic reporter he was 65 per cent businessman, 35 per cent footballer.

And sure enough, no sooner had we settled in his penthouse flat, with Fashanu stretching back on his high-backed, black-leather executive chair, than I discovered that he was eager to talk about his business, his promotion of African football, particularly his rescue of Zambian soccer after the horrific crash, but not at all keen to talk about what had happened to Mabbutt. 'I am trading with four companies and have other interests, connections in eight different African countries. I host a major television show, one of the top five in the country, viewed by 12 to 14 million viewers. I hope to start my chat show next year.'

Fashanu made no bones about the fact that fine business calculation determined his playing for Wimbledon. 'Alright Wimbledon trade on the fact that nobody loves us. I stayed with Wimbledon because I can pursue my own interests. Wimbledon always give me time to do my other projects. These things I could not have achieved if I was playing for Arsenal. Because managers there have this perception of the footballer that is blinkered: now sick as a parrot, or over the moon etc. I cannot lead my life like that. I like to express myself both on and off the field. Lots of players get up in the morning, kiss their babies good morning, go to the football club, train, come home in the afternoon and either watch videos or walk around the West End.'

Fashanu was different. He hardly ever trained and off the field he was the epitome of the football capitalist. When I suggested to Fashanu that the controversy with Mabbutt gave him a sort of Jekyll and Hyde character, the man who off the field dines with presidents and ambassadors but on the field plays a physical game that lands opponents in hospital or ends their career, he interjected: 'No, Jekyll and Hyde is too blunt, too tabloidy.'

There was almost a touch of bravado in the way he saw the whole Mabbutt incident. 'The Wimbledon style of play is like that. Other teams might have ten high balls knocked into the box, we will have 25 and the challenges go on outside the box as well. All those high balls and we've had two incidents. The thing that happened to Gary Mabbutt happens every day in football. Football is too fast, everything is based on aggression, everything is based on kick and rush. It is too fast.'

As he spoke he so distanced himself from the Mabbutt incident that he made it appear as if he was a neutral observer rather than the man at the centre of it. 'Sometimes it even frightens me how quick the game is getting. You haven't got a split second to make a decision. Wrong decision, wrong challenge and you are going to be pilloried. I say to football, wake up, that is what's going on.'

There had been calls for an FA enquiry on the use of elbows but as Fashanu saw it the concern was exaggerated. 'The game has been going for a hundred years. You tell me how many people have been killed by an elbow in the face? Injured, yes, killed, no.' For Fashanu an elbow in the eye was less lethal than a hamstring. 'Hamstring injury takes you out for nine weeks, fractured cheekbones take you out for four weeks.' However, his next comment revealed the incident had got home to him: 'One incident like that and they treat you as a murderer: Fash smashes skull, skull basher.'

But even if the Mabbutt incident had put him on the defensive there was no contrition. Far from apologising, Fashanu would not even admit it was clumsy. 'I am not saying it was a clumsy challenge. I will still challenge like that. I have an excellent disciplinary record. Well, you see, 17 years I have been in football. In those 17 years I have had two accidents. One where I bumped into a gentleman called John O'Neill.' The bump had resulted in O'Neill sustaining a ruptured knee which ended his career – he would later take Fashanu to court – but Fashanu balanced this against his own sufferings. 'I have also suffered a broken nose here and there but nothing to write home about. That in a career where I am supposed to be a robust striker is pretty good going. My disciplinary record is very good. I consider myself a gentleman.'

Now I learned that, contrary to the tabloid reports that had so intrigued me, he did not have an hour-long meeting with Mabbutt. He had never seen, let alone talked to Mabbutt. In fact, Fashanu did not get past the hospital's reception that night. At the time Fashanu was in the hospital Mabbutt lay five floors above being examined by the surgeons. Fashanu told me he had been misreported and he had spoken to Mabbutt's girlfriend: 'I went to see him after the match. His girlfriend came down and had a message for me. "Gary bears you no grudge at all. You could be the one. See you at the return. Rest easy." I sat for an hour with his girlfriend. I said, "I shouldn't have gone for the ball." She said, "How can you say that, because that means you mustn't be on the football field." Reporters called me up and I said, "I haven't spoken to Gary but his message was see you on the return". They reported I had actually spoken to Gary.'

But did he even have such an involved conversation with Mabbutt's girlfriend, or spend an hour with her that night as he claimed? Later when I checked with Mabbutt's girlfriend I found she had no recollection of the conversation and Peter Barnes, the Tottenham secretary, who was standing next to her as Fashanu arrived, said, 'I do not remember hearing any such thing. As for Fashanu being with Gary's girlfriend for an hour I cannot see how that can be. He wasn't there for more than five minutes, maximum.'

In some ways the most interesting feature of my interview was the way Fashanu brought it back to race; 'I am conscious I am black, you have to be better to do well as a black man. As a Nigerian, brought up by adopted white parents, I was a black person brought up in a white environment. No, I didn't feel like a zebra in a lion's cage but I knew I had to be better than a white person to do well. Be smart.'

He then gave this explanation for his image as a hard man of the game: 'The football image of black players was created many years ago because it was an era when there were lots of black players, people like Garth Crooks and other small players. Coaches would say you don't worry about them: little black player, give him a kick and he won't come back. Or it is too cold he won't want to play. Up comes John Fashanu – when you give him a good kick he enjoys it, comes back even stronger.'

It was revealing the way Fashanu saw colour in the whole Mabbutt incident. Fashanu was convinced that had he been white he would not have been subject to such media scrutiny. 'If this incident had happened to a white player it would not have been blown up. It is character assassination almost. As a black person I feel this veil over me. Any successful black person must bear that in mind. Somebody, somewhere is waiting to pull you down.'

Some time during our conversation Fashanu had invited me to join him for a ride to the Wimbledon training ground. When we got there we found Sam Hammam, the Wimbledon Chairman. Fashanu had said that he had been able to ride out this storm because he was not like other black players and because of Hammam. 'Had there been another black player his position would have been precarious. I was able to overcome it because I had the backing of my club chairman, Sam Hammam, a Lebanese, a very strong man. What a mountain of a man he is. Close friend of mine for many years. I cannot speak too highly of him. He is a great guy. Had he been an English chairman, no way would I have had such support, no way.'

As we made to leave the ground, Steve Howard of *The Sun* arrived and spoke to Fashanu. After he had gone Fashanu said to me, 'Watch that fellow. He will always stick the knife into you.' He then drove back to town and as were on the Westway he suddenly turned to me and asked, 'So why have *The Sunday Times* sent you to interview me? Because they want to play the ethnic card? Sometimes papers do that, they send their black reporters to interview a black personality and then get the guy to stick the knife in.'

I replied that my colour had never played any part in *The Sunday Times* asking me to cover a story and it struck me as a supreme irony that for the first time in 20 years of reporting I had been asked whether my racial origins had made a difference – the irony being that the questioner was a black. On the Sunday morning after the story appeared I got a call from Fashanu. He was not pleased with the article. 'You stuck the knife in, didn't you?'

'What do you mean?' I asked. 'I reported you accurately. Everything was taped right in front of you.'

'I am not denying I said those words. But it is how you presented it.'

'If you feel you have been misreported tell me what it is.'

'Yeah, you reported what I said. I am not denying the words, it is how you presented it. You stuck the knife in. Goodbye.' Then, after a pause, he said slowly, 'My friend,' in a tone which indicated he clearly did not see me as his friend. He then put the phone down.

Six months after this I met up with Fashanu again. This was in the summer heat of America and the press centre of the Pasadena Rose Bowl. Fashanu was there commentating on the matches and proud of the prowess of the African teams, particularly Nigeria, who came within an ace of beating Italy. I offered him my hand. He looked at it and said, 'You have some cheek in wanting to shake my hand.'

'Why? You are still not on about my article, are you? I reported you accurately. If you had any complaints why didn't you come back?'

'It is how you presented what I said, it was the way you were sticking the knife in. After what you did you have some cheek to offer your hand. I am not going to shake your hand.' Then, after a pause, he added, 'My friend,' in a tone which clearly indicated that our conversation was over.

So what explained Fashanu's feelings, his terror that the veil was always being pulled down over him? As he had told me while we were driving back to central London in his car, 'You feel the shadow, this veil over you. Somewhere, somebody is waiting to pull you down. Linford Christie wins gold, the next day headlines are of his brother arrested for fraud. I have seen it with our successful black people. You ask yourself why?'

Fashanu's invoking of Christie was significant. Christie seemed to share a similar fear of the veil being pulled down when in the summer of 1995 he broke down on television and announced he would not take part in the Atlanta Olympics. The pressures put on him by the media and the authorities, he claimed, had got to him.

Not that there is any comparison between Fashanu and Christie. Christie is a world-class athlete, perhaps the greatest sprinter Britain has produced; Fashanu is a journeyman footballer who will not long be remembered for his football. Fashanu may have had his moments in football, most notably being part of the Wimbledon team that upset Liverpool and won the Cup in 1988, preventing a second double for the Merseyside team. Christie has 30 international honours to his name, including nine gold medals, and is quite unique. He has defied the most cherished of sporting conventions – that as you grow old you grow worse – and done it in a sport, sprinting, where the ageing process can be so cruel. In his early twenties, when he should have been broadcasting his special talent, he was a gangling, indolent athlete – talented but more intent on playing dominoes – and going nowhere. As he has aged he has improved and in a sport where the young have a stranglehold, Christie won the Olympic Gold in 1992 when he was 33, and the following year at 34 the World Championships.

Christie would instantly be inducted into any British Hall of Fame, were such a thing to exist. Yet the way Christie wept on television and spoke of the lack of respect shown by the media and the authorities suggested that he, too, despite his enormous success, or perhaps because of it, carries traces of paranoia that Fashanu exhibits – although in Christie's case it springs from a very different well. With Christie it is a feeling that for all his great achievements he has not been shown enough respect. The cynic might say this all boils down to how much money he can make. His television outburst did come while he was in the middle of negotiations with the British Athletic Federation about how much he would be paid for taking part in races. The negotiations had not been going well and Christie was feeling sore. But whatever prompted the outburst, that a certain paranoia exists cannot be denied.

The mood was further soured by his displeasure about the sort of press he was getting, always a source of irritation with him. Just before the television show an article in *The Observer* had spoken of his powers waning. He was riled by the way the article highlighted his age. He is extremely sensitive about any reference to his age, seeing it as an attack on his ability and character, or worse, implying that he might have achieved success at a late age in sporting terms through unfair means. *The Observer* article had a cartoon of him wearing a vest marked 35 and approaching a bend marked Beware End of Road. The whole thing was compounded by the fact that an unauthorised biography was about to be released – his authorised biography emerged later – and in his mind it all added up to one thing: the world at large was not showing him enough respect, or nuff respect as the blacks call it.

Respect is an important word in the post-'60s black lexicon, the word and the meaning attached to it being drawn from the songs of Aretha Franklin which were much in demand during that seminal period. It is a word that symbolises the black demand for civil and political rights and to be put on a parity with whites. The importance Christie places on it can be seen from the fact that the company Christie has set up to market his activities is called Nuff Respect. Christie's angst was that despite his tremendous achievements, his standing as the most successful British sprinter of all time, he was not getting the respect he felt he deserved.

In the course of his television performance Christie shrewdly drew the contrast between the public adulation he received and what he saw as less than reverential attitude in the press and from the people who ran British athletics. Many of the journalists who regularly write on athletics vigorously defended the media's treatment of him, suggesting that he was being unfair in claiming that he got a bad press. One of the examples cited by Christie was a headline which said: 'Christie fails at last'. What sort of headline is that, demanded Christie? Isn't that demeaning? The television audience, always ready to believe that the media is keen to scalp celebrities, cheered. Yet was this in any way more derogatory, if at all, than the one during Bradman's heyday which said 'Bradman fails, scores 90'? The implication of the headline was that Bradman was always expected to score a hundred on every visit to the crease and that his failure to reach his own high standards, albeit by 10 runs, was newsworthy. Similarly, Christie's headline expressed surprise, and since news by definition is something that is unexpected it made sense, however much it made Christie feel that it did not show 'nuff respect'.

This, of course, was not the first time Christie had complained of lack of respect. His career has been marked by stormy press relations. In 1988, just before the Seoul Olympics, a *Daily Mirror* headline which criticised the performance of British athletes including Christie had him raging and over the years there have been other occasions. Christie's complaint is that not only his achievement in overturning accepted wisdom that a sprinter slows down with age never been properly appreciated but that he has also not been given enough credit for putting Britain on the world sprinting map and for being the first British athlete who has bridged the colour divide. Young white boys, as much as young black boys, see him as their hero and flock to him: they root for him when he runs and then, boosted by his wins, try to emulate him.

Following his television appearance he had another brush with the press as he flew out of Heathrow to attend an athletic meeting in Nuremberg. In the departure lounge he stormed at the press, in particular the clicking photographers, saying: 'If you lot want some then I will give you something different to write about. I don't want to see blood shed on the airport carpet, but if you want some . . .' No blood was shed but Christie complained to airport security about being hassled by photographers, further burnishing the image of a man who clearly felt he did not receive his due from the world. Part of the reason for his fragile state may have been caused by the fact that his mother was dying. She died a few days later.

One other comment which had clearly got Christie going was his unhappiness with the constant references to his lunch box. Just as he had won the Olympic Gold *The Sun*, focusing on his tight lycra shorts which emphasised his crotch, enquired, in that mixture of provocation and mirth that is the paper's hallmark, what does Linford Christie have in there? Then, having posed the question, it began to speculate in its characteristic style, mixing equal doses of smut and tastelessness, as to whether Christie put his bananas in there causing the crotch to become so prominent? Or, perhaps, his entire lunch box? This led to the paper dubbing Christie's crotch as the lunch box.

Christie, not surprisingly, was not amused and referred to it during his television performance. He saw it as ethnic stereotyping, building on the common white fantasy of the well-endowed black male. Matters were not helped by Jimmy Greaves, one of the two hosts of the programme, rather insensitively wondering if it would not be better if Linford did not wear such tight shorts. Christie, rightly, protested that he should not be judged by the shorts he wore. What mattered was not how he looked but what he achieved.

It is possible to feel a lot of sympathy for Christie on this issue and he does raise an interesting point when he asks whether newspapers would talk in this fashion of Sally Gunnell's breasts. But it is debatable how much *The Sun* see it as quite the simple race issue that Christie does. The way they refer to Christie's lunch box suggests a combination of mirth and stereotyping. Even as he announced his 'retirement' *The Sun* headlined the news as Christie retiring his lunch box and an editorial said both *The Sun* and the ladies would miss Christie's lunch box. It could also be said that such mockery is no worse, probably more tolerable, than the way *The Sun* so cruelly classified Graham Taylor as the turnip, an epithet that has stuck to him. Christie's race gave the issue of the lunch box an extra edge but if

Christie was white would it be any different? Given the way *The Sun* and the tabloid press works it remains doubtful.

When Christie's autobiography finally emerged it became clear that behind his railing against the media and complaints that he was not given enough respect was a man confused about his identity. Autobiographies by their very nature are self-serving but Christie's story must be the supreme example of the genre. Although like many first person stories of sportsmen it was ghost-written, it is almost impossible to establish from the book who the ghost-writer is. Nowhere does the name of ghost-writer Maurice Hamilton appear except for a reference to him in the acknowledgements, which are written like a poem and where Maurice is thanked along with some others but without any explanation as to why he deserves gratitude.

Christie would not be the first celebrity who would not be eager to highlight that somebody converted his words into a book. It is interesting to note that Christie's reticence on this subject is even more marked than that of Diana Modahl's, whose autobiography emerged a few months later. Although Modahl did not put her ghost-writer in lights she clearly identified that she had used a ghost-writer, albeit you had to hunt the copyright page to find it. Moreover, given the title of Christie's book – *To Be Honest With You* – such an attitude to his ghost-writer was quite revealing.

But then Christie's book is an altogether extraordinary read and not for the obvious reasons. There is, for instance, Christie's attitude to the police and race relations in the country. Following his televised anguish in the summer of 1995, there were some journalists – Richard Williams of *The Guardian* in particular – who felt that Christie had expressed the thoughts of a deeply wronged man – a man who had every reason to feel the weight of the white world's injustice to a black man. After all, when Christie had his first Mercedes was he not stopped and harassed by policemen who could not believe that a black man could drive around in such a car? Williams argued that the way Christie had been treated was abominable and that if the country could not find a place for him, one of its greatest ever sportsmen, then it did not deserve to have him.

Yet when it came to discussing the police in his autobiography, Christie does not describe the incident at all. His attitude to the police is that whatever problems he and his family might have once had, they have been long forgotten and were more due to a minority of bad policemen on the force. Most of the force were very good and Christie had long forgiven the people who had wronged him. 'I cannot sit back and dwell on those things because doing that will hamper my progress.'

However, in the very next passage he says that the younger police have lost touch with the community and longs for the good old days when a local policeman dealt with erring youngsters by giving them a clip round the ears rather than, as now, taking them to court and giving them a criminal record. The very next passage contains a general remark on race relations to which even the most right-wing person would subscribe: 'The problem with racism will always occur in any society where there are people of different creed and kind.' But Christie is comforted by the fact that with more than 60 per cent of the British athletic team black they are spreading the right message and uniting the country across the racial line. All this is very encouraging and comes early in the book (pages 36–37). But move on to page 163 and we are given this dismal conclusion about race relations: 'It is also very clear to me that racism, especially in Britain, has become institutionalised. That's how I honestly see it. I try to put myself in a position where it does not affect me too much but it's inevitable that we should have problems when more than one race or creed try and live together. In Britain racism is ingrained so cleverly that you can't do anything about it. If you are black and complain, the first thing they say is that you have a chip on your shoulder. There is no way round it. I know it exists; I know I am black. I don't have to go out and shout about it.'

Reading these two passages it is hard to resist the feeling that we are dealing with the experiences of two entirely different persons. But then to be fair to Christie the autobiography gives ample evidence of a man who does not know quite how to reconcile his very contradictory life.

In the early part of the book Christie dwells on his Jamaican background and presents what is almost a caricature colonial view of Britain – brought up to believe the streets were paved with gold etc. There are some sweet moments in this romanticised picture. His father, for instance, growing up in Jamaica, believed only black people went to jail and it was only when he came to England that he realised white people also went to jail. Christie describes how he was brought up to be always smart, disciplined, go to church, respect authorities and never leave home without a collar and tie – travelling for an indoor event against Germany at Dortmund, his first for Britain, he was shocked to see fellow athletes dressing in ripped-up jeans and dirty trainers. In his Jamaican school, when a teacher asked a question, the student was expected to raise his hand, stand and then answer. When Christie did that in his English school he was soon told to shut up and taunted as 'brain-box' by his fellow schoolmates. The overall picture Christie draws of his upbringing is of a man brought up to believe in John Major's Back to Basics philosophy. After pages of such moralising, it comes as a surprise to learn that his own life is almost a total repudiation of such values.

Christie makes no attempt to reconcile the glaring contradictions in his life. His attitude seems to be that the less he and others talk about this aspect of his life the better. He is so reticent about his personal life and it is dealt with so casually and confusingly that it is almost impossible to piece it together. After pages of a Back to Basics moralising we are told he has become a father, having made the friend of one of his sister's pregnant. But there is no mention of the girl's name. The next minute we are told of the great love of his life, the woman he now lives with. She is named and praised lavishly but we have to wait for another 200 pages to discover the name of the sister's friend he impregnated and the other woman who has borne his children. Even then the details are presented in such a fashion that the reader has to be quite a detective.

That Christie may not wish to highlight these relationships is understandable. An autobiography will naturally seek to present the person telling the story in the best possible light but the fact that he does not feel he had to explain why his life has not matched the Victorian values he would like all of us to follow suggests a man not at ease with himself. When such a man sees himself as a role model for youth the omission is quite staggering.

The context in which Christie mentions the names of the mothers of his illegitimate children is quite interesting. It comes in the middle of a rant against the press for highlighting his personal life. His is particularly annoyed that they come just about the time he is involved in major championships. Christie sees this as a form of disloyalty from the British press and contrasts it with the way the American press always supports their athletes. It would be reasonable to argue that the way *The Daily Mail* presented the articles – 'How Linford Christie put his family on the fast track to handouts from the Welfare State' – was inflammatory, highlighting the fact that his two illegitimate families were now receiving state handouts. But given Christie's high profile and his espousing of Victorian moral values it was a legitimate counterpoint. It raised the question, why does such a successful athlete, a role model for black and white kids, wail so much? And what does all his wailing amount to?

The most perceptive examination of this has come not in the mainstream press but by a black columnist in a black magazine. Writing in *Voice* magazine, just after Christie's television moan in the summer of 1995 – and in the same issue that dealt with the fallout from the Henderson article which merited front-page treatment – the columnist, Tony Sewell, put the whole Christie affair in a perspective that had clearly escaped everyone in the mainstream press. The article is worth examining in some detail. The headline on the front page of the weekly newspaper was 'Is Linford just a big girl's blouse?'. The headline on Sewell's piece read 'Quit the Whingeing'. The article that followed made it clear where this black columnist was coming from.

'It's summer. And with all its glorious sunshine you'd think it would be a time to be cheerful. Not for the very rich and privileged in our community – for the Black celebrities it's that time of year to start whingeing. And what makes it worse for me is that it's the brothers who are doing most of the moaning. It began with Christie's usual outcry about not enough money, not enough praise from the media and not enough worship for his sacrifice as Black role model. I have little sympathy for this and it lacks style. Linford Christie is no Martin Luther King; perhaps he needs to get a grip on the real meaning of his contribution. Sprinters are important but none feature in my top ten great Black Brits.

'What is worse about this whingeing is that years of bad politics have made us into "victim"-hoods instead of Robin Hoods. We need to get on the offensive and get a grip of our lives. But no one wants to listen to that message. They prefer to wallow in the bad news about Black people. This is encouraged by celebrities who are stinking rich and go on as if they were the first Black man on to the slave ship. In fact, if you want to be regarded as a super Black role model then you've got to have an above average whinge factor . . .'

Then after listing the black celebrities who go on whingeing, including Chris Eubank, who had been on the same television show as Christie and who acted as his cheerleader in a particularly obnoxious fashion, suggesting that the role of the press should be to behave as fawning camp followers of celebrity sportsmen, Sewell went on to say: 'These big babies are whingeing for the wrong reasons. Check them out! Are they complaining about the refugee problem in Rwanda? Are they pouring out their passions for people booted out of Britain? Many of them would stand up and tell you about the numerous charity functions they have given their blessings. However, their loudest whinge is not for these noble causes. It is for themselves . . . We whinge at the slightest trouble to fall our way. It is now the vogue talk about Black male oppression as if [it] were the latest perfume to come out of Paris. Yes, Black males get the rawest deal, but not at every count. Whingeing has to be a weapon that is used very sparingly or it loses its potency. You celeb guys make me ashamed to call me a "Black man". You'll be wearing high heels next – oh you are Carl Lewis.'

Sewell also made the significant point that compared to black men black women were much more mature: 'Black women on the whole have become much stronger in recent years. They have realised that whingeing expends vital energy which could be used in getting on with the task of getting ahead. This compared with the early days, when Black women used to be the biggest whingers in town. In those days confidence was low and the only way one could get a release from the madness of Britain was to get in a huddle and knock everything in sight – including each other . . . As I have said, she has moved from victim-hood to Robin Hood. Sadly, us guys are acting like silly girls, and we don't look good into the bargain.'

As it happened, just about the time Christie was whingeing, another black athlete, but a woman, was also in the wars. The athlete was Diana Modahl. Modahl shares with Christie a Jamaican ancestry – except Modahl was born in this country – and as a child she and her family always cheered Jamaican victories on the track. Like Christie there was a lot of Jamaica in her upbringing, but while Christie lays on the Victorian values with a trowel, Modahl's early story is more homely with many details about Jamaican cooking.

Where the two athletes have gone their different ways are the very contrasting manners in which they approached their athletic careers and the images they built up. Modahl, unlike Christie, was a dedicated athlete in her youth, so much so that she broke up with Derek Redmond, her first boyfriend, fearing it would interfere with her career, and until 24 August 1994, when it was revealed that she had failed a drugs test, she was the goody two-shoes of British athletics: girlish, devout, she organised prayer meetings in athletics villages and had an appealing, charming naïveté. Her husband, Vicente Modahl, wooed her by saying on their first encounter, 'You have such beautiful eyes, will you marry me?'

But then came the dramatic news from Victoria in Canada that Modahl was being sent home because she had failed a drugs test and suddenly Modahl, her world in tatters, joined Christie in believing that there was a conspiracy against her. Her autobiography, *Going the Distance*, spells out how the news shattered her world. The first 84 pages of her book, taking us to the fateful day, are blissful, the story of a girl who did good, worked hard and succeeded, complete with an almost gooey Barbara Cartland-style romance with a Norwegian. Then came her positive drugs test and her world fell apart.

Modahl has since worked hard to prove her innocence and succeeded. So much so that she has now come back as an athlete with her reputation restored. In the process she has indicated how fallible drugs tests can be.

This was demonstrated when BBC TV made a documentary showing how she proved her innocence and, perhaps even more conclusively, when she had a spread in *Hello* magazine in the sort of fawning article that magazine reserves for celebrity new mothers and their families. Modahl should have been pleased with *Hello*'s feature for it meant all her hard work, helped by Vicente and her heavyweight lawyers, who also advise Princess Diana, had succeeded. She had gone a long way to reinvent herself from the disgraced woman athlete of August 1994 to the martyr figure of today.

Yet, as her comments in *Hello* make clear and those in *Going the Distance* amplify, Modahl is bitter about the way she feels the athletics world and the press have treated her. Her grouse against the athletics bodies is understandable but that she should rail against the press – and this is where she becomes a Christie clone – is quite extraordinary. From the moment it emerged that Modahl had tested positive the press, certainly the sporting press, was unanimous that some dreadful mistake had been made. David Coleman was only one of the prominent journalists to spring to her defence.

I was then writing the Inside Track column for *The Sunday Times* and worked with Ian Chadband, the paper's athletics correspondent. Ian reported the confusion and anger of the British team and journalists in Victoria. As soon as it emerged that Modahl had been tested positive after what was, in effect, a practice race in Lisbon. The feeling that a mistake had been made grew to a grave suspicion that the Portuguese had cocked it up. You can't, ran the view, expect the Portuguese to get these things right. The doubts seemed to be confirmed when it was revealed that some weeks before anybody in Britain knew of the test results the Russians had heard rumours that a British athlete had tested positive. A Moscow paper had even printed the rumours.

The Russian connection was intriguing and made this a Britain versus nasty foreigners issue. After her Lisbon test, but before the results were known, Modahl had taken part in the Europa Cup where her victory helped Britain qualify ahead of Russia for the World Cup final. If Modahl were to be disqualified, so would Britain, and Russia would take her place.

Not long after this I got a call from a former *Sun* journalist who said he had heard from business contacts who often went to Portugal that soon after the Lisbon drugs test KGB men were seen in Lisbon. Needless to say I could not get to the bottom of the KGB story but by this time the Portuguese and the IAAF were more than a little dismayed by the mud being thrown at them in the British press. I was able to establish some of what had gone on in Lisbon and also reveal that Modahl's urine sample was found to contain testosterone/epitosterone equal to 42,08 value, more than three times that found in Ben Johnson.

Yet even when I revealed this story on the front page of *The Sunday Times* the belief was strong that it just could not be true. There was just no explanation as to how she could have had so much testosterone. After all, had not John Regis said Modahl was as an angel and angels do not take testosterone in any case not more than three times that of Ben Johnson.

Nobody in sport had ever been shown to have had so much testosterone and medical opinion was almost unanimous that the only explanation was that Modahl was ill. The following week the Modahl camp lent credence to such stories. A BBC journalist, Brendan Pittaway, who some months later made a powerful case for her defence in a radio programme, rang us at *The Sunday Times*. I had been joined by a colleague, Jonathan Rendall, on the story and Pittaway gave us to understand that we might be able to reveal the real reason as to why the tests showed such crazy figures. With Modahl in hospital undergoing tests for cancer, Pittaway rang Rendall and me saying she was almost certainly 'seriously ill' and hoped to give us confirmation. At one stage on the Saturday morning he seemed certain but he rang later that afternoon to say 'the lawyers have decided to put the lid' on the results of the test. This was just as well since the tests proved she did not have cancer. What she had were two minor conditions which might explain the levels of testosterone and details of these were leaked by Pittaway to another Sunday newspaper.

However, in her rant against the press Modahl ignores all this, or is not aware of it. She told *Hello*, 'It was very scary to read speculation in the newspapers that ovarian cancer might be the cause of such a high level of testosterone.' Scary, but a rumour emanating from her own camp.

Modahl's fashionable scapegoating of the press obscures the fact that her treatment by the athletics press was extremely favourable, almost heavenly compared to the way they dumped Paul Edwards who had also tested positive and had come back from Victoria on the same flight. For good measure Edwards, who was ill, came back on a stretcher with a blanket wrapped around him and looking very much like a criminal. Edwards was duly banned and although like Modahl he hired a law firm and even held a press conference to tell his story, he did not get anything like the press that Modahl did. Indeed, at his press conference, held at an expensive law firm, journalists were very sceptical of his story and could not wait to debunk it. He was seen as the bad boy without any redeeming qualities and although he has tried to clear his name it has been a fitful exercise which has gone virtually unnoticed.

This raises an interesting point. If this was indeed quite as much of an institutionalised racist country as Christie would have us believe, then Edwards, being white, would have had all the sympathy and Modahl none. In reality the reverse has been true, suggesting simplistic notions on race can be dangerous. So what explains the sort of angst Modahl and Christie have? What prompts their wail that they do not get fair treatment? Part of it is due to the natural and fashionable desire to blame the messenger for the contents of the message. The press may be useful and courted when the message is what you want to hear, but if the press should produce the wrong tunes they are held to be responsible, even if, as in Modahl's case, the press are merely relaying the notes provided by international bodies.

It is interesting to consider that such angst is not displayed by black rugby players. Here the attitudes of Jeremy Guscott or Victor Ubogu are particularly instructive. Guscott also has Jamaican ancestry but only on the paternal side, his father Henry having come here from Jamaica. If anything he has had a more troubled upbringing than either Christie or Modahl, having been thrown out of the house by his father when he was a teenager. He clearly does not get on with his father – his autobiography has a photograph of his mother but not of his father – yet there is little of the chippiness that Christie displays. He is even confident enough to publicise the name of his ghost-writer on the cover of his book and not pretend that he does not exist.

It could be said that this may reflect the fact that Guscott's game, rugby, is a middle-class one. But his background is hardly middle class: Henry is a hospital porter, although on his mother's side Guscott hails from Brits who helped found or at least maintain the empire. His great-grandfather formed the settlement on San Carlos in the Falklands and his mother, born in Madras, was part of the Raj. Stephen Jones, who wrote Guscott's biography, is convinced Guscott has no chips on his shoulder and also has a revealing story about Victor Ubogu. When England played the All Blacks, Shaun Fitzpatrick turned to Obogu and said, 'Right, black bastard, now show us what you can do.' Brian Moore, then writing for *The Sunday Times*, reported this to Jones, who is the paper's rugby correspondent. Jones was horrified. But Ubogu did not care and did not even want it reported. For Jones this seemed a sign of his incredibly relaxed attitude, one that he seems to share with his fellow Nigerian-born players such as Adebayo and Steve Ojomoh.

It is possible that there may be special factors at work here,. Like Guscott they play for Bath. Ubogu, Adebayo and Ojomoh even travel down in a limousine to Bath matches and Adebayo and Ojomoh, like Guscott, are West Country bred – Guscott born in Bath, Adebayo and Ojomoh brought up in Devon.

But there is something more than mere accident of birth or upbringing to explain why these rugby players are so different to Christie or Modahl. Unlike them they do not feel the need to advertise that they are English. They seem secure in their sport and their place in this society in the way Modahl and Christie are not. Modahl's wail as she sucessfullyfought the athletics bodies was: how could they do this to me after all I have done for my country? Christie has wrapped himself round the flag even more ostentatiously as if he fears if he does not it might be taken away from him. His book is replete with examples of his desire to wave the flag, literally and metaphorically, and how this has got him into trouble with the fussy athletics authorities. The apogee of this came in his television performance in the summer of 1995. Then he broadcast his patriotism with a fervour which had it been done by anyone else would have been considered offensively xenophobic but in Christie's case appeared eccentric.

According to Christie, British athletic officials had always looked askance when after his great triumphs he waved the Union Jack or even physically wrapped it round him. But, he asked, we are British, proud of it, why aren't they respectful of our feelings? Then he told a story his father had told him that no plane flying from the West Indies to England had ever crashed. The implication being that the West Indians coming to England were so fond of England and such was their love for this country, that no agency on earth, or the heavens, could stop them. What the significance of this story was he never explained but it seemed to underline the bewilderment of a man who had achieved so much but felt he did not belong.

We may never be able to understand Christie's angst but his raising of the patriotism issue does require us to look at the question Matthew Engel raised during the Henderson debate. Can we define a patriotism for a multi-cultural England with which all sportsmen and sportswomen and all sports lovers of whatever colour will be comfortable with?

CHAPTER TWELVE

Towards a New England

So how do we create a modern English sporting patriot?

At the height of the row about Robert Henderson's article on who should or should not play cricket for England, Matthew Engel wrote: 'This is a subject that goes far beyond sport. It ties in to our failure to make recent immigrants feel part of our society, to come up with a concept of British citizenship, something that has to involve both rights and responsibilities – and why any kind of patriotism in this country always seems to be either backward-looking or xenophobic . . . It is an issue that the Blair Government is going to have to address. Other countries manage it perfectly well. Migrants to Australia, of every race, are encouraged to become Australians – and are made aware of what that means – without losing touch with their individual natural heritage . . . International sport depends on its participants loving their country without hating anyone else's. If British sport is to succeed and, more important, British society is to succeed in the 21st century, then the notion of Britishness has got to be considered by serious thinkers, not left to polemicists and extremists from either side. John Major wanted to preside over a country at ease with itself. Alas, he has failed in that too, And this argument helps prove it.'

The argument Henderson raised was a phony one, yet the fact that Henderson was allowed to generate a debate shows that there is a real problem of inclusiveness. How can the English make people of different racial origins, who were once under their rule and to whom they taught games and often the values they know, be part of the family? And however curious Engel's treatment of Henderson's views might have been by posing the question in such a way he has presented a formidable challenge.

The challenge is formidable because the unease of the English sporting nation, perhaps even more than the political nation, is so manifest as to be palpable. The saloon bar view of the current state of English sport can probably be summed up as follows: 'Once we beat the world in everything. And why not? We had created these games and taught the foreigners how to play. Now we cannot win at cricket, football, rugby, you name it we are also rans. Yes, we hold wonderful tournaments. Cricketers from all over the world love to play at Lord's, but then they usually win there, same with footballers at Wembley, the rugby players at Twickenham, and if the tennis world and his wife looks forward to Wimbledon, even to get past the first round we have to make an Englishman of a Canadian. All right, so Frank Bruno wins a world boxing title, but these titles are not what they were. When Henry Cooper floored Muhammed Ali, or Cassius Clay, or whatever he called himself then, it meant something. Now everyone has a world heavyweight title.'

Not that the saloon bar analyst is anti-foreign or a sporting little Englander. What confuses him is that the wrong sort of foreigners are now beating England. If Australia were beating England in cricket, unwelcome as it would be, it could be said to be part of a historical process. After all, Australia won the first cricket Test and has more often than not beaten England. And if Scotland were to beat England in football or the All Blacks or Wales in rugby, that would be considered part of the traditional historical pattern of English sporting encounters. In any event all these countries – even the Australians and the New Zealanders – can be presented as part of the wider family originally hailing from good British stock. What is impossible to accept is defeat at the hands of Sri Lanka or Zimbabwe in cricket or by an African country in football. They are not foreigners whom the English sporting mind can easily accept as worthy opponents. It is when these countries defeat England that the man in the saloon bar, let alone the public bar, realises that the sporting empire has finally crumbled.

At this stage the pub analyst is apt to turn philosopher and his anger is directed at the players, for their insatiable appetite for money, and the administrators who are universally held to be doddery old fools or, in Will Carling's memorable phrase, 'boring old farts', capable of drinking vast quantities of pink gin but not much else. And however much Carling's view may be considered a caricature, in recent years sporting administrators have given the impression of rabbits caught in the glare of headlights, perpetually trying to perform an uncomfortable, if not impossible balancing act between players' demands and sponsors' needs; on the one hand trying to cope with claims for money from players and violence both on and off the field, and on the other, the high speed commercialism prompted by television moguls like Rupert Murdoch which is changing sport almost overnight and virtually making it an adjunct of television.

It is easy and tempting to say all will be well if we could go back to the ethos of amateurism, or the high moral purpose of *Tom Brown's Schooldays*. But, as we have seen, that supposedly high moral purpose was designed for an imperial race, meant to help them subjugate and administer blacks and browns who now not only claim equality but form part of the English sporting nation. In any case the image of the Victorian amateur has only been created with the help of a great deal of humbug, as W.G. Grace's cricket career shows. Grace railed against cricket following in football's footsteps and becoming a business, declaring; 'There is another thing I am afraid of: that is that cricket will be made too much of a business like football.' Yet he turned down a tour of Australia because he could not get £1,500 plus expenses. When he went on one in 1891 he received £3,000 plus all his expenses including the cost of a locum and an allowance for his wife and daughter who went with him. His first benefit raised £1,458, a marble clock and two bronze ornaments – not bad value in 1879 for a man supposedly an amateur. His second benefit four years later fetched £9,073.8s.3d, a very generous sum for the times.

W.G. Grace was hardly the first Victorian to be a bit of a hypocrite and recent research on Henry Newbolt, the man who gave us 'play up and play the game' – marrying valour in cricket with valour on the battlefield – shows that Newbolt's private life hardly mirrored the noble image he sought to promote. He had secret affairs with lesbian women and shrank from fighting in the First World War.

So if the Victorian past does not work, can the Australian present provide a guide? Engel would like us to take a leaf from Australia. But it is difficult for a polyglot, multi-cultural country to seek a common sporting identity. Australia, despite several decades of trying to forge a sporting nationalism, has not been entirely successful.

Australia's early sporting nationalism was built on the idea of racial identification with Britain. Britain of the south, earthy good old stock, John Bull junior showing John Bull senior how well it had learned the games created by John Bull senior were phrases that greeted Australia's initial sporting success. In 1877, after Australia had beaten England in Melbourne in the first-ever cricket Test, the *Australasian* wrote: 'The victory of the Australian Eleven over the English cricketers is no ordinary triumph. For the first time a team representing the cricketing prowess of England has been beaten on equal terms out of that country. The event marks the great improvement which has taken place in Australian cricket, and shows, also, that in bone as well as muscle, activity, athletic vigour, and success in field sports, the Englishmen born in Australia do not fall short of Englishmen born in Surrey or Yorkshire.'

Later that year as plans were made for the first-ever visit by an Australian team to England, the *Australasian* wrote: 'They wish to show John Bull that we can play cricket here as well as the old folk at home can. They are proud of their skill, as they ought to be, and wish to prove at Lord's and the Oval and other grounds in England that the colonials are worthy descendants of the good old stock from which they have come.'

Even as recently as the 1950s Australia identified with England and saw English visits in a wonderful filial glow. In *Elusive Victory*, the story of the MCC visit to Australia in 1950–51, E.W. Swanton described how Australia sympathised with Freddie Brown's team so strongly that Swanton was embarrassed by it. 'As to popular sympathy for the English team among Australians that was always strongly and often embarrassingly in evidence, particularly during the first three Tests. The climax of the feeling came at Melbourne, as it had done four years earlier. I had never known a crowd so generous to the enemy as that which watched the New Year Test at Melbourne on Hammond's tour (in 1946–47). In this second Test of 1950–51, over the Christmas holidays, there seemed hardly anyone among the fifty thousand present who was prepared to countenance any other result than a win for England. Indeed, I never expected to see again such a reaction to the ending of a Test match, least of all one that has been fought through with such even tenseness, to so close a conclusion. When the last England wicket fell the crowd just melted silently and sadly away while the victors, who had bowled and fielded more admirably to pull the game out of the fire stole quietly back to their dressing-room.' It was a wonderful image of John Bull junior weeping that it had defeated John Bull senior by 28 runs in a match which England had often dominated.

Australia has changed a lot since then. If Swanton on the 1950–51 tour was embarrassed by the warmth Australians felt for England, then by 1979 there had been such a revolution in Australian sentiments that I was astounded by the anti-English feeling, manifest even when England were not playing Australia.

It was the first season since the Packer peace, the inauguration of the now familiar Australian triangular World Series one-day matches, and England were playing the West Indies. In the English summer West Indies had retained the World Cup – at that stage the West Indies were considered supreme one-day players. After two World Cups they had yet to lose a single game, but had not yet won a Test series in Australia. England were expected to lose but in this opening match, with the final ball to be bowled they were in with a chance of a remarkable victory. The West Indians required three runs to win. Brearley – and those were the days before fielding restrictions and circles – sent everyone to the boundary, including the wicketkeeper, and the West Indies failed to get the runs they needed.

The Australians were aghast. During the match I had seen how the young Australians had mobbed the West Indian players, while generally ignoring the English, but tangible evidence that warmth had turned to something like real distaste came the next day. Then the papers made it very clear they saw this English victory as betrayal. And one Sydney afternoon paper even ran the headline 'Poms Sabotage the Series', criticising Brearley's field placing as unsporting and reflecting the Australian anger that England had defeated the West Indies. The Australians wanted a final between Australia and the West Indies, and, thwarted in this and by the fact that Lord's would not stake the Ashes for the Test series, they spent much of the Australian summer baiting Brearley, taking their cue from the Iranian hostage crisis. At that time, Ayatollah Khomeini's Iran held the staff of the American Embassy in Teheran as hostages which led to the popular American slogan, 'Free our people'. A popular Australian cricketing chant directed at Brearley – who, like Khomeini, had a beard then – was: 'Free the Ashes'.

The change in feelings towards England is perhaps natural given the way the children of immigrants from Southern and Eastern Europe and now Asia are beginning to emerge in Australian sport. While their presence is less evident in cricket (the only major East European-origin cricketer to emerge had to change his name from Durtanovich to Pascoe to make the grade) it is quite obvious in other sports such as soccer and hockey. In hockey the migration of Anglo-Indians has clearly raised Australia's hockey stock. As John Bull senior's sporting prestige wanes, so sports like basketball are becoming more prominent, indicating the influence of America. All this can only be accelerated as Australia moves towards a republic and begins to think of itself as an Asian-Pacific nation rather than the John Bull of the southern hemisphere. England can hardly reinvent itself like Australia in order to find an acceptable sporting patriotism and the difficulty is increased because while Australia is a country built on immigration, England is a country which is horrified by the very word. It is only in the last few years that it has even begun to accept, but with grave reluctance and some unease, that is has become a multi-cultural country. The different racial groups who now live here have very different historical traditions, some of them quite opposed to each other. The creation of the empire, not to say its ending, is little understood even by historians and can generate very different emotions in the various peoples who make up this island. In trying to marry such diverse cultures, you can get an awful lot of confusion.

Take the contrasting positions of Clive Lloyd and Bryan Gould.

It would be nice to think that Clive Lloyd is the sporting equivalent of the former Labour MP Bryan Gould. A New Zealander by birth, Gould was so readily accepted that he even stood for the Labour leadership but then, disillusioned by politics, returned to his native New Zealand. As a front-ranking leader in England, his New Zealand birth was little known in this country, let alone held against him. Perhaps it helped that he was middle class, hardly had a trace of an accent and was, of course, white.

Superficially Clive Lloyd has been treated just as well. In Lancashire cricket, where he sits on the committee, he is seen as a Lancastrian, he is also on the Sports Council and both Labour and Conservative parties have courted him as a possible candidate. Not many years ago, *The Guardian* featured him in a television advertisement in a bid to attract new readers. However, when he goes abroad he becomes a West Indian – he is now the West Indian manager and the match referee in the recent South Africa-England Test series. His West Indian teams, the most successful in the history of the game, are treated with great disdain and Lloyd remains for many people in this country the great enemy. He is seen as the man who by introducing four big, black fast bowlers ruined cricket and did his best to destroy this wonderful English game.

The very contrasting ways Gould and Lloyd have been treated by the political and sporting establishments may not entirely be a matter of race but, clearly, the fact that Lloyd is a black West Indian and Gould a white New Zealander who can trace his ancestry back to this country, in a way Lloyd cannot, must be a factor. If Engel's challenge is to be successfully met then we must somehow create a concept of Britishness which means the Clive Lloyd in sports is regarded in much the same fashion as Bryan Gould was in politics, his colour and origin making no difference to his status.

The problem in defining a patriotism is that you almost by definition need a new enemy. This is not a peculiar English problem. Poets and romantics of all lands may speak of their love for their country but in all countries love of one's country somewhere, somehow postulates hate for some other people or land. Patriotism, it has been said, is an inclusion strategy which must mean there is an outsider who has to be excluded. The story of English patriotism is full of such exclusions, the outsiders ranging from the Roman Church dating from Henry VIII's fallout with the Pope – Rome is still very much the enemy in Northern Ireland – to the constant and bitter disputes with France. Then, once Britain became an imperial power, millions ruled by Britain easily became the others. And now that the empire is no more the other has become the European Union. At various times others have also included the Scots, as for instance when John Wilkes was defining his brand of English patriotism, just after the Seven Years War.

As Linda Colley has described so masterfully in her *Britons: Forging a Nation 1707–1837*, until the Seven Years War and the Treaty of Paris in 11763, Britons saw themselves as pre-eminently a Protestant nation with Britain as a polity built on commerce, and as the land of liberty founded on Protestantism and commerce. Although even before the Seven Years War there was an extensive empire it was largely seen as a trading empire, a beneficent creation of a liberty-loving and commercial people and quite different to the Roman and Spanish empires, which were built on blood and conquest. The spoils of the Seven Years War made such assumptions untenable and made many intellectuals ponder: what made an English patriot?

Edmund Burke wondered how a strong presiding power, so necessary in maintaining a vast disconnected and infinitely diversified empire, could be compatible with traditional British liberties, and within a year of the Treaty being signed Edward Gibbon, mediating on the issue, decided to write *The Decline and Fall of the Roman Empire* as a lesson for the British. Engel would like to see a patriotism that offends no one, which may be by definition impossible, and has contrasted the patriotism of Michael Slater, who kissed the Australian badge on his helmet when he scored a hundred at Lord's, with the way, say, a Hick or a De Freitas would behave. 'It is hard, no, impossible to imagine either Graeme Hick or Phil De Freitas doing the same' – a lament that echoes the feelings of Linford Christie, who on coming here from Jamaica realised with horror that schoolchildren were not asked to recite the national anthem every day. But then such public displays would go against the grain of English character. The fact is that while Slater could with a single gesture define his Autralian-ness, the English find it impossible to define what being English means. In any case defining Englishness by reciting the national anthem may mean being anti-Scottish as was demonstrated during Euro '96. When England played Scotland, the English sang the national anthem and booed the Scottish Flower of Scotland anthem.

The week after Engel raised the question Ian Jack, also provoked by Henderson, went around asking people what they felt constituted Englishness. 'Nearly everybody had trouble with the idea of England.

Nobody mentioned Drake or Shakespeare or Nelson or the picture of Westminster on the HP sauce bottle.' So elusive was Englishness that Jack found it almost impossible to devise a satisfactory test to prove a person was English. He tried to set a series of questions: to be English do you have to like roast beef, be a master of English prose style, name every battleship that fought under the White Ensign in Jutland and live in England?

Jack could easily find a person like that but the problem was that while the person could answer yes to all those questions, and many more besides, not many would consider him unequivocally English, to use Henderson's wretched phrase. And the person's own Englishness might be equivocal. The person Jack had in mind was Nirad Chaudhuri, the 97-year-old Bengali-born author living in Oxford.

The fact is the English today have a problem defining Englishness. Look back on the definition of Englishness at the height of the empire and, as Naipaul has said, it comes across as a country striking an attitude, people at play, defining themselves in terms of how they should behave. Stiff upper lip, impeccable manners, fair and upright, always dressing for dinner. Now that the empire has gone this has been transformed, as John Casey says into a version of middle-class patriotism. 'It fervently supports the British boys and girls doomed to fail at Wimbledon and gamely but sadly acknowledges the prowess of Australian and West Indian cricketers when they triumph over England. Gardening, visits to the country houses and a lump in the throat at Spitfire flypasts go with this sort of patriotism.'

But, as Casey acknowledges, against this must be set the patriotism of the working class 'who mix it with jingoism and – yes – xenophobia. This country does indeed have a history of popular dislike of foreigners'. It led during the Napoleonic wars to a monkey that had been washed up from a wrecked ship at Hartlepool being hanged as a dangerous Frenchman. 'That,' says Casey, 'is what I call xenophobia.' And it can lead to curious results. So while other countries honour their flag the English flag is most often seen on the T-shirts and underpants of football hooligans.

There is an English patriotic streak which can avoid hating others. Alexander Pope expressed it best in 'Windsor Forest':

> O stretch thy reign, fair peace! from shore to shore
> Till conquest cease. and slav'ry be no more;
> Till the freed Indians in their native groves
> Reap their own fruits, and woo their sable lovers.

But it rarely went beyond the poetic imagination and with the empire gone the English seek other enemies to hate like the European Union. Alongside this hatred is an angst that while the other nations, even those who are part of the United Kingdom like the Scots, the Welsh and the Irish, celebrate their nationalism and their national days, the English do not seem to be able to do so without a mixture of boorish jingoism and xenophobia. St George may be the English patron saint but the flag and the symbolism has also been appropriated by the facists making many English uncomfortable with too close an identification with the day. It is now fashionable among some English to wail that they are the only people who do not seem to have nationalistic symbols. But they fail to realise that when flag-waving nationalism became fashionable in the 18th century the English lorded over the world and did not need to assert their identity. The peoples and countries ruled by the English struggled to define their nationalism against this overwhelming English power and were fearful that if they did not create meaningful symbols they would be suffocated by the English.

Could a possible answer lie in America?? The racial situation in America may be much worse than in this country but in sports there is no dearth of black American heroes, led by such stars as Michael Jordan and Magic Johnson. Despite the fractured nature of American society and its deep racial scars, these stars symbolise the nation and the American belief that sports can create a colour-blind society.

This is despite the somewhat depressing story of O.J. Simpson which suggests that while a black sports star could become a hero, if he falls he could polarise society widening the racial divide. Before 12 June 1994, Simpson was acclaimed by all sections of American society, more so perhaps by the whites, as his affectionate nickname of 'Juice' testified. Here was a sportsman of the highest class and pedigree whose life off the field matched his achievements on it. He had married a beautiful white woman, lived in Beverly Hills and played golf with the good and the great of American society including the President. Then came his wife's horrific killing, he was charged with murder and society polarised. Before the murder blacks might have felt he mixed a bit too much with whites, but once he was arrested they saw him as their champion while most whites had no doubt that he was a murderer.

As the trial progressed and Simpson used expensive legal help to save himself, most whites saw him as another celebrity who had the money to get the sort of justice denied to ordinary folk. When the largely black jury, after almost a year of court hearings, took only four hours to pronounce him innocent, the divide in society was clear to see: the blacks cheered, the whites gasped in disbelief. Yet despite his fall from grace, the American dream of sport promoting a colour-blind society lives on.

Here it is interesting to note the very different way English society has viewed Frank Bruno. Bruno has always been held in great affection in this country, at times rivalling the feeling Simpson used to generate in America before 12 June 1994, but these feelings for Bruno rise from a very different well. Where O.J.'s status as the All-American boy derived from his sporting prowess, Bruno has become famous not so much because of his sporting ability but in spite of it. Even those who were convinced Simpson had killed his wife cannot deny his sporting feats. In Bruno's case he has never been able to discard the tag of the manufactured boxer. His efforts to win a world title have been one long hard slog and if he was always assured of the public's affection it was not so much because his boxing impressed, let alone enthralled audiences, but because in defeat he always gave his all and conformed to that most reassuring of all English sporting images: the gallant loser.

Although he finally won a title, the affection for him is due to his ability to play the comic, the know what I mean 'Arry role, rather than awe at his natural sporting ability. Simpson advertised Hertz cars, which played on his fantastic ability to run, Bruno advertises HP sauce as a sort of comic relief. In this role he is accepted by everyone and the fact that he has a white wife – but then she comes across as a dependableworking-class white girl – helps rather than hinders.

The one good thing for Bruno is that, never having been raised to the heights that O.J. was before June 1994, should he err and fall it might not lead to the angst that Simpson's fall produced in America. The contrast between Simpson and Bruno also shows the very different ways the English and the Americans treat sport. Unlike Americans, the English, for all their love of sport, do not take it quite as seriously. Nor do they see it as a metaphor for life.

What, you ask, not even cricket? True, the game strikes a chord in a way that no other game does. And while it may be an exaggeration to say, as Neville Cardus did, that if everything in English life was destroyed it could all still be recreated provided a copy of the laws of cricket survived, the cosy images that many English have of their country – which can sometimes be a definition of Englishness – nearly all derive from village cricket. George Orwell summed it up when he described cricket as a game where 'the blacksmith is liable to be called away in mid-innings on an urgent job, and sometimes about the time when the light begins to fail, a ball driven for four kills a rabbit on the boundary'.

Cricket also has the power to produce imagery that can often be used to reflect national moods. During the war, as Italy fell but Germany was yet to be beaten, an MP got up in the House of Commons to declare: 'We have got Ponsford, now we have to get Bradman' – a reference to the prolific pre-war Australian batting partnership that so plagued the English.

In recent years, even as the English cricket world has agonised over the state of the game, buffeted by defeats at the hands of almost all countries including the minnows Zimbabwe, politicians have taken to invoking the game as if the very mention of cricket could define national values. John Major has used the imagery of cricket to describe the type of country he wishes to recreate and images of cricket figured prominently in both the recent Conservative leadership elections.

In 1990, when the Conservatives removed Mrs Thatcher, the seminal speech by Sir Geoffrey Howe that spelled her doom spoke of Mrs Thatcher being the sort of captain who broke her own opener's bat before they went out to the crease. The 1995 contest between John Major and John Redwood saw the Redwoods' campaign constantly pictured against a cricketing backdrop. He was urged to stand while he was at Lord's watching England play the West Indies and on the Sunday, barely 24 hours before he made his crucial announcement, he kept the journalists crowding round his house at bay while he finished playing his village cricket match. In the style which every cricketing wife would have recognised, and mimicking the TV series *Outside Edge*, Mrs Redwood served the waiting journalists tea and biscuits.

Even Michael Portillo, who was not a candidate but allowed his 'friends' to arrange an office which was his putative campaign headquarters, was forced to show his devotion to the game. Reacting to unfavourable comparison with Redwood's courage in opposing Major and comments that as a person of Spanish origin he did not identify with cricket and would probably be more at home in a bullring, he immediately had himself pictured at a cricket match. Unfortunately for him it rained.

But while these images are powerful, cricket is not quite as integral to English life as baseball is to Americans. No English prime minister would dare start an English season by bowling the first ball whereas American presidents have traditionally opened the baseball season by throwing the first pitch. In that sense the Americans are closer to C.L.R. James's Greeks. They see sport as part of the entertainment industry but also as a metaphor for life. In England there is fierce resistance to the idea that sportsmen are high-class entertainers who should be paid a lot of money and for all the soft-focus, nostalgic visions of countryside and village green cricket, the game is not seen as a metaphor for an English dream. To understand this consider two films, David Putnam's *Chariots of Fire* and Kevin Costner's *Field of Dreams*. There can be little doubt that *Chariots of Fire* is by far the superior film but although it is a wonderful recreation of sporting history it does not go beyond the story of Liddell and Abraham. Yes, Putnam raises questions of class, religion, race and gentlemen and players, but the film is not a metaphor for English life, rather a slice of 1920s England. On the other hand, Costner's *Field of Dreams* tells us how Americans fantasise about their future. A farmer on his uppers in the Midwest suddenly has a vision and converts his farm into a baseball field. In the process many of his problems vanish, he reconnects his life and rediscovers the American dream. Also, through a sort of magical process historic baseball wrongs are righted. Baseball heroes who through some misfortune or other never really got their due share of glory reappear and get another chance. Supervising all of this is the farmer's guru: a black professor who has been shunned by everyone – a symbol of the historic black exclusion from American society – but who proves an inspirational guide to the farmer. The film ends with a long line of snaking car-lights making their way to this recreated American dream. America, it proclaims, has found itself on the baseball diamond created on someone's field. It is very corny, very Hollywood, but it expresses the way Americans see sports. And despite the fact that the racial situation in America is much worse than in this country, such a view of sports does allow Americans to come together because both white and blacks see sport as a symbol.

The story of basketball and the black myth of basketball as jazz is just as instructive. Originally invented as a white man's game, a game of Scottish Calvinist inspiration at a college for Presbyterian missionaries in Springfield, Massachusetts, it was a winter sport, an indoor game, and the game's inventor, Reverend James Naismith, did not believe in playing to win. But now played by its great black stars it is more of an urban game and one American writer has seen it as a vehicle which helps us enter the mythic world of black experience. 'The game is corporate black life; improvisatory like black life, formal, yet casual; swift and defiant; held back, contained, and then exploding full of leaps and breakaway fluid spirits.'

To English ears this may sound like a gift for *Private Eye's* 'Pseuds Corner' but it underlines that the Americans take sport seriously in a way the English do not and cannot. Cricket may feature as a symbol during election contests but there is an element of jest and fun in the way the English portray it, with some of the jokes, like the game itself, very in-jokes which only the English understand. This explains why, despite all the millions of words written about cricket and other sports, sportswriters are never allowed into the mainstream of English literary life. There is no English equivalent of Ring Lardner, who started as a baseball writer and became a famous short story writer, or James Scotty Reston, who graduated from sports journalism to become a famous political columnist. The only modern journalist to make such a transition in this country has been Brian James. Bernard Malamud could write a novel based on baseball and Norman Mailer is only one of many American novelists who are proud of their writings on sport. *The New York Review of Books* regularly carries lengthy articles on baseball written by Stephen Jay Gould, who is a world-renowned palaeontologist by trade and spends his professional time studying life's uninterrupted 3.5 billion-year history on earth.

Against this all we have to offer is Brian Glanville. He is a considerable novelist in his own right but has had reason to complain that for all his literary achievements he is more famous for his football writing than for his novels. Albert Camus could pontificate about being a goalkeeper and not lose his right to be considered a serious novelist; Brian Glanville may write the most compelling novel but still not be taken seriously as a writer. In recent years some other prominent novelists have taken to writing about sports, most notably football, but they see it as a diversion. They appear to enjoy the thrill of posturing, even preaching their own brand of nihilism, with some of them thinking it is a bit of fun to write in praise of Eric Cantona's behaviour at Selhurst Park. For them it is all a joke, a laugh, a giggle – anything goes.

All this does is open the door for enemies of sport like Neil Lyndon who, writing in *The Spectator* on 29 April 1995, drew a horrific picture of the country's infatuation with sport. He had calculated that in 1993–94 the BBC had carried 1,387 hours of sport, an average of more than three hours 48 minutes every day of the year. Lyndon asked: 'What are the wider consequences of so much attention being concentrated on sport by so many people and by so much of the communications media? What does it do to a people and a culture to fixate with games? . . . [it] expresses the general *zeitgeist* of this generation of men for whom sport is appealing chiefly because it is neutral, uncontentious, morally uncomplicated, a political black hole. It is without any dimension of ethical or ideological interest. It never gets old because heroes of sport are always young. It is also sexually obvious which may be why so few women are taken with sport and why it is reassuring to the sexually uncertain . . . What might be called the haute bourgeois culture had evidently had its chips. Does anybody today seriously hope, as Keynes used to hope, that all people and all human consciousness might be elevated and ennobled if everybody equally received the benefits of high art?'

C.L.R. James would have an easy answer to Lyndon: go back to the ancient Greeks and learn how sport is integral to their life and how they turned out mighty philosophers and thinkers which shaped Western thinking while devoting a good deal of their time to sports. However, the answer to Lyndon's lament that the Keynes idea of high art ennobling life is no longer accepted is that it was a 19th-century idea which was one of the casualties of the First World War. The literary and cultural critic Paul Fussell, in his book *The Great War and Modern Memory*, observed that the First World War established irony as the dominant mode of British literature and experience, overturning the 19th-century belief in inevitable progress. In poetry it has meant a tradition from Thomas Hardy to Philip Larkin, in novel from Evelyn Waugh to Martin Amis, and on television comedy it has established ironic icons such as Tony Hancock, Wilfred Brambell as Steptoe, Warren Mitchell as Alf Garnett, John Cleese as Basil Fawlty and Richard Wilson as Victor Meldrew, men who are misunderstood and use sarcasm as their natural turn of speech. Basil Fawlty or Victor Meldrew could never see anything as high art without trying to mock it.

This blends in easily with the English desire for self-deprecation and a wish to make even complex issues cosy and comfortable. So during the Second World War the Defence of the Realm Act becomes DORA and a five-year tax-exempt saving plan becomes TESSA. Cosiness can stretch to such an extent that recently there have been advertisements by Prudential, the giant insurance company, saying: 'Now that you have had TESSA for five years, why not try Prudence?'

There is also in certain sporting circles an element of sporting self-hatred matching the political self-hatred that George Orwell identified in pre-war left-wing circles. In pre-war politics it meant often taking the sides of almost anyone who disagreed with the establishment view in this country, in sport it can mean always accepting that any team from a Latin country will have more flair than an English soccer team or any cricket team from the sub-continent more naturally wristy players than their English counterparts. To try and smooth all these elements into one sporting patriotism, where the sporting nation could be at ease with itself, seems an almost impossible task.

Yet a start must be made. The starting point must be some attempt to educate our press, and particularly our tabloid press, not to treat every sporting contest as a national battle of wills. The tabloid treatment of England's matches with Spain and Germany during Euro '96 is the latest example of such an attitude. They can, of course, claim to be following established history. The war had barely ended when, in the winter of 1945, the Moscow Dynamo team visited this country and led George Orwell to conclude that sporting contests, far from generating goodwill, can often increase bad feeling. The Russians upset their British hosts by seeking neutral referees and also claiming that the Arsenal team that faced them was really an English team when the English claimed it was a league side. Interestingly,

The News Chronicle, then strongly pro-Russian politically, was most bitter about the Russians on the sports pages, leading Orwell to comment that 'sport is an unfailing cause of ill-will'.

Orwell's warnings have been borne out very amply since then, but in recent years a more worrying trend has emerged. The English tabloid press, and even some broadsheet newspapers, seem to go out of their way to denigrate all foreign sporting countries. The World Cup draw saw some of the home countries pitted against Moldovia and other outposts of the former Soviet empire. *The Daily Mirror* ran a column of postcards from these countries. But instead of witty, warm, even affectionate, pieces they were uniformly hostile. *The Mirror* had gone to players who had visited these countries and obviously hated the experience. These players warned how awful the countries were and how terrible it would be to play there.

Now if these were countries Britain was at war with one could understand such coverage. This was a prelude to a sporting contest meant to generate goodwill, yet here was a national newspaper, months before the games were due to take place, painting the most unattractive, bleak picture of these lands. One reason could be it made good copy, another that it fed English distrust of the foreigner. It could also be that underneath the hatred there is a strong sense of resentment, a bitter and rancid feeling of loss that this country, which once created all these games and gave them to the world, no longer rules the world of sports. If that is the case then it seems that the English sporting world which once suffered from a sense of superiority is now burdened with a terrible weight of inferiority.

It would help if we could acknowledge that while England created the games the world plays it did not popularise them. Indeed, the English were surprised that others took them up and at times it seems the English have never recovered from the fact that foreigners aspire to play games invented by the English. Individual Englishmen may have spread the game, English sporting institutions did little to spread the nation's sporting culture. Football became a world game not because of the FA but because of FIFA, more so in recent years when FIFA has taken the game to Africa and other continents.

In cricket, until the 1980s the English, in the shape of the MCC, ran international cricket with the President of the MCC also President of the International Cricket Conference. And how well did the MCC spread cricket? In more than 100 years of international cricket only seven countries gained Test status, the seventh being Pakistan because it was created as a breakaway new country from an existing Test country, India. In the last ten years two more have joined and it is only now, with an independent ICC, free of the MCC, that efforts are being made to bring other countries into the game. The United Arab Emirates participation in the World Cup is almost classic. This is a team of Indians and Pakistanis playing in the desert. However, unlike the colonies created by the English, these Indians and Pakistanis in the desert do not rule the place, they merely work there. They are similar to the many expat Englishmen who have lived in places like Argentina or even America. Yet the cricket played by such expat Englishmen, although it has led to many MCC visits to these countries, has not produced a team that can play in the World Cup. No team has emerged from their ranks to challenge the world. Now, in less than 20 years, a team has come from the desert and plays well enough to take part in the World Cup. Of course this has meant enlarging the World Cup, perhaps adding matches that may not quite be as testing as the ones in previous World Cups. True, there may have been ulterior motives in increasing the size of the competition but how else do you spread the game, how do you reach out to parts of the world the game has never reached?

Yet the English reaction to this has been to mock it. Are the preliminaries to the World Cup not a farce, asked Gary Lineker on the Sunday that the Indians held the opening ceremony. Yes, agreed the BBC reporter in Calcutta in a resigned voice, suggesting it was the sort of thing that one had to now put up with. But mock it as they might, the fact is that these workers from the sub-continent, some of them of peasant background, often illiterate, have done more to spread the game than their much more sophisticated English cricketing colleagues.

They have been able to do so because, unlike the English, they are not burdened with inventing the games or snared in an impossible dichotomy, a problem that was well expressed by H.R. James, Principal of Calcutta's Presidency College in the early part of this century, when lecturing his Indian students. He warned them that while they could be Indian patriots they should not be anti-English. 'One thing that patriotism in Bengal should not do is to direct the national spirit into an attitude of hostility to British rule. There would be something I should call patricidal in such an attitude.' Given that India was then ruled by Britain, and that an Indian patriot would have to demand British withdrawal, it was an almost impossible condition. It was like a father claiming the right of parenthood over the child but denying the child any rights over him.

But the Raj saw no dichotomy and high Raj officials often described their Indian collaborators – and there were many of them – as men of 'wide citizenship', praising them for choosing what they called the 'hard road' of collaboration. The reality was that if anybody chose the hard road it was the nationalists who suffered imprisonment while the collaborators' 'hard road' also meant high salary and all the privileges that went with serving under the British. The absurdity of the Raj position can be seen if we note that nobody would liken those who served Vichy France during the Second World War as having taken any hard road in collaborating with the Nazis. As we have seen, it was this inability to square the promise of political citizenship with the diametrically opposed reality on the ground that contributed to the fall of the Raj.

Perhaps I am asking too much of sportsmen and sports administrators to understand all this. After all, eminent historians of the British Empire do not seem to want to tackle the subject. Look at an article in the February 1996 issue of *History Today* by Professor Max Beloff, Emeritus Professor of Government and Political Administration at Oxford. This looks ahead to a new *Oxford History of the British Empire*. Beloff's article is described as second thoughts and a provocative assessment of the achievements of the Empire but it proves dull, boring and predictable and, what is more, Beloff nowhere considers the central dilemma so succinctly presented by Chaudhuri: why did the British confer subjecthood but withhold citizenship, the central rock on which the Empire ultimately floundered. If Emeritus Professors at Oxford cannot even being to consider this question, and instead revisit old, tired arguments and present them as provocative second thoughts, then it is too much to ask humble sports people to be radically adventurous.

In any case some of the argument is academic as the English cannot turn the clock back and can do little to remedy their failure to spread their own sporting inventions. It would not be in their nature to suddenly become sporting evangelists and it would do little good now. But it is still not too late to send signals that might help convince us, if not the wider world, that English sport can develop an international outlook. Some of the gestures could be very simple but very effective. For instance, the FA when seeking a new chairman could have appointed Bobby Charlton. Wouldn't that be much better than ignoring him, as happened with Bobby Moore? Even two weeks before his death he was just another ex-player, often seen sitting at the back of the stands in some press box commentating for radio on a game. It was only after his death, news of which coincided with the dreadful murder of a little child by two Liverpool boys, that his deeds were remembered. Then much attention was focused on his gesture of wiping his hands before he shook the Queen's on that memorable afternoon when England won the World Cup. That mark of respect and thoughtfulness by Moore, in contrast to the shocking scenes from Liverpool, was seen as the measure of England's decline and fall. Moore was almost canonised as representing a different, nobler Britain. Yet the nation waited until his death to bestow such glory on

237

one of its greatest sporting sons. Surely something can be done while these people are still alive?

It need not be more than in a symbolic capacity but it will send a message to the world at large that sportsmen who represent all that is best in this country's sports are part of the administration of the game. It is a supreme irony that Charlton is often used by foreign countries such as Japan to help in their bid for the World Cup but is without any similar recognition in his own land. It is nothing short of scandalous that Charlton is not even a FA councillor, and it is part of the English sporting tragedy that he is unlikely to come anywhere near Lancaster Gate.

The Brazilians understand the need for such human sporting symbols well enough as witnessed by their use of Pele as their ambassador. The fact that Pele represents Brazilian sport does not cure all its problems, but the message it sends about Brazil is powerful and beneficial. A similar message needs to be sent and the goodwill generated can be used to try and lay the first bricks of a sporting nation which, as Engel says, is at ease with itself, which appreciates what its ancestors created, accepts that people from all over the world have not only taken up this nation's creations but may outperform the children of the founders, and learns to compete without hating. It is a big task but it needs to be begun now.

If this is not attempted then we, once the others but now part of this country, who were first drawn to the glow of the wondrous English sporting world will always be like children peering at the shuttered door of the confectionery shop. And we will have to echo Ian Jack's view that the English operate a club into which nobody can gain admittance: 'The English were then a magical race; you couldn't buy, speak, write or bribe your way into membership, because the members could never quite define what the qualifications for membership were other than being a member already.'

If that is indeed the case then the English have become like the ancient Hindus and how ironic it would be if I and people like me had travelled all this way only to find that we were back in our old, discarded world. Perhaps it would serve us right for making the journey in the first place. But then I had no choice. Who could have resisted that photograph in *The Times of India* of Ron Hendry holding the championship trophy and Peter Baker the FA Cup as Tottenham's double team made its way through North London? I certainly couldn't.

POSTSCRIPT

As I write, the trails of sporting and national glory produced by Euro 96 have been more than wiped out by the sense of misery generated by the failure in Atlanta. Sandwiched in between, has been the decision by a London jury, that Imran Khan did not libel Ian Botham.

All these events may appear unrelated, but there is a common, underlying theme of sporting nationalism, and the English reaction to them reveals a nation as confused as ever about its sporting identity. The failure at Atlanta produced the most nationalistic response, equating sporting failure with national failure. As the medal table showing Britain just ahead of Kazakhstan and way behind even Cuba, Turkey and Greece flashed on the screen, the question was: Okay, we accept we are not as good as the USA or Russia, or even France, but beaten by *Cuba*, what has gone wrong?

There were the usual calls for more government action, more demands for money, but little or no acknowledgement that British sport these days is actually quite well funded, with a lot more soon to be available – at the rate of £300m a year – when lottery money starts coming through. In any case, every Olympics leads to a post-mortem resulting in a committee or sports body being set up to try and produce excellence. Few bothered to check that Britain never manages to win more than about three or four gold medals – their best since 1924 has been six gold medals in Melbourne, back in 1956.

The angst reflected hurt national pride, the feeling that the country which had given the world all these games was, now, as so often, being left behind by the others – the teacher, as ever, was being surpassed by his pupils. The question nobody asked was: what do we mean when we say 'give the world the games'? Just as during the euphoria over Euro 96 – barely less than a month before the Atlanta let-down – nobody asked what we meant by 'Football is coming home'?

A good slogan, a good song, and certainly one that galvanised the English nation. But who was 'coming home' when England played Scotland at Wembley? As a sporting contest it was an intensely nationalistic occasion with the English singing the British national anthem, the English fans booing Scotland's *Flower of Scotland*, and The British Broadcasting Corporation behaving more like the English Broadcasting Corporation.

Yet days before the match, John Major had launched a major political offensive against Labour's devolution plans – an offensive that led Labour to change their tack – and pledge to fight the election on the indivisibility of the union. So, when John Major applauded England's performance and publicly acknowledged the nation's debt to Terry Venables, the England coach, what nation was he talking about? Did his remarks mean he accepted the nation was, in practice, divisible?

It could be argued that to dwell on such differences is pedantic. In any case, there is sporting nationalism and real nationalism. We have one British political nation but different British sporting nations. And in football it suits everybody for Britain to have the unique honour of having four national sporting teams, something that not even the old USSR, which was allowed separate seats in the United Nations for 'countries' like the Ukraine, could claim. But if that is so, how can we, the very next month during the Olympics, take up the nationalist argument of failure on the sporting field equalling national failure, more so at a time when political boundaries in the sporting sense, are being blurred?

Britain fields a table tennis player who played for China, a British woman – through marriage – represents Italy, and two of the Greek medal winners were until recently Albanians and Russians, who have, with the unfreezing of the Soviet bloc, at last been able to claim their Greek ancestry.

And what kind of sporting nationalism was on display in the law courts, when Imran Khan, representing Pakistan, fought Ian Botham representing England? Khan's witnesses included present and former England captains and a former England player, all former Cambridge blues. This was a case that to an extent, represented a duel between Pakistan and England, but, at times, it came over more as a case of Oxbridge Middle England coming together against Botham, who could be seen as representing the populist *Sun*-reading English working man. Imran, as I have said, was the ultimate example of the civilising influence of this country's sporting imperialism.

Why does all this matter? It matters because it is important for this country to make sense of its unique sporting heritage if it wants to produce a more successful sporting nation, representing the various tribes and communities from different parts of the world that now inhabit this island. Failure to understand its past, and use it to build its future, means the country often presents a very split sports personality. It both claims too much, and too little. When it suits us, we claim to be the nation that created the games the world plays, but when the tune changes, this is the country paying the price for being the first, the country which by creating these games, and giving them to the world, made a rod for its own back.

This country can either behave like the sporting Roman, the country that gave games to the world, and bask in the glory to its sporting children and their successes, or it can behave like a chippy, angst-ridden, second-hand nation, which feels hard done by, and is envious of other countries who copied the games this country invented, but now play them more successfully than the mother country.

I would, as I have argued in this book, much prefer the Roman approach. It would do honour to this country's sporting past, and be a launch pad for a successful sports nation – successful on the field and at ease off it. Recent events have not encouraged me to think such an enlightened approach is likely.